Francis Hutcheson

On Human Nature

Reflections on our common systems of morality
On the social nature of man

Edited by
THOMAS MAUTNER

T0371451

CAMBRIDGE
UNIVERSITY PRESS

CAMBRIDGE UNIVERSITY PRESS
Cambridge, New York, Melbourne, Madrid, Cape Town, Singapore, São Paulo

Cambridge University Press
The Edinburgh Building, Cambridge CB2 8RU, UK

Published in the United States of America by Cambridge University Press, New York

www.cambridge.org
Information on this title: www.cambridge.org/9780521430890

© Cambridge University Press 1993

First published 1993
Reprinted 1994, 1995
This digitally printed version 2008

A catalogue record for this publication is available from the British Library

Library of Congress Cataloguing in Publication data
Hutcheson, Francis, 1694-1746
On Human Nature / Francis Hutcheson ; edited by Thomas Mautner
p. cm
Includes bibliographical references and index.
Contents: Reflections on our common systems of morality–On the social nature of
man.
ISBN 0 521 43089 5 (hc)
1. Ethics. Modern–18th century. 2. Social ethics. 3. Man. 4. Hutcheson, Francis,
1694–1746. De naturali hominum socialitate. English. 1993 III. Title.
B1501.05 1993
171'. dc20 92–23820 CIP

ISBN 978-0-521-43089-0 hardback
ISBN 978-0-521-05710-3 paperback

Francis Hutcheson (1694–1746) was the first major philosopher of the Scottish Enlightenment, and one of the great thinkers in the history of British moral philosophy, influencing Hume, Kant, and his pupil Adam Smith. He firmly rejected the reductionist view, common then as now, that morality is nothing more than the prudent pursuit of self-interest, arguing in favour of a theory of a moral sense. The two texts presented here are the most eloquent expressions of this theory. The *Reflections on our common systems of morality* insists on the connection between moral philosophy and moral improvement, and was a preview of his first major work, the *Inquiry* of 1725. The lecture *On the social nature of man*, arguing against the psychological egoism of Hobbes, appears here in an English translation for the first time. Thomas Mautner's introduction and editorial apparatus provide a mass of new information, helping to give the reader a sense of the intellectual climate in which Hutcheson lived.

Francis Hutcheson

On Human Nature

Contents

Appendices

Preface

Francis Hutcheson (1694–1746) is one of the great names in the history of British moral philosophy, yet his writings are not easily available. Of his writings on moral philosophy, the two pieces here presented have been even more inaccessible than the rest. The first, a preview of his *Inquiry*, here called *Reflections on the Common Systems of Morality*, was omitted from the 1971 facsimile edition of the collected works. The second, his inaugural lecture on man's natural sociality, here given the title *On the Social Nature of Man*, has remained comparatively inaccessible because it was published in Latin. It is presented here in an English translation for the first time.

When researching relevant material for this edition, other pieces by Hutcheson, published in his lifetime but not included in the facsimile edition of the collected works, came to my notice. One is a letter, published in a French translation, in which he protested against some unfavourable remarks by the reviewer in *Bibliothèque Angloise* 13 (1725). It is not included here, as an English version of it has recently been published in an article by David Raynor. For further detail, see p. 82 below. Another item is a letter on conic sections in *Bibliothèque Raisonnée des Ouvrages des Savans de l'Europe* 14 (1735), intended to draw favourable attention to a new work on the subject by his colleague Robert Simson, professor of mathematics. This letter does not fall within the scope of moral philosophy, so it is not included here. It is interesting, however, to note that in geometry, as in moral philosophy, Hutcheson favours the ancients over the moderns. There is also an *exercitatio* of 1740, later included in an Italian anthology designed for students of jurisprudence. For further information, which also explains why it is not included here, see the bibliography under books and articles [Anon.], *Variorum* ... There is also an item attributed to Hutcheson by Caroline Robbins ('When it is that colonies may turn independent', in Caroline Robbins, *Absolute Liberty*, ed. B. Taft, Hamden, Conn.:

Archon 1982, p. 140). It is a short preface to the three-volume edition of Henry More's (1614–87) *Divine Dialogues, containing disquisitions concerning the attributes and providence of God*, which was published 1743 by the Foulis press in Glasgow. This attribution is, however, very doubtful. The actual text of the preface does not point in Hutcheson's direction, and I am not aware of any other grounds for this attribution. The preface reveals familiarity with the major philosophical writers. It is signed by `The Editor': no doubt the printer, Robert Foulis, who may well have written it. He was a very able and well-educated person, and after the formation of the Glasgow Literary Society some years later he frequently presented papers on learned subjects at its meetings (see Richard Duncan, *Notices and Documents illustrative of the Literary History of Glasgow*. Glasgow [Maitland Club] 1831, p. 16).

Much of the work on the present edition of the *Reflections* was done during a stay at the Social Values Research Centre of the University of Hull in February 1989. I wish to thank its Director, Professor Brenda Almond, for her great kindness in providing for me a friendly and hospitable working environment, and am greatly indebted to her for her very helpful advice both on the content and on the style and organisation of the rather wide-ranging editorial material.

The idea of preparing an English version of Hutcheson's lecture on man's social nature first occurred to me in connection with work undertaken during a stay as a Fellow in the Institute for Advanced Studies in the Humanities at the University of Edinburgh in 1981. The sojourn offered much intellectual stimulation in an agreeable setting, and I am very happy to have this opportunity to acknowledge my gratitude to the Institute.

The translation of the *Lecture* began life as a draft of my own, but for its present publishable form I am heavily indebted to Colin Mayrhofer of the Department of Classics, the Australian National University, who also identified the classical poetry quoted in that text. I am most grateful to him for his generous assistance.

I also wish to express my sincere gratitude to M. A. Stewart of the Department of Philosophy, University of Lancaster, who, in response to many inquiries, kindly and knowledgeably provided information on many obscure points.

David Fate Norton of the Department of Philosophy, McGill University, and Knud Haakonssen, of the Department of the

History of Ideas, the Australian National University, each took great trouble to review, with great care and great expertise, an earlier draft for the introductory essay. They gave very generously of their time and offered much helpful advice, for which I am most grateful.

Sylvia Deutsch, Research Assistant in the Department of Philosophy, the Australian National University, was of great help in tracking down source material, and provided much support through her friendly, intelligent, and highly professional work.

The final version of the translation of the *Lecture* benefited from extensive comments, based on a meticulous review by an anonymous publisher's reader which I had the good fortune to receive; they were offered 'in the spirit of a collaborator and contributor', and so were the very helpful comments on the other parts of the penultimate version of this book. The name of this generous reader was subsequently communicated to me, and I am pleased to be able to address my warmest thanks to Michael Seidler, of the Western Kentucky University, to whom I remain much obliged.

Method of reference

It was the custom of the time to give books lengthy descriptive titles. They served the same purpose as that now served by publishers' blurbs, and newspaper advertisements would usually reproduce the wording of the title-page. Hutcheson followed this convention, as can be seen in the bibliography, and this is why convenient abbreviations are needed for his writings. Hutcheson himself used this method and explained:

> In the References [...] the Inquiry into Beauty is called Treatise I. That into the Ideas of Moral Good and Evil, is Treatise II. The Essay on the Passions, Treatise III. And the Illustrations on the moral Sense, Treatise IV.(*Essay...*, 1st edn, 1728 p. xxii; 3rd edn, 1742 p. xx.)

In this book, his first major work will be referred to as *T1&T2*, or as *Inquiry*. The first part will be called *T1*, or *Inquiry into Beauty*, and its second part *T2* or *Inquiry into Virtue*. The second major work will be referred to as *T3&T4* or as *Essay and Illustrations*. Its first part will be called *T3*, or *Essay*, and its second part *T4* or *Illustrations*. *Reflections* will refer to the two instalments in *The London Journal* of November 1724, as reproduced here, and *Lecture* to the present translation of *De naturali hominum socialitate oratio inauguralis*, the inaugural lecture on the social nature of man, delivered in November 1730 and published in the same year. I shall also use *System* for his *System of Moral Philosophy*, posthumously published in 1755 but finished in 1737, and, when appropriate, 'Compend' for the Latin and English versions of his *Short Introduction to Moral Philosophy*.

All eighteenth-century dates are given in the new style only, so that the calendar year is taken as beginning on 1 January, and not 25 March.

In other respects, standard conventions are adopted, among them the use of square brackets to indicate editorial additions, omissions, comments, etc. Quotation marks are used to indicate that an expression is mentioned rather than used, though occasionally italics are employed for this purpose. In quotations, spelling and punctuation has been preserved, whilst the use of capitals and italics has been modernised.

I have tried to keep the footnotes short. For this reason, some notes have been made into appendices. Some of these deal with matters which, although peripheral to the main argument, may be of interest to some readers. There is also some additional information in the bibliography.

Abbreviations

BLC   The British Library, *General Catalogue of Printed Books*

DNB   *Dictionary of National Biography*

ING   Pufendorf, *De iure naturae et gentium*

NUC   *The National Union Catalog* (U.S.A.)

OHC   Pufendorf, *De officio hominis et civis*

The following refer to Hutcheson's works. See p. xii above, and for further particulars, the bibliography

Compend   *Short Introduction to Moral Philosophy* (1747) and the Latin originals (1742; 1745) .

T1   *Inquiry into Beauty*

T1&T2   *Inquiry*

T2   *Inquiry into Virtue*

T3   *Essay*

T3&T4   *Essay and Illustrations*

T4   *Illustrations*

Introduction

Hutcheson's life and work

Francis Hutcheson inspired David Hume, Adam Smith, Immanuel Kant, and many other eminent moral philosophers. Their fame eventually overshadowed his, and he is now comparatively little known.

Hutcheson's grandfather had, like so many other Scottish Presbyterians, settled in Ulster, where he served as a minister. His son John Hutcheson (d. 1729), the father of Francis, followed him in the same calling. Francis Hutcheson was born in Armagh on 8 August 1694.

His studies began a local school, where he acquired a sound grasp of classical languages, and were continued in a `dissenting academy', one of the schools at more advanced levels which had been set up primarily for the education of students who for religious reasons were unable or unwilling to attend the educational institutions of the Church of England; the universities of Oxford and Cambridge and Trinity College in Dublin being foremost among these. At the age of sixteen Hutcheson moved to the University of Glasgow where, after a year of study, followed by a year's break, he undertook theological studies for for another four years. Having successfully concluded these studies he returned to Ireland, and was made a probationary minister. Not long after, he accepted an invitation to set up an academy in Dublin.

The new venture was a success: Hutcheson even had to find an assistant teacher to help out. During his time in Dublin he also became associated with the circle around Robert, Viscount Molesworth (1656–1725). Molesworth had been on friendly terms with the third Earl of Shaftesbury (1671–1713) and there can be little doubt that it was through him that Hutcheson took notice of and became influenced by Shaftesbury's philosophy.[1] Molesworth also

---

[1] Robbins, `When it is that colonies may turn independent' in Caroline Robbins, *Absolute Liberty* (ed. B.Taft), Hamden, Conn.: Archon 1982, p. 155: Molesworth's

encouraged Hutcheson to publish, and it is probable that he may have helped to have the *Reflections* published in *The London Journal*. It was here that Hutcheson also became friendly with Edward Synge (d. 1762), who later became a bishop in the Church of Ireland, that is, the established Anglican Church. They were both thanked by Hutcheson in the Preface to the *Inquiry*. Also associated with this circle was Hutcheson's close friend James Arbuckle, to whose writings some further reference will be made in the following account.

By the time Hutcheson left Glasgow he was well regarded for his academic ability, and his publications from 1725 soon established his reputation. When the professor of moral philosophy, Gerschom Carmichael, died in 1729, Hutcheson accepted an invitation from the university to fill the vacant chair, which he took up in the autumn of 1730. It was then that he delivered the inaugural lecture included in this volume.

Hutcheson spent the rest of his life in Glasgow, with occasional visits to Ireland. He was very popular with students and colleagues, indeed with most people, except the orthodox, who disapproved of his liberal theological tendencies. On one occasion, in 1738, there was even a prosecution (unsuccessful) before the Glasgow Presbytery for alleged deviations from the Westminster Confession, a document ratified in 1647, to which all ministers of the Church of Scotland were obliged to subscribe.

He was very well liked as a teacher; in Glasgow, he pioneered lecturing in English.[2] His regular classes, and those open to the general public, were consistently well attended. One popular series of lectures, mentioned by William Leechman, whose memoir is the main primary source of biographical information, was given on Sunday evenings and dealt with Grotius's *De veritate religionis Christianae* (On the truth of the Christian religion).[3] He complained that teaching duties and other academic matters did not give him the uninterrupted time he needed to write an improved treatise on

---

influence was a catalytic agent conveying English influence to Hutcheson. The contact with *The London Journal* is discussed in Appendix 16, p. 159.

[2] This is described as a new departure, at p. 64 in William Robert Scott, *Francis Hutcheson. His Life, Teaching and Position in the History of Philosophy*. Cambridge: Cambridge University Press 1900. Reprint: New York: Kelley 1966. According to Robbins *Absolute Liberty*, p. 154, Carmichael had occasionally done likewise.

[3] See William Leechman's preface to Hutcheson's *System of Moral Philosophy*. See also p. 9.

moral philosophy. He did, however, finish the manuscript to his *System* in 1737 (posthumously published by his son in 1755, with a dedication to Synge), and published a compend on moral philosophy, and one on metaphysics. A sudden illness struck him down on his birthday in 1746.[4]

Among Hutcheson's students, the one who rose to greatest eminence was Adam Smith (1723-90), the author of *The Theory of Moral Sentiments* (1759) and *An Inquiry into the Nature and Causes of the Wealth of Nations* (1776), who also later held the Glasgow chair in moral philosophy.

In histories of philosophy, Hutcheson is regularly mentioned together with Shaftesbury as a representative of the theory of a moral sense. Many aspects of that theory are still topical and currently the subject of a keen philosophical debate: for instance, the question of the ontological status of moral qualities, and the question of similarity or difference between such qualities and the secondary qualities, such as colours, for instance.

As a critic of egoistic theories of motivation Hutcheson preceded Joseph Butler (1692-1752) and David Hume (1711–76), and deserves an equal place with them in this part of the history of thought. As a critic of rationalist theories of ethics he anticipated Hume. Hume's writings on moral philosophy frequently echo Hutcheson's arguments and even his turns of phrase.

Political writers took note of Hutcheson's statements on matters of political morality, to be found mainly in his *System*, and cited him frequently. Anthony Benezet (1713–84) did so in his argument against slavery. Activists in the cause of American independence, like Francis Alison (1705–1779), professor in Philadelphia, who used his compend as a textbook, were influenced by him. And – as persuasively argued by Garry Wills in his *Inventing America* – when Thomas Jefferson drafted the American Declaration of Independence, Hutcheson may have been his chief source of inspiration.[5]

---

4 The information above is chiefly derived from Scott, whose biography, published almost a century ago, has not yet been superseded. For details about Hutcheson's publications, see the bibliography.

5 On Alison, see David F. Norton, `Francis Hutcheson in America', *Studies on Voltaire and the Eighteenth Century* 154 (1976) 1547-68. There are far-reaching similarities. Wills's claim that there was a direct and distinctive influence has, however, been hotly disputed. See e.g. Gordon S. Wood, `Heroics', *New York*

When dealing with ideas and their history, different levels of opinion can be distinguished. We can for many periods and societies identify something that can be styled a climate of opinion, a prevailing or at least very influential political or religious ideology; it enters into the mentality of a society, into the spirit of the times. This is particularly significant in the case of Hutcheson, for it was at this level that Hutcheson desired to bring about important changes in moral beliefs and attitudes.

At another level, however, there are the theories proposed by the learned in ancient and modern times, theories which are beyond the immediate concern or grasp of a wider public. At this level are to be found, for instance, theories of moral ontology, concerning questions of what kind of reality can be ascribed to moral qualities and relations, and theories of moral epistemology which try to determine whether moral truths can be known, and if so, how.

Hutcheson's theory of a moral sense, for which he is best known, belongs to this second level. That theory is not, however, elaborated in our two present texts, nor does either of them have much to offer on the closely related topic, under debate recently, of whether or not he should be interpreted as a moral realist.[6] The texts here presented deal with ethical matters and questions of moral psychology which are much closer to the more popular level of moral thought. The moral sense is mentioned neither in the *Reflections*[7] nor in the *Lecture*.

This is why Hutcheson's moral epistemology and ontology will receive only marginal attention in the following introduction.[8] The comments on his ideas will be confined mainly to the topics

Review of Books 28, no. 5 (1981) p. 16. There is a very useful list of contributions to this debate on p. xiii in Leidhold's translation of *T2* and in his notes.

[6] `Realism' is the term currently in vogue. Near-synonyms are `objectivism', `cognitivism', and `factualism'. The term `realism' was actually used at the time, though not in exactly the same sense. For Shaftesbury, `realism, in respect of virtue' is the opposite to moral positivism, i.e. to the view that morality has its basis in an act of (divine) legislation (*The Moralists* II, 3, in *Characteristics*, vol. II, pp. 52ff.).

[7] Noted by Wolfgang Leidhold, who actually argues in his *Ethik und Politik bei Francis Hutcheson*, Munich: Alber 1985, p. 21, that the moral sense is not a central theme in Hutcheson's thought.

[8] There is a very useful list of recent discussions of these topics in J. Schneewind (ed.), *Moral Philosophy from Montaigne to Kant*, Cambridge: Cambridge University Press 1990, p. 524.

discussed in these two texts. Although prepared for different purposes and occasions, they have a common message: a decisive rejection of important doctrines which present human nature as selfish and corrupt, and a strong affirmation of the contrary, positive view.

The present first section of the introduction will be followed by an account of the contemporary intellectual scene which formed a setting for Hutcheson's thought, as it comes to expression in the two texts, except for some matters specific to the *Lecture* which are dealt with in the editorial overview of that text. The next section presents his own position, while the last two sections review some contemporary reactions to his ideas and discuss the present-day relevance of some aspects of this eighteenth-century debate.

The intellectual environment

The rejection of the view that all our actions are ultimately self-interested was perhaps what mattered most to Hutcheson. His position can be better understood once we understand why it could be so significant. To this end, a view of the intellectual landscape in which he was situated will help. First to be considered are the religious and moral notions that were inculcated in most people early in life.

Man's natural corruption

When considering the way people are and the things they do – human characters and actions – some will seem to us indifferent: neither good nor bad. But as for the rest, we inevitably divide them. We approve of some, disapprove of some; some are admired, some despised.

There have been times and places when this apparently natural way of thinking has met powerful opposition. The division into good and bad is rejected. In its place comes a different doctrine, one which denies that any human character or action can be good. Human nature is essentially flawed. The basic contrast is no longer that between the good and the bad. The only distinction that can have any application in real life is that between two ways in which the bad appears. The bad may appear in disguise, masquerading as something good; or it may appear undisguised.

This view seems at first sight to be strongly supported by the facts. The difference, it has been said, between an optimist and a pessimist is simply that the pessimist is better informed.

On reflection, it is, however, not so easy to formulate this pessimistic doctrine in a coherent way. In order to make good sense it needs an implicit contrast with a possible alternative. One cannot seriously deplore the absence of the good unless its existence is at least conceivable.

Some moralists and satirists who adopted this outlook, to be further discussed below on pp. 14ff., concede this when they allow that genuinely good actions or characters *are*, after all, possible – though extremely rare. In mitigation, let us say that they compensate with their wit for their lack of consistency.

Theologians and pessimistic metaphysicians are a little more consistent.[1] They do not allow any of it even at the outer boundary of the natural and human world, that is, in the realm of very high improbability, but relegate it to a supernatural or metaphysical realm. Yet a critic could complain that the difficulty remains unresolved: the difference is only that the genuinely good is no longer said to be extremely rare but rather extremely remote.[2]

Some of these writers also tried to argue for this pessimistic view by turning the theory that all motivation is selfish into a conceptual truth.[3] The consequence of that move is, however, rather awkward: unselfish motivation can no longer be regarded as highly desirable, albeit improbable or miraculous. It becomes altogether impossible. The theory now suffers from a serious tension: the contrast between selfish and unselfish is both implied and denied.

Leaving aside the difficulties there may be in giving this pessimistic or indeed misanthropic outlook a coherent formulation, there can be no doubt that views of this kind have exercised a powerful influence in past and present times. They were very important in the moral and religious thought in Hutcheson's time.

Man's natural corruption: theologians

The doctrine of man's natural corruption is central to many strands of Christian thought, but was given particular emphasis by Luther and Calvin. An authoritative formulation of a strand of Calvinist theology was given by the Synod of Dort (Dordrecht) 1619, when it condemned, in five points, the less forbidding Arminian doctrine.[4]

---

[1] Pessimistic metaphysicians: e.g. Schopenhauer and Eduard von Hartmann.

[2] This is a central part of Ludwig Feuerbach's analysis in *Das Wesen des Christentums* [The essence of Christianity] 1st edn 1841: in religious thought, all positive human qualities are taken away from man and instead ascribed to a being who does not belong to the human and natural world.

[3] See p. 72.

[4] Arminius's five condemned articles and the Canons of the Synod are in P. Schaff, *The Creeds of Christendom*, vol. III, New York: Harper 1877, pp. 545ff.

Incidentally, it was not only the doctrine that was condemned. The same fate also befell the leadership of the Arminian party: one of them, Grotius, spent some years imprisoned in the Loewestein castle.[5] The five points were:

(1) The nature of man, owing to Adam's fall, is totally depraved. Nothing good can come from him without God's gracious intervention. (2) God decided *before* creating the world which people would receive salvation. (This is the doctrine commonly known as supralapsarianism. The number of persons saved might be very small. These are God's elect.) (3) Christ's sacrifice on the cross redeemed the elect only. (4) God's grace is irresistible, so that salvation is independent of any decision by the person elect. (5) Those destined for salvation cannot forfeit it.

This rather rigorous version of Calvinist theology was the one prevailing in the Church of Scotland. It had been set down in the Westminster Confession of 1647, which served as the Kirk's doctrinal standard.

Leechman's statement, mentioned above on p. 4, that Hutcheson lectured on Grotius's defence of the Christian religion, would at first sight suggest to us merely that Hutcheson wished to promote Christian knowledge. But we can now see that more is implied. These Sunday lectures dealt with a book whose author had been a leading opponent of the theology of the orthodox-conservative Evangelical party in the Church of Scotland. There is a clear hint that Hutcheson's sympathies lay with those whose theological sentiments were more liberal, and who were soon to become known as the Moderate party. This was indeed the case.

The moderate reaction against Calvinist theology had started earlier in England with theologians often described as latitudinarians, a term which at the time was mostly used disparagingly by their opponents. Among these moderates were Edward Stillingfleet (1635–99), John Tillotson (1630-94), and other churchmen, including Cambridge Platonists like Benjamin Whichcote (1609–83), Henry More (1614–87), and Ralph Cudworth (1617–88). Important to them was the view that good and evil are not measured by God's will but

---

[5] Hugo Grotius (1583–1645). He escaped, with the courageous assistance of his wife, hidden in a trunk supposedly containing books only. He then made his way to Paris, where he wrote *De jure belli ac pacis* (On the law of war and peace), 1st edn 1625, the work that has established his reputation as the father of international law. See also p. 51.

are so essentially and unalterably'[6]

They shared a distaste for the puritan doctrine of salvation and its implications, a doctrine involving justification by faith alone, imputed righteousness, and absolute predestination. Similar views slowly gained acceptance among the Scottish and Irish Presbyterians, and Hutcheson became their most significant early advocate.

To return to our theme: man's natural corruption. The Westminster Confession (16, 7) asserts:

> Works done by unregenerate men, although for the matter of them they may be things which God commands, and of good use both to themselves and others; yet because they proceed not from a heart purified by faith, nor are done in a right manner according to the Word, nor to a right end, the glory of God; they are therefore sinful and can not please God, or make a man meet to receive grace from God. And yet their neglect of them is more sinful and displeasing unto God.[7]

Article 13 of the Thirty-Nine Articles of the Church of England, which define the theological doctrine of that church, declares similarly:

> Works done before the grace of Christ, and the inspiration of His Spirit, are not pleasant to God, forasmuch as they spring not of faith in Jesu Christ, neither do they make men meet to receive grace, or (as the school authors say) deserve grace of congruity: yea, rather, for that they are not done as God hath willed and commanded them to be done, we doubt not but that they have the nature of sin.[8]

Why is it that good works, like helping victims of misfortune, even at great personal cost, do not please God? If we were to accept strictly the passages just quoted, we would, for instance, find nothing in the story of the good Samaritan that would suggest that his action was pleasing to God; rather, it would have to be regarded as sinful.[9]

---

[6] Here, use has been made of the account in J. Spurr, `"Latitudinarianism" and the Restoration Church', *Historical Journal* 31 (1988) 61–82.

[7] The whole document is in Schaff, *The Creeds of Christendom*, pp. 600ff.

[8] E. Gibson, *The Thirty-Nine Articles of the Church of England*, London: Methuen 1897, p. 415.

[9] The parable in the gospel, Luke 10:29–37, does not seem to convey this message,

One possible answer is that God demands that human actions be
motivated by a personal relationship to God. This relationship may
be described in terms of obedience and submission or it may be described in terms of love and devotion. This required relationship
cannot occur without faith in Christ. A person who acts well, but
fails to satisfy this kind of demand, cannot be saved. Many good
people, virtuous pagans and even, it seems, good Samaritans, will
come to a sticky end.

One could leave it at that. No matter how good and honourable
a person's motive and action may be, if the relationship to God is
absent, the person rightly deserves utter condemnation. This could
make God seem to be absurdly jealous, or completely inscrutable,
and his commands would, from our point of view, seem morally
arbitrary.

The reaction against this theological view could take different
forms. One writer, Henry Dodwell (Jr), commended, with apparent
sincerity, throughout his book *Christianity not Founded on
Argument*,[10] a complete *sacrificium intellectus*, as for instance in this
passage:

> The exactest observer of moral law is a vile and wretched sin-
> ner in God's account, as long as he proceeds by human lights
> and motives and upon the strength of mere ethics only. Nay,
> even his most virtuous actions themselves are highly criminal
> and displeasing to God, as long as he continues in such a dis-
> position of mind, as they are undoubtedly of a nature corrupt
> and unregenerate. *For whatsoever is not of faith is sin.*[11]

Dodwell thought that to expound would be to expose, and·

---

but we are here concerned with certain theological doctrines.
[10] London (1st edn 1741) 2nd edn 1743 p. 16. The motives of the author, Henry
Dodwell Jr (d. 1784) are discussed in *DNB* and in John Mackinnon Robertson, *A
History of Freethought*, vol. II, 4th edn London: Watts 1936, p. 744. There were
those who discerned no satirical intention, e.g. the writer in *Bibliothèque Raisonnée*
29 (1742) p. 451, as noted in Johann Anton Trinius, *Freydencker-Lexicon*, Leipzig
1759.
[11] My italics. The biblical quotation is from Rom. 14:23, here used facetiously in a
sense that the apostle might not have intended, but which nevertheless has
patristic authority: `Augustine and many others, accepting that *pistis* means faith
in the basic Christian sense, have understood Paul to be enunciating the doctrine
that works done before justification and all works done by pagans can only be
sin', C.E.B. Cranfield, *A Critical and Exegetical Commentary on The Epistle to the
Romans*, 2nd edn Edinburgh 1983, p. 728.

thereby reduce to absurdity. There can be no doubt that his intention was parodical.

In the same vein, Henry Fielding (1707–54) has Shamela report a sermon by Parson Williams with feigned ingenuousness:

> people very often call things Goodness that are not so. That to go to Church, and to pray, and to sing Psalms, and to honour the Clergy, and to repent, is true Religion; *and 'tis not doing good to one another, for that is one of the greatest Sins we can commit, when we don't do it for the sake of Religion.* That those People who talk of Vartue [sic] and Morality, are the wickedest of all Persons. That 'tis not what we do, but what we believe, that must save us. . . [12]

These two passages restate the doctrine of the established churches which was quoted above, though in a different tone of voice. Dodwell and Fielding were probably influenced by another writer, Pierre Bayle, about whom more will be said shortly.

So far, the doctrine, presented parodically or in earnest, has been simply that whatsoever is not of faith has no merit. If the question were asked *why* this is so, various responses can be given. One is that asking such a question is itself sinful, a sign of pride which arrogantly expects a doctrinal tenet to be made intelligible, a symptom of man's corrupt state. A second kind of response, already mentioned, is that faith is necessary for the relationship that God demands from man. But there is a third kind of response, compatible with the second and standardly assumed to be implicit in it. It is a response which makes the doctrine more intelligible by adding an important premiss: a person's motive and action will be essentially flawed, because, without the required relationship to God, all actions are ultimately dictated by self-love. Actions of that kind lack genuine merit, and *therefore* cannot please God. This view is present in the writings of Luther and Calvin. All beneficent acts, for instance, are tainted with underlying motives of selfishness, and this is why they have no merit. Bayle formulated it brilliantly:

> I desire it may be observed, that speaking of the good morals of some Atheists, I have not ascribed any true virtue to them.

---

12 My italics. Henry Fielding, *Shamela*, ed. D. Brooks-Davies, Oxford: Oxford University Press 1980, p. 336. In Fielding's *Tom Jones*, Thwackum expresses similar sentiments.

Their sobriety, chastity, probity, contempt of riches, zeal for
the public good, good offices to their neighbour, neither pro-
ceeded from the love of God, nor tended to honour or glorify
him. They themselves were the principle and end of all this:
self-love was the only ground and cause of it. They were only
shining sins, *splendida peccata*, as St Augustin [*sic*] says of all
the good actions of the Heathens. I have therefore done no
prejudice to the true religion by what I have said of some
Atheists.[13]

Bayle's intentions were, and remain, a matter of controversy.[14]
His professed view was that all the efforts of our reason to cope
with religious doctrines are doomed to failure. He did not, however, put forward an alternative view which could accommodate
the demands of reason: he did not opt for atheism, deism, or some
alternative variant of more orthodox theology. Instead, he adopted
a fideistic stance: the voice of reason must be silenced and faith un-
questioningly embraced.

Man's natural corruption, the absence of genuine merit in the
character or the actions of human beings in their natural condition,
is, then, due to the fact that all motivation is flawed by being ultimately self-interested. If this flaw can be removed at all, it is only
through God's gift of faith, that is, only by supernatural intervention. But if supernatural, that is miraculous, intervention is left
aside, and man's natural condition alone is to be considered, then
there is always self-love[15] at bottom: all motivation is selfish, all
selfish motivation rules out merit, therefore no human action has
any merit.

Man's natural corruption: satirists

Theologians were certainly not alone in holding that everything
noble and generous is disguised selfishness, that our virtues are
nothing but splendid-looking vices, and that all love is self-love. A
long line of moralists, among them Montaigne, Charron, Hobbes,
Gracián,[16] Jacques Esprit,[17] and Rochefoucauld, had done their best

---

[13] On Pierre Bayle (1647–1706) and on the quotation, see appendix 1 on p. 148.
[14] See appendix 2 on p. 149.
[15] On the terminology, see appendix 3 on p. 149.
[16] Baltasar Gracián (1601–58), author of *El discreto* (1646), translated as *The Compleat Gentleman* (2nd edn 1730); not identical with the twelfth-century Benedictine

to demonstrate, often in a satirical vein, the deceptiveness of what passes for honesty, benevolence, and other kinds of disinterested virtue.

In England, the best-known moralist and satirist was Bernard Mandeville (1670–1733). His *Fable of the Bees* created quite a buzz among the reading public in the 1720s. The similarity between the outlook of satirists like himself and the theological view did not escape notice. Quite to the point is the comment that Mandeville 'supports one of the tenets of our religion, the natural corruption of human nature, unless assisted by divine grace'.[18]

The satirists differed from the theologians in that their perspective tended to be secular and thus excluded any recourse to miracles – in this instance the miracle of divine intervention that alone can produce genuine goodness of character or conduct. But it was agreed that in the natural state genuine virtue, which necessarily involves disinterestedness, in the form of disinterested benevolence, is, if not impossible, at best very rare. It would involve going against human nature as it actually exists. With few exceptions – perhaps none – what looks like genuine virtue is spurious virtue, pretence, hypocrisy.

Hutcheson was aware of the affinity between the two kinds of writers, the theologians and the satirists. In a comment on Mandeville, he wrote:

> He has probably been struck with some old Fanatick Sermon upon Self-denial in his youth, and can never get it out of his head since. 'Tis absolutely impossible on this Scheme, that God of himself can make a Being naturally disposed to Virtue: for Virtue is Self-Denial, and acting against the Impulse of Nature.[19]

A similar diagnosis was proposed by Adam Smith, who had

---

monk Gratianus, the compiler of Canon Law.

17 Jacques Esprit (1611-1678) was the author of *De la fausseté des vertus humaines* [On the deceitfulness of human virtues] (1678). Rochefoucauld used to seek his comments when drafting his own maxims and reflections.

18 In *The Monthly Mirror* (1803), as quoted in F.B. Kaye's edition of *The Fable of the Bees*, vol. II, p. 438. The same point is made by Bernard Harrison, in his *Henry Fielding's Tom Jones. The Novelist as Moral Philosopher*. London: Sussex University Press/Chatto & Windus 1975, p. 75: 'Mandeville ... far from being the genial sceptic he appears on the surface, is at bottom a curious type of radical puritan.'

19 *Hibernicus's Letters*, p. 407, at the end of Letter 47, dated 19 February 1726.

studied under Hutcheson:

> Some popular ascetic doctrine which had been current before
> his [Mandeville's] time, and which placed virtue in the entire
> extirpation and annihilation of all our passions, were [sic] the
> real foundations of this licentious system.[20]

The two kinds of theory considered so far have in common the
view that action not motivated by self-interest is contrary to human
nature. For such action to occur, something like a miracle is necessary, according to the theologians. According to the moralising
satirists, if such an action occurs at all, it is an extremely unusual
event. What the two views have in common is a reluctance to admit
that human action is ever inspired by genuine benevolence. Logi-
cally the two views are of course quite different, as just mentioned,
but they share two central assumptions. One is that with the qualifications explained above, all motivation is self-interested. The
other is that self-interested action can have no merit, that there is an
opposition between morality and self-interest.

Morality identified with self-interest

Another theory, current at the time, and an important element in
the intellectual climate that confronted Hutcheson, also included
the assumption that all motivation is self-interested. But it did not
put morality in opposition to self-interest. On the contrary, morality
was identified with self-interest. Right action consists in the prudent pursuit of one's interests; wrong action is sheer folly; it consists in action detrimental to one's own interests. It is now time to
consider this view more closely.

Why not commit a crime if it pays? Or, in Shaftesbury's words:
why be honest in the dark?

The early eighteenth century was a time when an increasing
number of writers tried to give religion and morality a philosophical basis, that is, independently of any appeal to the authority of
Christian revelation. All that was needed was a rational theology[21]
which would establish the existence of God, a future state (after

---

[20] Adam Smith, *Theory of Moral Sentiments* (1st edn 1759), pp. 485–6; (1976) p. 313.
   The word 'system' was often used in the way that we now use 'theory'.

[21] Also known as natural theology, or natural religion.

death), and the just distribution of rewards and punishments in that state. Then there would be an obvious answer to the question: why be moral? The answer was regularly given in terms of rewards and punishments in a future state.

According to Herbert of Cherbury (1583–1648), traditionally regarded as the originator of deism,[22] this doctrine was one of the five fundamental tenets which could be firmly established by the light of reason unaided by divine revelation.

Those who differed from the more radical deists by admitting both reason and revelation as means by which truths of religion could be known gave the same reason for being moral. As Hutcheson put it:

Now the greatest part of our latter moralists establish it as undeniable that all moral qualities have necessarily some relation to the law of a superior of sufficient power to make us happy or miserable and ... that we are determined to obedience to laws ... merely by motives of self-interest...[23]

On this view, which can appropriately be labelled prudentialist,[24] there is nothing sublime or very difficult about morality: all that is needed is a plain common sense that can look beyond immediate satisfactions and take a long-term view. Prudence and rationality are often identified.[25] In the same way that a sensible person will make an effort, often successfully, to change unwholesome eating or drinking habits because of the long-term adverse effects on his physical well-being, so he will try to modify his conduct in order to conform to the rules of morality, that is, the laws laid down by God, because of the very long-term and extremely adverse effects on his physical and mental well-being in a future state.

---

[22] Deism is defined in Samuel Johnson's dictionary as 'the opinion of those that only acknowledge one God, without the reception of any revealed religion'.

[23] T2, Introduction. 1st edn 1725, p. 104f.; 2nd edn 1726, p. 114f.; 3rd edn 1729, p. 107f.; 4th edn, 1738 p. 108f.

[24] See below, e.g. p. 72 and p. 116.

[25] An interesting identification of rationality and self-love, on the one hand, sociality and benevolence on the other, was drawn by Henry Grove (1684–1738). See appendix 4 on p. 149.

Advice to a young lady

There was nothing esoteric about this outlook. It was constantly urged on the public at large, in sermons, pamphlets, and books. At this more popular level there is, for instance, a short piece, slipped into a contemporary journal, entitled `Advice to a young lady in a few select moral Maxims'.[26] The ninth of them reads:

> Religion is much out of fashion, but be assured that those who disregard heaven, can never be depended upon; duties without sanctions have very little or no force on us.

Note the last two words: `on us'. The view is that all of us, and not just some others, some weaker brethren, need religion as a reason for being moral. The advice to the young lady is not political: it does not say that the doctrine of a future state is politically and socially indispensable, or at least useful, which was succinctly summed up by Voltaire's *Il faut de l'enfer à la canaille*. The advice presents a reason for doing one's moral duty.

The influence of this outlook was so pervasive that it is worth our while to stop to consider a few representative statements from leading philosophers like Samuel Pufendorf (1632–1694), John Locke (1632–1704), and Gottfried Wilhelm Leibniz (1646–1716), and from a few others whose place in the history of these ideas is less prominent.

Samuel Pufendorf

It was Pufendorf's view that if religion, especially the fear of divine punishments, were removed,

> no one would practise works of mercy or friendship without having the assurance of glory or reward.[27]

This is quite an extraordinary statement. Every act of friendship, every charitable act, must have an ulterior motive: the agent must have in view some private benefit! Pufendorf also held the view that without fear of divine punishment there can be no such thing

---

[26] *The Present State of the Republick of Letters* 6 (1730), p. 449.

[27] remotis poenis divinis ... Nemo quoque opera misericordiae aut amicitiae foret exerciturus, nisi gloriae aut emolumenti explorata spe. *De officio*, 1, 4, 9.

as a conscience. This is the outlook of the moral philosopher whose popularity was probably unequalled in the earlier part of the eighteenth century.[28]

John Locke

Locke held Pufendorf's writings in very high esteem, and the basic role of self-interest in his own ethical theory in the *Essay Concerning Human Understanding* (1690) is obvious. Here is an illustrative statement from Locke:

> The [ancient] philosophers, indeed, shewed the beauty of virtue; [...] but leaving her unendowed, very few were willing to espouse her. [...] But now there being put in the scales on her side, 'an exceeding and immortal weight of glory' [2 Cor. 4,17]; interest is come about her, and virtue now is visibly the most enriching purchase, and by much the best bargain. [...] The view of heaven and hell will cast a slight upon the short pleasures and pains of the present state, and give attractions and encouragements to virtue, which reason and interest, and the care of ourselves, cannot but allow and prefer. Upon this foundation, and upon this only, morality stands firm, and may defy all competition.[29]

Gottfried Wilhelm Leibniz

Locke thought well of Pufendorf: Leibniz did not. But there was no disagreement on the question of moral motivation, and he did agree that a theory that left an afterlife out of account would be inadequate:

> [T]o set aside here the consideration of the future life [...] and to be content with an inferior degree of natural law, which can

---

28 Klaus Luig, `Zur Verbreitung des Naturrechts in Europa', *Tijdschrift voor Rechtsgeschiedenis* 60 (1972) 539-57 has a list which includes 146 different editions (including translations) of Pufendorf's *De officio* (1st edn 1673) before 1789, and not even this list is complete. Among them was a translation into English by Andrew Tooke, under the title *The Whole Duty of Man According to the Law of Nature* (1st edn 1691; 5th edn 1735). For information on books entitled *The Whole Duty of . . .*, see appendix 5 on p. 150.

29 *The Reasonableness of Christianity* (1st edn 1695), ¶245 *ad fin*. There are very similar statements in Samuel Clarke. See p. 25 below.

even be valid for atheists, [...] would mean cutting off the best part of the science of [natural law] and suppressing many duties in this life as well. Why, indeed, would someone risk riches, honors and his very existence on behalf of his dear ones, of his country, or of justice, when, by the ruin of others, he could think only of himself, and live amidst honors and riches? Indeed, to put off the enjoyment of actual and tangible goods simply for the immortality of one's name and for posthumous fame – for the voices of those whom one can no longer hear – what would this be if not magnificent folly?[30]

Leibniz makes explicit reference to the noble sentiment, *dulce et decorum est pro patria mori*,[31] a standard topic in this debate. Allusions to it were common, and occur in many of the writers to be considered in the following.

Leibniz also mentions some lines in Horace, to be found here on p. 96, which, as we shall see, were regularly quoted by those who wanted to reject a mercenary approach to morality. But Leibniz uses these lines not in order to deplore a mercenary mentality, but to articulate what a rational one would have to be: without a future state there would be no reason for being moral.

From the great number of other writers who insisted on the necessity of rewards and punishments in a future state, Basil Kennett (1674–1715), George Berkeley (1685–1753), and Thomas Johnson (c1703–37) can be selected as representative.

Basil Kennett

There is a typical statement in the `short' introduction to the first translation into English of Pufendorf's major work, *On the Law of Nature and Nations* (1st edn 1703).[32] The introduction is unsigned, but there can be no doubt that the author is the translator-in-chief, Basil Kennett. The author takes a favourable view of moral demonstrations of a future state, mentions Pascal by name, and proposes arguments (pp. 16f.) inspired by Pascal's Wager,[33] so it is a most

---

30 *The Political Writings of Leibniz*, ed. P. Riley, Cambridge: Cambridge University Press, 2nd edn 1988, p. 67. This comment on Pufendorf was written in 1706.

31 `It is agreeable and fitting to die for one's country.' Horace, *Odes*, iii, 2.

32 Twenty-seven closely printed folio pages! This introductory essay was omitted in the 2nd edn (1710). The quoted passages are from pp. 10f. and p. 13.

33 Briefly, an argument that belief in God is the only safe and sensible way out of

plausible assumption that the introduction is written by Kennett, who was the translator of Pascal's *Pensées*.[34]

Kennett was a Fellow of Corpus Christi College in Oxford, and eventually President. He served as chaplain to the factory in Leghorn 1706–13.[35] He was widely known as the author of *The Antiquities of Rome* (¹1696), for a century the standard handbook.

> Did nature so contract the prospects which religion open's [*sic*] to our view, as to let death close the scenes and shut out all beyond, to expect so unprofitable an honesty, would be to look for the stream, when we stopp'd the fountain. All the reasons and measures of acting, which arise from the temporal condition of things must be finally resolv'd into interest: to which tho' Virtue points out the safe and infallible path, yet Vice, as better skill'd in by-ways, is too often the more expeditious guide. [...] Virtue would be thought a kind name for abject weakness, and innocence, the apology of a coward [...] Where would we here [i.e. hear] of one that would oppose injustice and oppression, when his own effects were out of danger; and by affording shelter to others, draw the storm upon himself? Would any man stand in the breach, who had but one life to support his courage? Would not to succour distressed innocence be true knight errantry? Would there be such virtue as fortitude, except on the stage?

Without a future state, the law of nature would have no obligation, and to sacrifice oneself for fame would be `folly insupportable'. In substance, Kennett's view seems entirely to coincide with that expressed in the quotation from Leibniz above.

George Berkeley

Berkeley's lasting fame derives from the bold immaterialism which

---

uncertainty: if the belief is false little or nothing is lost, but if it is true the gain is immense.

34 Blaise Pascal's (1623–62) view of human nature was unflattering and had much in common with that of both the theologians and the moralists. He is more extreme than Hobbes: by nature, all men hate each other. `Tous les hommes se haïssent naturellement l'un à l'autre' (*Pensées*, no. 134, p. 1126, ed. Chevalier; no. 207, p. 162, ed. Tourneur and Anzieu).

35 *factory*: an establishment carrying on business in a foreign country; a trading station for a merchant company.

he developed in works written in his twenties. His originality and independence of mind was also shown in his challenge to Newton's infinitesimal calculus, in his writings on the contemporary political and economic situation in Ireland, etc. But on the present subject-matter, he saw no reason to deviate from the common view:

> Tully[36] has long since observed, that it is impossible for those who have no belief in the immortality of the soul, or a future state of rewards and punishments, to sacrifice their particular interests and passions to the public good, or have a generous concern for posterity.[37]

Thomas Johnson

Yet another typical statement is provided by Thomas Johnson, Fellow of Magdalene College in Cambridge. He edited Pufendorf's *De officio* with copious annotations, and published a few works on theology and moral philosophy. His view on the *dulce et decorum* is again the standard one:

> For a man to hazard his life for the good of his country, is a noble and exalted instance of Christian heroism; because 'tis setting aside the consideration of a present less evil, for the sake of obtaining a future greater good; since he is well assured that his light affliction, which is but for a moment, worketh for him a far more exceeding and eternal weight of glory. 2 Cor. iv.17. But however truely great this would be upon such a prospect; yet, if we set aside the consideration of a future reward, and all is supposed to be at an end when this perishing scheme is closed, I must insist upon it once more, that it would be madness and folly to part with one grain of happiness here. Whatever fine things may be said of *the brave spirits of the ancient Pagans*, I must think, that such of them as

---

[36] At the time, the custom was to refer to Marcus Tullius Cicero by his middle name. The reference is probably to the first book of Cicero's *De natura deorum* [On the nature of the gods]. It was often quoted in this context, for instance by Archibald Campbell (see p. 75) in his *Enquiry into the Original of Moral Virtue*, Edinburgh 1733, p. 424 note: 'Atque haud scio an, pietate adversus Deos sublata, fides etiam, & societas humani generis, & una excellentissima virtus, justitia, tollatur.' [I wonder whether mutual trust, human society, or the most excellent virtue of justice can remain if religion is abolished.]

[37] *Essay towards Preventing the Ruin of Great Britain* (1st edn 1721) in *Works*, vol. VI, at p. 79.

gave up their lives upon a fantastical notion of honour, without any hopes of a future reward, made a very foolish bar-
gain, unless they thought the disgrace and obloquy of refus-
ing to act as they did, would have made life not worth the
enjoying it, if they had refused.[38]

And so one could go on. It is no exaggeration to say that opinions of this kind had gained a firm hold in the public mind. They
were common among a large number of writers with Anglican or
Presbyterian affiliations, and we will review below (pp. 65ff.) some
who asserted or re-asserted them in response to Hutcheson.

A historical excursion

The apparently mercenary character of Christian ethics remained
on the agenda. Thus, a position very close to Hutcheson's was elo-
quently expressed by another eminent thinker in the following
statement about `so-called Christian morality':

> It holds out the hope of heaven and the threat of hell, as the
> appointed and appropriate motives to a virtuous life: in this
> falling far below the best of the ancients, and doing what lies
> in it to give to human morality an essentially selfish character,
> by disconnecting each man's feelings of duty from the inter-
> ests of his fellow-creatures, except in so far as a self-interested
> inducement is offered to him for consulting them.[39]

The underlying view in all these statements is that all motivation is
self-interested.

This theological view differs from the one introduced earlier.
There we encountered the doctrine that natural man *cannot* be
moral. Now we have the doctrine, addressed to natural man, that it
is in his interest to be moral, that he ought to be moral because it
pays: it is clearly assumed that he *can* be moral. A subtle tension
will arise if the two doctrines are considered to belong to the same
system of belief. But this is a difficulty best left to the theologians.

---

[38] *Essay on Moral Obligation*, London 1731, p. 63.
[39] John Stuart Mill, *On Liberty* (1st edn 1859): Dent (Everyman edn), p. 109; Penguin
1974, pp. 112f.; Cambridge University Press 1989, pp. 50f.

What makes an action right?

So far, we have considered problems of motivation. There were also questions about right and wrong conduct, and about what it is that makes an action right.

One answer to the last question was that given by theological moral positivism, also known as the Divine Command theory of morality: the view that the wrongness of an action consists in its being prohibited by God, and its rightness in its being permitted or commanded by God.

This view is closely connected with the doctrine of man's natural corruption: our intellect and our will is not capable of discerning the light of nature and follow it properly in our judgements and decisions. Left to us is only submission and obedience to divine revelation.

Theological moral positivism was vehemently attacked by many writers for being intellectually untenable and morally repugnant. It was intellectually untenable because, as Hutcheson pointed out, statements like `The laws of God are just' would, on this view, turn into insignificant tautologies, which they are not.[40] It was morally repugnant, as eloquently expressed in an indignant statement by Arbuckle a like-minded friend of Hutcheson in a letter to Molesworth:

> We are debauched in the very first principles of our morality. [...] it is orthodox divinity[41] to make fear the principle of human actions, and the bare will of an absolute Lord the standard of rectitude. We must love God and keep His commandments. And why? Because God has commanded us to do so. All our obligations must be enforced by the scourge. And on this hopeful principle we build both our religion, and morality. Judge then, mylord, what fruits of virtue and true honesty can be produced in the minds of people, that have never been used to any other culture.[42]

---

[40] Tautologies of the type `God commands what he commands'. T2 (1st edn 1725) 7, 3, pp. 253f.; (4th edn 1738) 7, 5, p. 275. Hutcheson was certainly not the first to argue this. See note 43 below.

[41] *divinity*: theology.

[42] Letter from James Arbuckle to Viscount Molesworth of 13 February 1723, in: Historical Manuscripts Commission. *Reports on Mss in Various Collections*, vol. VIII (1913), p. 355. See also M.A. Stewart, `John Smith and the Molesworth Circle', *Eighteenth-Century Ireland* 2 (1987) on p. 101.

Many other writers took a similar view; according to Leibniz, most writers of any importance agreed.[43] Take for instance Samuel Clarke (1675–1729). Among English philosophers active in the early decades of the eighteenth century, Clarke's renown would have been overshadowed only by that of his close friend Isaac Newton (1642–1727). He was at the centre of keen theological and philosophical debautes because of his boldly rationalist natural theology and his heterodox anti-trinitarianism. On our present subject matter, he wrote:

> that which is Holy and Good ... is not therefore Holy and Good, because it is commanded to be done; but is therefore commanded by God, because it is Holy and Good [... The] Law of nature has its full obligatory power, antecedent to all consideration of any particular private and personal reward or punishment.[44]

Clarke advocated a rationalist theory to explain wherein the rightness or wrongness of an action consists: there are, in the nature of things, objective moral fitnesses discernible by human reason.[45]

The theory now under discussion is a theory of what it is that constitutes moral *rightness* and *wrongness*. The question, discussed already, of what *motive* there can be for complying with the demands of morality, is of course different, and on that question Clarke adhered to the standard view by his insistence on the doctrine of sanctions in a future state. There was no inconsistency in this. He agreed with the many writers already cited that there can be no motive for complying with the demands of morality without a superior power who is able and willing to impose sanctions for non-compliance.

There is a complication at this point. The standard view was, and remained until Kant, that there can be no obligation without laws

---

[43] G. W. Leibniz, *Theodicy* (1st edn 1710), London: Routledge 1952, ¶182. He mentions Plato's *Euthyphro*. Others who agreed were Grotius, Henry More, Cudworth, Bayle, Shaftesbury, etc.

[44] *A Discourse Concerning the Unchangeable Obligations of Natural Religion*, London, 1st edn 1706, p. 110.

[45] This theory is exposed to the now classical objections that were first made by Hutcheson, although they are best known in the form that Hume presented them. See *T4*, section 2, and Hume's *Treatise of Human Nature*, ed. Selby-Bigge and Nidditch, Oxford: Oxford University Press 1978, Book III *Of Morals*, part 1, section 1.

backed by sanctions.[46] Thomas Johnson, for instance, could assert[47] that with very few exceptions – only Grotius and Samuel Clarke, according to him – all the leading writers shared the view that there can be no moral obligation without rewards and penalties: Stillingfleet, Locke, Pufendorf, Barbeyrac, Cumberland, Samuel Parker.

This concept of obligation was closely linked with motivation. But if the assumption is made that God commands that a certain rule of conduct be obeyed and attaches sanctions for non-compliance, if and only if the rule of conduct is in itself of the right kind, then it can be inferred that there will be an obligation to do A if and only if doing A is right. This no doubt tempted some thinkers to collapse the distinction between obligation and rightness, and Clarke's view that actions can be intrinsically obligatory seems to be a case in point. But on that view obligation and motivation become separate notions, and Clarke did indeed insist on the necessity of a future state.

A historical excursion

Later, Immanuel Kant (1724-1804) was to observe that deriving morality from a divine will would be grossly circular if that will is defined in terms of moral attributes; but if it is not,

> the concept of God's will remaining to us – one drawn from such characteristics as lust for glory and domination and bound up with frightful ideas of power and vengefulness – would inevitably form the basis for a moral system which would be in direct opposition to morality.[48]

Objections of this kind remained commonplace in nineteenth-century thought on morals and religion. Examples are not hard to find. Here is a violent reaction from John Stuart Mill (1806–73):

---

[46] `All obligation arises from some law'; `obligation antecedent to all law is a contradiction and flat absurdity'. Daniel Waterland, *The Nature, Obligation, and Efficacy of the Christian Sacraments considered* (1st edn 1730) in *Works* (1st edn 1823) vol. V, pp. 431–549, on p. 443, or (3rd edn 1856), vol. IV, pp. 51–148 on p. 61f. On this eminent theologian, more will be said on pp. 70f. below.

[47] *Essay on Moral Obligation* (1731), p. 43. On Johnson, see above, p. 22.

[48] *Grundlegung zur Metaphysik der Sitten* (1st edn 1785), p. 443 (in the pagination of the Academy edition). The quoted passage is taken from H.J. Paton's translation, *The Moral Law*, London: Hutchinson 1948.

so preposterous a doctrine ... the infinitely mischievous tendency of a theory of moral duty, according to which God is to be obeyed, not because God is good, nor because it is good to obey him, but from some motive or principle which might have dictated equally implicit obedience to the powers of darkness. Such a philosophy ... must extirpate from [men's] minds all reverence, all admiration, and all conscience, and leave them only the abject feelings of a slave.[49]

Again, the Swedish philosopher Viktor Rydberg (1828-1895) wrote of `the so-called theological standpoint in moral philosophy' that it tends to the enslavement of mankind, to the destruction of the human sense of justice and morality, and to power-worship, servility, and selfishness.[50]

These attacks on the theory have a continuous history, and reappear constantly in most introductory philosophy texts. What is curious, however, is that the authors of these textbooks seem to have a problem when it comes to naming defenders of this theory. Who are the writers whose authority, influence, or sheer number makes them deserving of such a crushing refutation? It is not easy to think of an answer.

Some information can be gleaned from a review of Cudworth's posthumously published *A Treatise concerning Eternal and Immutable Morality*.[51] It has a list, in effect Cudworth's own, of `those who regard all morality as positive, arbitrary and factitious only'. Such writers are said to subscribe to one of the three kinds of fatalism: the materialist (Epicurean), the Stoic, or the theological (predestinationist) variety. The list names a number of ancient sophists and materialists, and ends with the words `Hobbes and divers Modern Theologians'. Cudworth did, however, make Ockham a joint defendant with Hobbes.

Again, in the polemical debate between Archibald Campbell[52] and those accusing him of heterodoxy, Campbell in one pamphlet

49 From a review, written in 1833, of R. Blakey, *History of Moral Science*, reprinted in Jerome Schneewind (ed.), *Mill's Ethical Writings*, New York: Collier 1965 p. 73.
50 V. Rydberg, *Filosofiska föreläsningar*: Leibniz' Teodicé [Philosophical Lectures: Leibniz's Theodicy], Stockholm: Bonnier 1900, pp. 43–6.
51 In *The Present State of the Republick of Letters* 7 (1731), in the abstract of Edward Chandler's preface to Cudworth's treatise at pp. 66–9.
52 *The Report...* Edinburgh: Lumsden and Robertson 1736, pp.56 ff. About Campbell, see below p. 75.

accuses his accusers of holding the opinion `that the laws of nature are no other but mere arbitrary institutions', and cites Cudworth at length in his rejection of that view.

One could find many more examples which are now forgotten or, if rediscovered, regarded as rather ephemeral. But if we are to confine our view to the great thinkers, we could almost suspect that the object of the attacks is fictitious, or at most of limited significance. It is at any rate perfectly obvious that for all the greatness of Ockham and Hobbes, the continuity and vehemence of the attacks on the position ascribed to them is out of all proportion to any influence they may have had in propagating it.

The true explanation must be sought elsewhere: the persistence and the strength of the opposition shows that what is rejected is not merely a theory proposed by this or that great thinker. The real target is a religiously backed moral authoritarianism which has been a significant part of our cultural heritage.

There has for long been a tendency to read the great philosophers of the past as if they were primarily conducting a great debate among themselves. The present case illustrates the shortcoming of such a method of interpretation.

The place of the debate

We have now considered some theories of human nature which were extremely influential in the early eighteenth century – and not only then. As observed by a writer in *Journal de Trévoux*, in England as in France it had become fashionable to bring in self-love everywhere and make it the primary motive, the only principle of the conduct of the heart.[53]

This was a fashion not solely among the learned, not confined to the school and the pulpit. Hutcheson's writings, including the *Reflections* and the *Lecture*, related to the contemporary debate on questions of ethics and religion, a debate conducted in books, pamphlets, articles, and reviews in magazines and even in newspapers, sermons, coffee-house conversation, and so on.

In Britain in the 1720s, this debate was not merely a minor

---

53 *Journal de Trévoux* 26 (1726), p. 2175: `[E]n Angleterre ainsi qu'en France, la mode est introduite de mêler par tout l'amour propre, d'en faire le premier mobile, l'unique principe de la conduite du coeur humain.' From the review of *Inquiry*, about which see also p. 81.

academic-theological side-show of little interest to the public at large. On the contrary, it attracted considerable public interest. Some contemporary comments can serve as confirmation.

Shaftesbury had observed that the activities of `the writing church militant' attracted keen public interest, and that this was evident from the way in which people involved in publishing conducted their trade. The publishing of books and pamphlets on religion and morality had become a very profitable business, so profitable indeed that booksellers in their unscrupulous quest for material gain could be suspected, at least in jest, of fomenting theological controversy. Shaftesbury likened them to a glazier who, in order to ensure a thriving business, tosses a football to a bunch of street-urchins on a frosty morning.[54]

He made this remark in the early years of the eighteenth century. It seems that the trend persisted. Some twenty years later, one writer observes that even the ladies and gentlemen of fashion at Bath, `that place of Gallantry and Intrigue',[55] who used to engage in `free discussion both of Religion and Politicks' had `entirely discarded [Politicks,] and Religion engrosses the whole Attention and Conversation of the Beaux and Belles'.[56]

The impression that questions of religion and morality had a central place in the public mind is again confirmed in the preface to the first issue of *Bibliothèque Raisonnée*, published in Amsterdam by Wetstein & Smith.[57] The editors of the new magazine noted the

---

54 *Miscellaneous Reflections*, 1, 2 *ad fin.*, in Shaftesbury's *Characteristics*, vol. II, p. 165.

55 Flirtations, clandestine amorous liaisons, etc. *An Essay upon Modern Gallantry* London 1726, explains facetiously (pp. 10f.): `By Gallantry, in the modern sense of that Word, is to be understood, a constant Application to the good Works of Adultery and Fornication; or the prevailing Art of debauching, by any Methods, the Wives and Daughters of any Men whatsoever, especially those of our dearest Friends, and most intimate Acquaintances.'

56 *Fog's Weekly Journal* no. 36, 31 May 1729, pp. 1f. These initial remarks are followed by an outline of a deistic view which has a great deal in common with that of Rousseau's Savoyard priest some thirty years later. The writer, who uses the initials A.R., takes exception to this modern view of religion and morality. On the whole, journals which, like *Fog's*, were in opposition to the Walpole government tended to be theologically more conservative.

57 William Smith, a friend of Hutcheson, had become a partner by marriage and had removed to Amsterdam. This magazine was to continue where the earlier sequence of *Bibliothèque Universelle et Historique*, *Bibliothèque Choisie*, *Bibliothèque Ancienne et Moderne* had been discontinued. Those magazines had all been edited by Jean Le Clerc (1657–1736), who in 1728 suffered a stroke which ended his long career as a writer and editor (see *Bibliothèque Raisonnée* 16, pp. 344ff.).

need for a journal in the French language that could be published in liberty in Holland, the only free country in Europe (except Great Britain), a journal which could also counterbalance the one-sidedness of the national magazines. In France, they continued, interests in art and *belles-lettres* were predominant, and

> In Germany, jurisprudence is much cultivated and compilations are extremely fashionable. In England, all the professions meddle in theology, and for every work of literature, medicine, politics, mathematics or philosophy, you will find twenty others dealing with religion.[58]

The fact has been noted;[59] to explain it would take us too far afield. The familiar fusion of personal and political commitments that can be seen in the adherents of modern ideologies had its parallel in the combination of religious and political party zeal in eighteenth-century Britain, where many of the writings on religion and morality had political overtones.

In France, religious and political concerns were similarly interwoven. The acute conflict between Jesuits and Jansenists was as much political as theological. Ironically, in their bitter struggle they overlooked the spread of deism and even atheism. Because of the censorship, such ideas were often not published in print, but communicated less visibly through the proliferation of manuscript copies clandestinely distributed. This did not happen in Britain, where, as in the Netherlands, there was a high degree of press freedom. This explains the greater flourish and extent of the public debate on religion and related topics.

---

[58] *Bibliothèque Raisonnée* 1 (1728), pp. ixf.: `En Allemagne, on cultive beaucoup la Jurisprudence, & les Compilations y sont extrémement à la mode. En Angleterre, toutes les Professions se mêlent de Théologie, & sur un Ouvrage de Belles Lettres, de Medecine, de Politique, de Mathématique, ou de Philosophie, vous y en verrez vingt autres dont la Religion sera le Sujet.' – `Philosophie' denotes here theories of mind and matter generally: what is now called metaphysics, physics, and psychology.

[59] As observed by Charles B. Realey, *The Early Opposition to Sir Robert Walpole 1720–1727* [= University of Kansas Humanistic Studies 4, nos 2-3], Lawrence, Kansas 1931, p. 93, the scandal of the South Sea Bubble (1720–21) occupied the public mind for a while, but the newspapers and public interest soon reverted to `that perennial subject of debate, religion ... even in the midst of the South Sea crisis, attention could be turned to a religious issue with very little effort'.

Hutcheson's contribution

In the *Reflections*, Hutcheson first makes observations on the *effects of the current systems of morality*, and then divides his discussion into two main parts: one dealing with *moral motivation*, the other with the *precepts of morality*. It will be convenient to follow this sequence.

The role of moral philosophy

It was a powerful attack on the writers on morality of his time that Hutcheson launched when he first appeared in print. Does this moral philosophy have a morally improving effect on those who study it? Does it enhance their sense of well-being? The answer to both questions, Hutcheson believed, must be negative. People who are unfamiliar with the systems of morality do not seem to be worse off, morally or psychologically.

Hutcheson obviously expected a great deal from the systems of morality. They ought to have an improving effect: a proper grasp of them should make a person psychologically more harmonious and morally more upright. If such beneficial effects were not discernible, one would suspect a defect in these systems. As we are told by his biographer William Leechman,[1] he 'regarded the culture of the heart as the end of all moral instruction'. The moralist has to engage more than the intellect of his audience.

In the beginning of the *Reflections* he makes this point quite explicitly: the question is whether those conversant with 'the modern schemes of morals' are *morally better* in their dealings with others and whether they are *happier* and more harmonious. His view is clearly that moral philosophy, the 'systems of morality', ought to have an improving influence.

This is the way in which religious teachings are regularly

---

1 In his preface to *System*, 1755, p. xxxi. Nevertheless, Hutcheson made a clear distinction between lectures and sermons. See appendix 6 on p. 151.

judged. Moral philosophy was subject to similar expectations by all the ancient schools of philosophy, however much they differed in other respects. On this point, the consensus lasted, and even at the time when Hutcheson wrote it would be difficult to find any writer who had explicitly distanced himself from that view.

The view is, then, that an adequate moral philosophy should

1 have practical applicability, and not merely provide theoretical descriptions and explanations;
2 bring psychological harmony or peace of mind to those who were susceptible to its influence;
3 have beneficial effects on the way people relate to one another.

The role of moral philosophy: comparison with Hume

It is of interest to compare this with the view taken by David Hume (1711–76), the greatest of the British philosophers of the eighteenth century. He was strongly influenced by Hutcheson in his own moral philosophy and had much in common with him: the most obvious instances being the critique and rejection of egoistic theories of motivation and of ethical rationalism.[2] It is therefore all the more interesting to observe the striking contrast in their view of the role of moral philosophy. This contrast can be said to mark a turning-point and a new departure in the history of moral philosophy.

It was Hume's ambition to develop a *science* of morals. But no science can, as such, help people to *feel* good or to *be* good, and indeed moral philosophy is, in his view, an inquiry only indirectly concerned with moral instruction or self-improvement. This modern, more limited conception of what moral inquiry can achieve has since become the one generally adopted. It is very different from Hutcheson's.

Hutcheson and Hume were not unaware of this difference between them. Hutcheson raised the matter when asked by Hume to comment on Hume's manuscript of Book 3 (*Of Morals*) of the *Treatise of Human Nature*. In a letter,[3] in which Hume responded to Hutcheson's comments, he pointed to the different tasks of the

---

[2] See appendix 7 on p. 152.
[3] See appendix 8 on p. 153 for a longer extract from this letter.

moralist and the metaphysician. He compared the distinction to that between a painter and an anatomist, and insisted that there ought to be a division of labour. The painter/moralist can represent virtue in engaging colours. The anatomist/metaphysician cannot do that. But this is not to say that he can be of no help to the painter:

> the most abstract speculations [i.e. those of `the anatomist'] concerning human nature, however cold and unentertaining, become subservient to *practical morality*; and may render this latter science more correct in its precepts and more persuasive in its exhortations.[4]

To return to Hutcheson: his assumption that moral philosophy ought to have an improving effect was generally shared. His view that something would be amiss if it failed to have a beneficial influence on people's conduct and sense of well-being would not have seemed strange to his contemporaries.

Rejection of egoism and moral positivism

As one author notes:

> Central to Hutcheson's philosophy was the confidence he places in human nature. There is much truth in the point of view that the Scottish Enlightenment `was essentially a reaction against the theological spirit which predominated during the seventeenth century'.[5]

This was a theological spirit which made God inscrutable and arbitrary, from the standpoint of human reason. With it went a theological moral positivism which Hutcheson rejected, as already noted on p. 24 above.

He did, however, spend more of his philosophical energy on the

---

4 In short, the `anatomist' of morals may have little talent for the task of moralising, but his work can help the moralist, as Hume argued in his *Treatise*, 3, 3, 6, *ad fin.*, where he re-used parts of this letter.

5 J. K. Cameron, in his contribution to R.H. Campbell and A.S. Skinner (eds.), *The Origins and Nature of the Scottish Enlightenment* (1982), in which he emphasises the part played by the theological controversies in the early eighteenth century in creating a more enlightened outlook among many clergy and academics. The quoted words are from H. T. Buckle.

refutation of the view that all motivation is self-interested, arguing against it in all his writings on moral philosophy,[6] including the *Reflections*. The refutation of this view, which has been labelled 'psychological egoism' in more recent times, was for Hutcheson a major concern. He maintained that there was such a thing as disinterested concern for others, expressed regret that

> this disinterested affection may appear strange to men impressed with notions of self-love· as the sole motive of action, from the pulpit, the schools, the systems, and conversations regulated by them[7]

and went on to present a number of objections. He strongly agreed with Shaftesbury, that a virtue that needs reward is not worth rewarding.[8]

Hutcheson had become convinced that a change was needed in the moral outlook purveyed by most theologians and philosophers. This would also affect political philosophy. The rejection of psychological egoism would have implications for theories of politics and human society. This is hinted at in the *Reflections* and can be clearly seen in the *Lecture*, where Hutcheson argues at some length against the theories that would base human society on nothing more than individual self-interest.

As will be shown, the new outlook that Hutcheson advocated would follow a middle course between theological and secularising theories. The guiding light would be provided by the brightest and best of the ancients. He announced this in the beginning of the *Reflections* and in the title-page advertisement of his first book. In the preface, he wrote:

> The chief ground of his [the author's, i.e. Hutcheson's] assurance that his opinions in the main are just, is this, that as he took the first hints of them from some of the greatest writers of antiquity, so the more he has conversed with them, he finds

---

[6] As noted by many commentators, e.g. William T. Blackstone, *Francis Hutcheson and Contemporary Ethical Theory*, Athens, Ga.: University of Georgia Press, 1965, p. 6, and Henning Jensen, *Motivation and the Moral Sense in Francis Hutcheson's Ethical Theory*, The Hague: Nijhoff 1971, pp. 13 and 15.

[7] T2 2, 9.

[8] The formulation is from Scott, *Francis Hutcheson*, p. 154, summing up Shaftesbury's opinion in part II, section 3 of the *Essay on the Freedom of Wit and Humour*.

his illustrations the more conformable to their sentiments.[9]

The targets of Hutcheson's criticism: theological and secular

Hutcheson's favourable estimation of the ancients did not, how-ever, include the philosophical tradition originating with Epicurus (341–270 B.C.). The Epicurean philosophy was conventionally rejected. For a number of reasons, it had long been considered to have an appeal only for hardened *esprits forts*. It was materialistic. It advocated a practical atheism: gods do exist, but they are utterly separate from and unconcerned with human affairs. It was hedo-nistic, declaring pleasure to be the highest good. It also proposed a hedonistic theory of motivation: in all action, the agent is motivated by the prospect of pleasure.

The Epicurean tradition was alive and well when Hutcheson wrote. In England, Thomas Hobbes (1588–1679) was constantly denounced by his critics for adhering to it, ultimately on the ground that it was not compatible with Christian beliefs.

And yet, the theory of *motivation* ascribed to Epicureans and Hobbesians was not easily distinguishable from that of many orthodox theologians, a fact which some of them were even pre-pared to concede. It was, then, only natural for Hutcheson to indi-cate, that his objections affected both this doctrine of the Epicureans and Christian moralists. In the *Essay*, he was to introduce the dis-tinction between selfish and benevolent desires with the comment that

> this distinction has been disputed since Epicurus; who with his old followers, *and some of late, who detest other parts of his scheme*, maintain [sic], `that all our desires are selfish: or, that what every one intends or designs ultimately, in each action, is the obtaining pleasure to himself, or the avoiding his own private pain'[10]

and refers in a footnote to Cicero, *De finibus*, book 1, which gives an outline of Epicureanism. The same reference reappears in the intro-duction to the *Illustrations*, where the theory is said to have been

---

9 *T1&T2* (1st edn 1725), p. xi; (4th edn 1738), pp. xxf.
10 *Essay* 1, 3; my italics.

'revived by Mr. Hobbes,[11] and followed by many better Writers'. A hint of whom he had in mind is given in the later editions of the *Illustrations*, where, after mentioning Hobbes, Hutcheson inserted `Rochefoucaut [sic] and others of the last century'.

The relative importance of the two rejected standpoints

It is appropriate to compare Hutcheson's attitude to the theological use of psychological egoism with his attitude to the more secular and satirical uses of that theory.

In the introduction to *Illustrations*, Hutcheson asserts that for some Christian moralists, `the prospect of private happiness is the sole motive of election'. The quotations above give ample support to this claim, and it is clear that the views that he wanted to reject were certainly not invented by him for that purpose. They were widely held, also by writers whose interests were more secular, but who likewise presented egoism as nothing but realistic common sense, like John Trenchard (1662–1723), co-author of *Cato's Letters*. Most of these essays were political, but some did discuss topics of religion, superstition, morality, etc.

> In the larger sense of the word, I think it impossible for any man to act upon any other motive than his own interest: for every pursuit that we make, must have for its end the gratification of some appetite, or the avoiding of some evil which we fear; and, in truth, when we say that any man is self-interested, we mean only that he is not enough in his own interest.[12]

A patron reaps satisfaction from obliging the objects of his kindness, and by making them more devoted to himself – which can be to his own future benefit.[13]

Other moralists of the more worldly kind presented similar views as a combination of realism and satire. One of them, who

---

[11] *T4* (1st edn 1728), pp. 207f.; (3rd edn 1742), pp. 210. See appendix 9 on p. 153.

[12] [Trenchard, John and Gordon, Thomas,] *Cato's Letters; or, Essays on Liberty, Civil and Religious, And other important Subjects.* 3rd edn. 4 vols. London 1733. Facsimile reprint New York: Russell & Russell 1969, letter no. 117 (first published 23 February 1723), vol. IV, pp. 96 ff. See appendix 16 for more information relating to these essays.

[13] For a discussion of the confusion, here quite explicit, between different kinds of egoistic theory, see p. 72 below.

provoked much wrath and much delight, depending on the reader's point of view, has already been mentioned. He was Bernard Mandeville, the notorious creator of a *succès de scandale* with the expanded 1723 edition of his *Fable of the Bees*.[14]

On the title-page of his first two treatises (1st edn 1725) Hutcheson made a point of advertising that the work contained a defence of the principles advocated by Shaftesbury against Mandeville. He also came out against Mandeville in three essays in *The Dublin Weekly Journal* in February 1726.[15]

How significant was this polemic against Mandeville for Hutcheson? To begin with, it is worth noticing that the reference to Shaftesbury and Mandeville was dropped not only from the second issue of the first edition (designated 1725(B) in the bibliography) but also from the second edition, which has the imprint 1726, although actually published already in October 1725, and from all the subsequent editions. The omission can be seen as an indication that the fashionable worldliness of some moralists was not a central concern for him, but that he regarded the polemic against Mandeville as a side-show of secondary importance.

Admittedly, some of the change of the title-page could have a different reason. In the preface to the later editions of *Inquiry*, Hutcheson expressed regret that Shaftesbury had taken exception to some aspects of Christianity, and that some persons had used him to justify their debauched theories and practice. In the *Lecture*, Hutcheson also signals that he does not completely endorse all the views of his philosophical master.

In Kaye's admirable edition of *The Fable of the Bees*, Hutcheson is described as Mandeville's most persistent opponent.[16] Taken in its strict sense, this statement only implies that *other* opponents of Mandeville were less assiduous, although it can easily be taken to suggest that Hutcheson saw this as his central aim. Jensen seems to suggest just that. He omits any mention of the conflict between Hutcheson's teachings and orthodox theology, and by this omission together with his statement that `there is hardly a work by

---

14 Followed by a further edition the year after, no doubt promoted by the judicial condemnation of the book. In T2, 1, 6 Hutcheson refers to the `3d Edition' of this work: this is probably the one dated 1724.

15 For some publication details, see appendix 10 on p. 154.

16 F. B. Kaye's edition of *The Fable of the Bees*, vol. II, p. 345, note 1. The change of wording on the title-pages of the *Inquiry* is not mentioned.

Hutcheson in which space is not devoted to attacking Mandeville's cynical egoism'[17] he creates the impression that Hutcheson's *only* aim was to refute Hobbes and his followers, such as Mandeville. The same impression is also conveyed by D. D. Raphael and many others, most recently A.-D. Balmès, who claims that under the influence of Hobbes, Mandeville, and Locke, egoism and relativism were the dominant moral theories.[18] Statements like these serve to play down Hutcheson's opposition to an influential religious doctrine. They were anticipated long ago by Victor Cousin:

> Hutcheson appeals to matters of fact and demolishes easily the philosophy of the London wits, the philosophy of the free-thinkers who thought of themselves as being the avant-garde of the human intellect, and had no idea that they were falling behind and returning to speculations many times refuted, as they confused moral with natural good and reduced all virtue to self-interest, motivated solely by hopes and fears.[19]

This is very implausible. Obviously Hutcheson had Hobbes, Mandeville and other reputed free-thinkers in his sights, but it is hard to believe that his full-scale philosophical campaign was conducted only in order to refute that kind of writing. After all, in the passage cited above at p. 34 he mentions first and foremost the pulpit and the schools, i. e. places where religion is at the centre. It would be natural for Hutcheson to have the climate of opinion fostered by religious teachings as his main concern. Turco concurs: Hutcheson's main target is the moral legalism of orthodox theology, and not Mandeville.[20]

---

17 Jensen, *Motivation*, p. 14.

18 Raphael, *The Moral Sense*, pp. 23, 31. For Balmès, see the introduction to her recent translation of Hutcheson's *Inquiry*, p. 8.

19 'Hutcheson, appuyé sur les faits, bat aisément en ruine la philosophie des *beaux esprits* de Londres, la théorie des *libres penseurs*, qui se croyaient à l'avant-garde de l'esprit humain et ne se doutaient pas qu'ils ramenaient en arrière, et revenaient à des spéculations mille fois convaincues d'extravagance, en confondant le bien moral avec le bien physique, en réduisant toute vertu à l'intérêt, et en lui donnant pour mobile unique la crainte et l'espérance.' (*Philosophie Ecossaise*, 3rd edn, Paris: Librarie Nouvelle, 1857, p. 86.)

20 Luigi Turco, 'La prima Inquiry morale di Francis Hutcheson', *Rivista Critica di Storia della Filosofia* 23 (1968) 39–60; 297–329, at p. 41: 'Va subito notato che, malgrado quanto esplicitamente suggerisce il frontespizio dell'Inquiry, il maggiore obbiettivo polemica dell'opera non è la Fable of the Bees, ma il legalismo morale dell'ortodossia religiosa.'

Behind this neglect of what must have been a major concern for Hutcheson is probably, at least in the case of Cousin, a certain apologetic tendency. It is likely, however, that what has led many commentators astray is a false principle of interpretation. It is rashly assumed that those attacked by a respectable philosopher must themselves be philosophically respectable.

Comparison with Butler

It is instructive to compare the concerns of Hutcheson and of Butler in this respect. Their theories have much in common. There are obvious affinities in their attacks on psychological egoism and hedonism, although for a long time the critique and rejection of these views have been more frequently associated with the name of Butler, whose first published statement came in his *Fifteen Sermons* 1726.[21] The book soon attracted attention in Dublin. Arbuckle, discussing the writings and sermons of ancient and modern theologians, singled out Butler for special praise:

> one of the best and most rational Volumes of Discourses I ever saw in my Life, I mean that lately published by Mr. Butler, the worthy Preacher of the Rolls.[22]

Hutcheson, who of course spent the 1720s in Dublin, would soon have become familiar with Butler's sermons, and indicated publicly his good opinion of them.[23] There seems to be no evidence that the two ever met, or had any direct contact,[24] but similarities between their theories have often been noted. One writer observes:

> [Butler's] view of things as a whole may be summed up in the

---

21 'This day is published Fifteen Sermons' according to an advertisement in *The London Journal* no. 359, 11 June 1726. Hutcheson's *Inquiry* had appeared in late February 1725 (or, according to Scott, *Francis Hutcheson*, p. 31, somewhat earlier that year).

22 *Hibernicus's Letters*, no. 101, 18 March 1727.

23 In the preface to *T3&T4* (1st edn 1728), p. xix. This passage was omitted in the 3rd edn 1742.

24 In Campbell and Skinner (eds.), *Origins*, T. Campbell states on p. 168 in his 'Francis Hutcheson, "Father" of the Scottish Enlightenment', that the two may have met in Dublin, and refers to Scott, pp. 26ff. But Butler is not mentioned on those pages, and Scott nowhere suggests that there may have been any meeting. I am not aware of any correspondence between the two; moreover, it seems that Butler never left England and that Hutcheson never went there.

one word 'teleological'. Human nature is a system or constitution, the same is true of the world at large; and both point to
an end or purpose. This is his guiding idea, suggested by
Shaftesbury, to whom due credit is given; and it enables him
to rise from a refutation of the selfish theory of Hobbes to the
truth that man's nature or constitution is adapted to virtue.[25]

It is not necessary to compare their theories here, or to discuss
the extent to which Hutcheson in his later writings was influenced
by Butler. But whatever similarity there may be between parts of
their theories, their aims and concerns were different.

Socially and ecclesiastically Hutcheson was closely associated
with the Presbyterian community in Ireland and Scotland. From an
early age (the standard anecdotes are all in Scott) he seems to have
reacted against the prevailing narrow theological spirit. It is only to
be expected that theologically inspired aberrations would concern
him much more than secular ones.

Butler's location was within the Church of England. The aberrations that concerned him, and many other Anglican clergymen,
were different. Frequently deplored was the fashionable ridicule of
the idea of disinterestedness and the prevalent 'prejudice against
public spirit'. Butler mentions 'that scorn, which one sees rising
upon the faces of people who are said to know the world, when
mention is made of a disinterested, public-spirited or generous
action'.[26]

The complaints against mocking worldliness and cynicism were
not uncommon among the Anglican clergy. Berkeley, for instance,
complained similarly that

> a cold indifference for the national religion, and indeed for all
> matters of faith and divine worship is thought good sense. It
> is even become fashionable to decry religion; and that little
> talent of ridicule is applied to such wrong purposes, that a
> good Christian can hardly keep himself in countenance.[27]

And, as we might expect, he complains, like Butler, that 'talk of

---

25 W.R. Sorley, *A History of English Philosophy*, Cambridge: Cambridge University
   Press (1st edn 1920) 1951, p. 163.
26 *Fifteen Sermons* (ed. T.A. Roberts), The Preface, ¶38, or *The Works of ... Joseph
   Butler*, Oxford: Clarendon Press 1874, vol. II, pp. xxiv, 142, 153.
27 Berkeley, *Essay towards Preventing the Ruin*, p. 70.

public spirit [is...] a matter of jest and ridicule [and is ...] treated like ignorance of the world and want of sense'.[28] Berkeley is no doubt describing what he experienced in the ambit of Anglicanism. He very accurately indicates this by referring to `the national religion'. Lukewarm, indifferent, or cynical attitudes towards religion were less evident among Roman Catholics, Presbyterians, and other dissenters.

To return to the main theme: whilst Butler had moved from his dissenting background to join the established church, Hutcheson remained in the Presbyterian fold. This, I suggest, explains the differences in emphasis. Butler had more occasion to observe the men of the world,[29] and the sterner kind of theology was not favoured in his church. For Hutcheson, who taught in Presbyterian institutions, fashionable worldliness would hardly be a pressing problem. He became involved in the theological conflicts that raged among the Presbyterians in Ireland and Scotland, and would have had few occasions to be upset by the mocking scepticism of the men of the world.

It is of course a matter of relative emphasis. The attempt to find a middle way between two extremes is well described in these words:

> In this state of affairs, when wit and refinement were associated with irreligion and libertinism, and religion and morality appeared inseparable from a sour, puritanical or hypocritical temper, there was a need and an opportunity for someone to work out a new intermediate culture, less cynical than that of the gentleman and less austere than that of the puritans.

This is how Basil Willey described the project that Addison and Steele had undertaken in the *The Spectator* (1711–14) and elsewhere.[30] It is a description that also fits Hutcheson, although his project was carried out at a more rigorous philosophical level. One

---

28 Berkeley, *Essay*, p. 82. There is much to suggest that these complaints were not unfounded. In Lecky's view, indifference or hostility to religion was indeed increasing in this period. See W. E. H. Lecky, *A History of England in the Eighteenth Century*, London: Longmans (1st edn 1892) 1910, vol. III, pp. 12f.

29 `... he was a man of affairs, with ample opportunity to become acquainted with the ways of the world'. E. Sprague, `Butler, Joseph', *Encyclopedia of Philosophy* (ed. Paul Edwards), New York: Collier–Macmillan 1967, vol. I, p. 432.

30 Basil Willey, *The English Moralists*, London: Chatto & Windus 1964, p. 238. On Hutcheson's view of Addison, see p. 49, note 47, and p. 57, note 64.

thing must, however, be added. Not only would the intermediate culture he sought be less cynical than that of the gentleman and less austere than that of the puritans, but it would also be less mercenary than the theologians allowed. He did reject the theories associated with the names of Epicurus, Hobbes, La Rochefoucauld, and Mandeville, and yet it is easy to understand that for him it was much more important to reduce the pervasive influence of oppressive and mercenary religious teachings.

Hutcheson's arguments against psychological egoism

Hutcheson did not merely reject psychological egoism, the theory that all action is motivated by self-interest: he produced *arguments* designed to refute it. He did so in the present two texts, and indeed in all his writings on moral philosophy. Only a sketch will be given here.

Some of the arguments have a simple structure. Hutcheson appeals to common sense and common *experience*, which are incompatible with psychological egoism in that they provide clear examples of non-egoistic motivation. Other arguments depend on the incompatibility between psychological egoism and certain *moral* assumptions. Of these, it is possible to distinguish two kinds.

One kind, prominent particularly in the *Reflections*, is designed to show that considerations of interest cannot give rise to the virtue that the moralists standardly try to inculcate. The point is made conditionally:

> *If* you want to retain your doctrine of virtue, you cannot consistently retain your egoistic theory of motivation.

The other side is, so to speak, left with a choice: give up your egoistic theory, or give up your moral theory. Since, in Hutcheson's opinion, the second alternative could hardly be taken seriously, the arguments can normally be put categorically:

> *Since* we want to retain our doctrine of virtue, we cannot consistently retain the egoistic theory of motivation.

When dealing with certain objections to his view, Hutcheson does, however, employ yet another type of argument. He makes use of a *teleological* theory, and introduces a distinction between what is conforming to nature and what is contrary to nature. It will be useful to consider some of the arguments more closely.

Irrational motivation

In paragraph 6 of the *Reflections*, Hutcheson refers to `a very ingenious author' who has argued that men's practices are very little influenced by their principles. We are perfectly capable of acting contrary to what we ourselves believe to be in our best interest. The appeal is to common experience: people often act against their best interests, from motives distinct from rational prudential self-interest. We can all be prey to emotional impulses, some of them irrational or self-destructive. It follows that not all our actions are motivated by self-interest.

The `very ingenious author' was Pierre Bayle who had argued this point at great length in his letter on the comet[31] and other writings. Chapters 135 and 136 of his *Pensées diverses* are headed *Pourquoi il y a tant de différence entre ce qu'on croit et ce qu'on fait* and *Que l'homme n'agit pas selon ses Principes*. He notes that people do not act in conformity with their convictions, not even about what would be to their private benefit, refers to Ovid's *Video meliora proboque, deteriora sequor,*[32] and tries to explain it.

There was no need for Hutcheson to mention Bayle by name as the proponent of this view. He could take it for granted that the reading public knew. Other writers did likewise. The following statement from a review article[33] provides one instance:

> We cannot say that every thing in this piece is new, The author of a book intitled: *Les Pensées sur les Comètes* ... has very justly [correctly] shewn us, in that ingenious performance, how much men in their manner of living deviate from their principles.

---

[31] *Pensées diverses*, 2nd edn, Rotterdam: Leers 1683. An early English translation has the title *Miscellaneous Reflections Occasion'd by the Comet which Appeared in December 1680*.

[32] `I see which is the better and approve of it, and yet I follow the worse.' Ovid, *Metamorphoses* 7, 20–21. Similar points are made in Note G to the article *Ovide* in Bayle's dictionary (2nd edn 1702).

[33] Of Mandeville's *Enquiry into the Origin of Honour*, in *The Present State of the Republick of Letters* 9 (1732), on p. 32.

In later works, Hutcheson did not use this Baelian argument again. The reason may have been that, to many people, Bayle's theological opinions and the sincerity of his professions seemed dubious, so that reliance on a view for which he was well known might easily give rise to suspicion. Some accused him of heterodoxy; others even of atheism. Even today the question of what his beliefs were remains a matter of dispute.[34]

The reason why Hutcheson did not subsequently use Bayle's argument may, on the other hand, have been the fact that Bayle's objection, ingenious as it is, differs from Hutcheson's preferred line of argument. Both writers argue that there are motives other than prudential self-interest. But where Bayle points to the influence of *irrational or self-destructive emotional impulses,* Hutcheson draws attention to the influence of *benevolence, distinct from rational prudential self-interest.*

Appeals to common moral opinion

In the main, Hutcheson's objections to psychological egoism are by way of a direct appeal to the common experience of immediate unselfishness, and to common sense, which does not hesitate to acknowledge its possibility. The appeal to common sense relies on the way we normally think, the way we normally respond to the way people act. One case in point is this: how do we regard a person who regulates his conduct entirely by an account-statement of his profits and losses in this world or the next? This is the question raised in paragraph 12 of the *Reflections.* We certainly do not have a high opinion of that kind of personal character. And if people really were like that,

> we should never find a man who could entertain such a thought as *dulce et decorum est pro patria mori.*[35]

The argument is that our praise of a noble self-sacrifice is entirely different from our praise of prudent rationality.

Another argument proposed by Hutcheson against prudentialist egoism is this. Suppose that the happiness of another person was clearly and obviously nothing more than a means to promoting

---

[34] See appendix 2 on p. 149.
[35] Horace, *Odes,* iii, 2. See footnote 31 on p. 20 above.

one's own advantage. Let us say that a wager had been laid so that one would win a vast sum of money if and only if that person was happy. We assume that the fact of the person's happiness or misery can be ascertained. One would then desire the happiness of that person. It is clear, however, that *this* desire for the happiness of another person, a desire which arises because the happiness of the other person is necessary and sufficient for one's own advantage, is entirely different from what we normally understand by benevolence. For benevolence, as we commonly understand it, is a virtue; but the desire that another person be happy so that one can benefit by winning the wager is not considered virtuous, rather, it is morally neutral.

There are quite a number of appeals to common experience,[36] for instance in paragraphs 22ff. of the *Lecture*. To mention only a few, Hutcheson refers to the love of offspring, the pleasures related to giving favours, the sense of gratitude, the immediate sympathy we feel even when our own interests are in no way affected, for instance when reading about events in distant ages and nations, and so on. Of particular significance is the discussion in paragraph 27 of the *Lecture* concerning the attitude of a man facing the absolutely indubitable prospect of imminent annihilation. In this thought-experiment, self-interest is ruled out. So is the prospect of pleasure at the future fulfilment of one's desire. And yet, a concern for the welfare of relatives, friends, or even mankind at large is not ruled out.

These appeals to actual or hypothetical experiences lead to the conclusion that

> There are, therefore, in man benevolent affections, which are immediately and often exclusively directed towards the happiness of others.

What has now been sketched is not the whole of Hutcheson's case against psychological egoism: in the *Lecture* he also deals with possible or actual replies to his arguments. We have, however, seen what *kind* of considerations he brings to bear against psychological egoism.

---

[36] As a curiosity may be mentioned Balmès's assertion, in the introduction to her translation, that Hutcheson 'deconstructs'(!) egoism by the accumulation of counter-examples.

So far, the arguments do not rely on general philosophical principles, but on what can be established by ordinary observation and reflection. As observed by David F. Norton, Hutcheson's method is observational; he urges us to quit the disputes of the learned and observe man in his common settings. This is also Leidhold's view. Hutcheson's objections all rely on statements whose truth can only be determined through self-observation. As Leidhold further observes, Hutcheson himself agreed that the opposite view was self-consistent although it failed to fit the facts of common experience. But Leidhold sees this appeal to experience as a weakness, detracting from the cogency of Hutcheson's objections – a debatable view.[37] The claim, often met with in the literature, that Hutcheson 'employs a Lockian epistemology to counter Hobbes's claim that all human action is self-interested'[38] is therefore doubtful. Furthermore, his reliance on a natural teleology, next to be considered, is certainly not Lockean.

Appeals to teleology

The evidence against psychological egoism provided by common experience is, it may be argued, by no means unequivocal, since there is very strong contrary evidence. Unprejudiced observation of human affairs, the argument goes, will create a strong suspicion, or even a firm conviction, that there is no such thing as genuine benevolence, and that all that passes under that name is spurious, or at best an unnatural artifice.

Doubts of this kind are introduced in the *Lecture* as objections requiring an answer. Why, it is asked, should good-will be regarded as more natural than ill-will? In the natural course of events, both can be observed to occur. To overcome such objections, Hutcheson employs a natural teleology: the view that a certain purposiveness, discernible by observation, is inherent in the nature of all things of a given kind. It is only to be expected that things will occasionally deviate from their proper course. An obvious example is the contrast between health and illness: health is the proper condition of a living being, illness a deviation. Similarly, the data of

---

[37] David F. Norton, *David Hume, Common-Sense Moralist, Sceptical Metaphysician*, Princeton, N.J.: Princeton University Press 1982, p. 65; W. Leidhold's translation of *T2*, p. xxv; Leidhold, *Ethik und Politik*, pp. 81ff.

[38] T. Campbell, `Francis Hutcheson', p. 168.

experience that support the egoistic theory are said to show only
that nature will occasionally depart from her proper course. Hume
noted Hutcheson's reliance on teleological assumptions, and disapproved:

> I cannot agree to your sense of *natural*. It is founded on final
> causes;[39] which is a consideration, that appears to me pretty
> uncertain and unphilosophical.[40]

When adopting this teleology, Hutcheson is influenced, as in so
much else, by Shaftesbury. The view is of course to be found in
Plato and Aristotle, and again in Cicero, who expounds it elo-
quently. It is in marked contrast to the modern philosophy of
Hutcheson's time: neither Descartes nor Locke accepted this part of
Aristotelianism, and the claim that one could by observation establish the proper purpose of things was rejected by them.

With Aristotle and the Stoics on his side, Hutcheson opposes the
stance taken by Pufendorf and Hobbes. 'We ought to judge nature
from her intention or perfect state',[41] he urges in the *Lecture*, against
Pufendorf, who explicitly states that by the state of nature he
understands not the best or most proper condition, but the condition in which men would be in the absence of, or in abstraction
from, various human inventions and institutions.[42] This concerns
the nature of society. As for the nature of man, with its various
kinds of impulses, some for better, some for worse, the same principle applies.

Hutcheson's critique of current theories concerning the precepts of morality

The precepts of morality were treated in accordance with a tradi-

---

39 *final cause*: a purpose or end, inherent in a thing or in its functioning.
40 From the letter to Hutcheson dated 17 September 1739, quoted in part in
   appendix 8 on p. 153.
41 Aristotle, *Politics*, 1, 2. T3 6, 7 suggests the same view of what is properly to be
   regarded as natural: nothing should be esteemed as characteristical of a species,
   but what is to be found among the best and most perfect individuals of that
   species. Cf. Cicero, *Tusculan Disputations*, I.xiv.32: 'num dubitas quin specimen
   naturae capi deceat ex optima quaque natura?' [Can you doubt that properly our
   ideal of human nature should be formed from the finest natures we meet with?]
42 *INC* 2, 2, 1. This has also been observed in J.-F. Spitz, 'Le Concept d'état de nature
   chez Locke et chez Pufendorf', *Archives de Philosophie* 49, (1986) 437–52, on p. 438.

tional division[43] used by Pufendorf in his textbook *De officio hominis et civis*, a frequently reprinted and frequently imitated best-seller.[44] Duties to God, to self, and to others are dealt with, in that order.

Duties to ourselves

When the subject-matter is divided up in this way, the word `duty' could easily mislead, and it could be preferable to use a different terminology to distinguish between the three areas of moral concern. This is particularly clear when we follow Hutcheson's discussion of the `duties' to ourselves. Of the three kinds of duty these get most of the attention in the *Reflections*. The discussion of them deals with questions of the right way to lead one's life so as to become a well-balanced, harmonious, and happy person; in short, how to achieve personal well-being. Hutcheson complains that this part of ethics was poorly treated by the scholastics, and subsequently neglected. This, he says, is a great omission, since `amidst Peace and Wealth, there may be sullenness, discontent, fretfulness, and all the miseries of poverty'.

Today, it would seem strange to bring this in under the heading of `duties' or moral rules at all – we tend to think of this as a *moral* matter only insofar as others are affected by our condition. Personal growth and the development of a sense of well-being are rather seen as belonging to the domain of psychology: self-development is no longer seen as a *moral* endeavour. Still, books on popular psychology, showing the road to self-improvement, *are* best-sellers, books on religion and morality *were*; the reasons for their success may be very similar.

There was, then, the general expectation, more or less vague, that the systems of morality ought to help people both to *be* better and to *feel* better, although, in Hutcheson's view, the current systems of morality left much to be desired in this regard. For one thing, he wished to encourage a certain outlook on life that he found in the best ancient writers, a mentality different from the one pervading the society in which he lived and, because of the predominant

---

[43] See appendix 5.

[44] See note 28 on page 19. - Hutcheson's attitude to Pufendorf merits further study. He regarded him as an important writer on moral philosophy and recommended his writings to his students. But on certain topics he differed, as is clear from the last paragraphs of the *Reflections* and some of the arguments in the *Lecture*.

influence of Calvinist theology. What he reacted against was a glum or dour view of life, a morose attitude of pervasive gloom, ill-humour, and sourness of temper. Such a mentality, far from being conducive to a happy and contented life, is indeed incompatible with it. The right kind of moral philosophy, he believed, would help us to overcome the cheerless and depressed mental condition induced by a certain kind of religious and moral environment, and would help to make us more harmonious and capable of a sense of joy.

As an illustration of what Hutcheson had in mind, we can select one of Arbuckle's *Hibernicus's Letters*.[45] It is an elegant piece of moral writing that makes its point gently, though firmly. Its edge, to put it colloquially, is against the killjoys of this world, against the kind of person who is hostile to and incapable of any cheerfulness.

The motto is from Seneca:

Humanius est deridere vitam, quam deplorare; adjice, quod de humano quoque genere melius meretur qui ridet illud, quam qui luget.[46]

Sir,

I have seen in some of your former papers a large essay upon *Laughter*,[47] which gave me very good hopes of your favourable attention ...

There is an unaccountable humour which prevails among some persons professing an extraordinary degree of devotion and piety, of not only banishing out of their own conversation every thing of mirth and gaiety,[48] but imposing a dismal countenance, and a reserved, if not sullen behaviour, upon all their acquaintance, as the sole condition of enjoying any share in their good opinion. A cheerful temper is with them a mark of want of Grace ...

---

45 Letter no. 34, dated 20 November 1725. *Hibernicus's Letters* pp. 272ff. The author is Arbuckle himself.

46 It is more human to laugh at life than to weep at it; moreover, the man who laughs at mankind deserves better of it than does the one who bewails it. Seneca, *De tranquillitate animi* (On peace of mind) 15, 3.

47 The reference is to Hutcheson's three *Letters* on that subject, in which he attacks Hobbes's account of laughter, and expresses regret that the author of *The Spectator* no. 47 [Addison] had adopted it.

48 Arbuckle's complaint echoes ¶4 of the *Reflections*.

> It has been my misfortune to reside for some time, in the
> quality of chaplain, with a very honourable and religious
> family, but unhappily far gone in this distemper; ...

The author of the letter goes on to complain of the excess of melancholy and austerity – the constant reminders of our mortality, etc.
and continues:

> But pray, where is the connection betwixt seriously regarding
> our latter end, and living as if we had our gravestone always
> before our eyes? Our business here is to do all the good we
> can... The best preparation for death is a virtuous life; and
> there can be no virtue without action, nor any action truly
> virtuous, which does not flow from a ready and cheerful
> mind.

> ... several passages of Holy Scripture are perverted, to justify
> this disconsolate sorrowful temper of mind.

Towards the end the author adds in mock resignation:

> If all this should not be able to prevail with some serious
> people to be pleasant themselves, it should at least influence
> them to make some charitable allowances for those of a more
> blithe and jocund constitution.

These are extracts from what might appear as a somewhat slight
and light-hearted *jeu d'esprit*. It does have a more serious under-
tone. It is sheer misery to be confined to the company of humour-
less associates, or to a society where people never smile.

Cheerfulness is a good example to illustrate the difference
between rival conceptions of morality. It was then thought to be
within the ken of a moral system,[49] but today, it is not a virtue
mentioned in textbooks or courses on ethics.

One contemporary expression of the tendency to confine
morality to duties towards others is given by John Gay:

> virtue generally does imply some relation to others: where self

---

[49] It is included among the virtues in Hume's *Enquiry Concerning the Principles of
Morals* (1st edn 1751), (ed. L.A. Selby-Bigge and P.H. Nidditch), Oxford: Oxford
University Press 1975. Hume also mentions " . . . that gloom and melancholy so
remarkable [i.e. noticeable] in all devout people". *Dialogues Concerning Natural
Religion*, (ed. N. Kemp Smith), 2nd edn. London: Nelson 1947, p. 226.

is only concerned, a man is called prudent (not virtuous) and an action which relates immediately to God is styled religious.[50]

With the emphasis Hutcheson places on benevolence in his moral theory, he does at times give the impression of being susceptible to the influence of this conception.

Duties to others

It is not only by neglecting 'duties to ourselves' that the scope of morality has been unduly narrowed. Even the remaining duties, those to others, have become far too narrowly conceived. Hutcheson complains towards the end of the *Reflections* that 'our later moralists' concentrate exclusively on rights and on perfect external duties, like the 'civilians', that is, legal writers. These paragraphs call for a few comments.

The tendency of which he complains had developed through the influence of the writers on natural law. Natural-law theory had become the core of moral philosophy, and was often regarded as synonymous with it. According to a historiography that had become widely accepted at the time that Hutcheson wrote, the theory was considered to have originated with Grotius's (1583–1645) *De jure belli ac pacis* (On the law of war and peace, 1st edn 1625) and to have been fully developed by Pufendorf (1632–94) in his major work *De jure naturae et gentium* (On the law of nature and nations, 1st edn 1672) and in his textbook, already mentioned above, *De officio hominis et civis* (On the duty of man and citizen, 1st edn 1673). These works were extremely influential. Their authors were generally regarded as the leading modern moral philosophers, and familiarity with them would be a matter of course for everyone who had studied at a university or an academy or who was interested the systems of morality.[51] So, for a

---

50 John Gay, *A Dissertation Concerning the Fundamental Principle of Virtue or Morality*, (1st edn 1731), in J. Schneewind (ed.) *Moral Philosophy from Montaigne to Kant*. 2 vols. Cambridge: Cambridge University Press 1990, vol. II, p. 404.

51 In *Passive Obedience* (1st edn 1712), *Works*, vol. VI, p. 43, Berkeley refers to 'men of so great note as Grotius and Pufendorf'. In a draft of 1719(?) for a speech in the Irish House of Lords, Molesworth wrote: 'I have not studied our common laws, much less our statutes; so much the worse for me. I wish I had. But I have read and known something of constitutions and the rights of nature and nations. I am

contemporary reader, the passing reference to the Law of Nature at the beginning of the *Reflections* would have been self-explanatory.

The conceptual scheme developed in the writings of Grotius and Pufendorf had gained wide currency. These are some of its salient features. Every person is by nature free and equal and has by nature a sovereign realm. Every trespass on this realm is an injury, a wrong. Every injury makes the use of force against the offender permissible. Rights in the proper sense come into being by voluntary acts. Rights thus created form part of the person's realm. Every violation of a right is therefore also an injury, a wrong. To every right properly so called corresponds a duty in another party to respect that right. It follows that every non-fulfilment of such a duty is an injury and justifies the use of force. The technical term *perfect duty* is defined as a duty whose non-fulfilment makes the use of force morally permissible. An *imperfect duty* is a duty whose non-fulfilment does not make the use of force morally permissible. Some writers, including Pufendorf, also devised the concept of an imperfect right to correlate with this kind of duty.

These concepts and postulates are at the basis of this 'theory of justice', which is often called Modern Natural Law Theory.

In particular instances, insistence upon the fulfilment of a perfect duty can be morally undesirable, for instance, if a wealthy creditor avariciously seeks to dispossess a poor but honest debtor. In such a case, the creditor may be said to have a 'right to do wrong',[52] and it is these rights, and the perfect duties corresponding to them, that Hutcheson called external. This topic is further illustrated in *System* (3, 1, 7, p.164):

> But this *shadow of right* [Hutcheson is referring to the superiority of husbands over wives] is no better than those which any insolent conqueror may extort from the vanquished; or any unjust sharper may obtain by some imperfection or iniquity of civil laws; or by the weakness, or ignorance, or inadvertence of one he is contracting with. To take advantage of such laws or forms, without regard to equity and humanity, must be entirely inconsistent with an honest character.

---

not quite unacquainted with Grotius and Puffendorf ... ', Historical Manuscripts Commission, *Report*, 1913, p. 283. He mentions them without explanation, since he could expect these two names to be well known to his audience.

[52] Though of course he has no right to *commit a wrong*.

Hutcheson's main complaint about rights-theories does not, however, depend on the undesirability of exercising these external rights. His complaint, one which he seems to have been the first to articulate, and which has often been heard subsequently, is directed against the tendency to identify moral theory with a theory of rights, and against the view that respect for a person's rights is the only important kind of moral consideration. His adverse comment on rights-theories is also of special interest because it is only in the *Reflections* that his negative attitude is made explicit.

Grotius and Pufendorf would of course have agreed that a theory of justice does not have the answer to *all* moral questions of right and wrong. But they tended for various reasons to emphasise perfect duties and the rights from which these spring, and devote much less attention to the imperfect ones. This is because the initial impulse, especially in the case of Grotius, was not to give a complete treatise on ethics. The same is true also of Hobbes, whose influence on Pufendorf is unmistakable. The primary concern was political, and the primary aim was to develop a theory of the conditions for peaceful co-existence.

The drift of Hutcheson's argument in the second part of the *Reflections*, the part dealing with the precepts of morality, is that moral philosophy has become more and more narrowly conceived. Duties to God have been relegated to theology, duties to ourselves have been neglected, and so have duties to others, except the perfect ones.

What is wrong with rights-based moral systems?

Why is this tendency misguided? Hutcheson's view is that a moral theory that confines itself to being a theory of rights, thereby confines itself to the conditions that justify coercion. A person whose response to the requirements of morality takes him no further than to the observance of rights has only reached a moral minimum. Such a person will observe only those rules whose transgression makes coercion morally permissible.

It is of interest to note that this argument presupposes a conceptual connection between the concept of a right and the permissibility of coercion in case of violation. A mentality for which such a minimum is sufficient is bound to be servile and mercenary:[53] for such a minimal virtue, impunity is the maximal reward. This is the note on which the *Reflections* ends; it resumes the one struck at the beginning with the verses from Horace, again confirming a debt to the best ancient writers.

Hutcheson's middle way

The dissatisfaction with moral theories to which the doctrine of rewards and punishments in an afterlife is essential could have made materialism, epicureanism, and atheism seem possible and indeed attractive alternatives. But at the time it would have taken considerable strength of mind to carry through a theoretical programme of that kind. Quite literally, one would have had to be an *esprit fort*. It would also have been advisable to be of independent means, or to have reliable patronage.

There was, however, a third way. Shaftesbury had pointed towards it, Hutcheson followed. As was observed earlier,[54] it can be characterised simply: it was the way that led back to the ancients. Hutcheson advertises this turn at the beginning of the *Reflections*. But it is also indicated in the first letter of his 'Reflections upon Laughter':

> The learned world has often been told that *Puffendorf* had strongly imbib'd *Hobbes's* first principles, altho he draws much better consequences from them; and this last author, as he is certainly much preferable to the generality of the *School-men*, in distinct intelligible reasoning, has been made the grand instructor in morals to all who have of late given themselves to that study: hence it is that the old notions of *natural affections*, and kind *Instincts*, the *sensus Communis*, the *decorum*, and *honestum*, are almost banish'd out of our books of morals; we must never hear of them in any of our lectures for fear of *innate ideas*: all must be *Interest*, and some selfish view; laughter itself must be a joy from the same spring.[55]

He certainly made no secret of it. The advertisement is there, on

---

[53] The merits of this objection will be discussed below, p. 61.
[54] See p. 34.
[55] *Hibernicus's Letters*, pp. 78f. First published in *The Dublin Weekly Journal*, 5 June 1725.

the title-page of the first edition of *Inquiry*: `the ideas of moral good and evil are established, according to the sentiments of the ancient moralists'. These words are followed by a quotation from Cicero's *De officiis* 1,14.[56] This is a feature of central importance in Hutcheson's moral philosophy.

Behind Hutcheson's wish to find a middle course between theological and secularising theories, with the guidance of the best ancient writers, lay a strong *moral* impulse. Here was the alternative to the unpleasant choice between radical free-thought and a morality of self-interest. His rejection of the latter is particularly marked in his choice of the lines from Horace in the beginning of the *Reflections*. The `principles of the ancients' to which he appealed would rule out legalistic and mercenary conceptions of morality.

Hutcheson did not see any difficulty in reconciling those principles with Christian religion, properly understood:

> It is certain that almost all the heathen moralists agreed with him *who spake as never man spake*,[57] that virtue consists in love, gratitude, and submission to the Deity, and in kind affections towards our fellows, and study[58] of their greatest good. All sects, except the Epicureans, owned that kind affections were natural to men; and that consulting the general public good of the whole, as it was the surest way for each individual to be happy, so it was *vita secundum naturam*, or *secundum rectam rationem*.[59] The Epicureans of the better sort, however they denied any affection distinct from self-love, yet taught the same way to private happiness, by reasons like to those used by Pufendorf, only without consideration of the providence of the Deity, or a future state.[60]

This is Hutcheson's reply to those who might complain that the moral theories of those pagans were incompatible with Christianity, and that if those theories were mentioned at all in university courses for students, many of whom would enter the ministry, it could only be for purposes of refutation. For Hutcheson, the virtues of virtuous pagans are genuine, and, as just

---

[56] For the full text see p. 170.
[57] John 7:46.
[58] *study*: efforts in support of, promotion.
[59] *vita* ... : life according to nature, or according to right reason.
[60] *Hibernicus's Letters*, p. 381. The letter, the first of the three discussing Mandeville, is dated 4 February 1726.

quoted, `it is certain that almost all the heathen moralists agreed with him who spake as man never spake'.

The style: ancient elements

Hutcheson's own moral theory has much in common with that of the ancients. But so too does his *style*, the form in which that theory is presented. His writings carry frequent allusions to the ancient philosophers and poets. In this, there is an expression both of his personal taste and of the spirit of the times:

> He read the historians, poets and orators of antiquity with a kind of enthusiasm and at the same time with critical exactness. He had read the poets especially so often that he retained large passages of them in his memory, which he frequently and elegantly applied to the subjects he had occasion to treat in the course of his prelections.[61]

Hutcheson's predilection for the ancient writers was obviously genuine, but it was at the same time consonant with the dominant trend of literary and polite writing. The French quarrel between the ancients and the moderns had found its first widely audible echo in England with Sir William Temple's *An Essay upon Ancient and Modern Learning* in 1690, which favoured the ancients, as did subsequently Swift, Addison,[62] and Pope. The defenders of the moderns had less of an impact than their counterparts in France.

The appreciation of the ancient writers was general, and references to them had virtually become a literary convention. Addison and Steele graced every issue of *The Spectator* (1711–14) with a motto from a classical author. The essays from this journal were frequently reprinted in the eighteenth century.[63] Hutcheson was familiar with them:[64] few if any members of the reading public

---

61 William Leechman, Preface to Hutcheson's *System of Moral Philosophy*. Glasgow and London 1755, pp. xx–xxi; *prelections*: lectures.

62 *The Spectator* 160 (1711).

63 Usually in sets of eight volumes. Apart from translations into French, Dutch, and German, *BLC* has thirty-six entries for the period 1714–1814, to which can be added many reprints of selected essays. It was not unusual for sets of essays first published in journals to be reprinted, e.g. *Cato's Letters, Hibernicus's Letters, The Letters of Atticus* (by Thomas Cooke), etc.

64 Addison's essay in no. 47 is discussed in the first letter on laughter in *The Dublin Weekly Journal* 1726. Other references can be found in *T1, T3,System*, etc. All the

were not. The *Spectator* essays had many imitators, and *Hibernicus's Letters* was only one of them, with a few lines of Latin poetry or prose adorning each essay.

No writer's name occurs more frequently in Hutcheson's writings than that of Horace. We can safely assume that he shared Arbuckle's appreciation:

> [Horace] is one of the authors of antiquity who can never be too much admired, for the beauty and variety of his compositions, the delicacy and justness of his reflections, and the inimitable art he has of always appearing new every time he is read; being every where so rich in sense, that we are perpetually making new discoveries in him, and may constantly apply to him *Milton's* character of that noble species of writing,

> Where more is meant than meets the Ear.[65]

The content: ancient elements.

Turning now from aspects of style and taste to the content of the theory, the lines from Horace, quoted at the beginning of the *Reflections*, are of special interest. By quoting these lines, with their edge against mercenary principles of conduct, Hutcheson actually signals his appreciation not only of an ancient writer, but also of a modern one. Many of his readers would notice that he in this way associates himself very closely with the views advocated by Shaftesbury, in whose *Essay on the Freedom of Wit and Humour*, in the *Characteristics*, some of the lines from Horace are quoted at the end of part 3 as a reinforcement of the preceding paragraph:

> I know, too, that the mere vulgar of mankind often stand in need of such a rectifying object as the gallows before their eyes. Yet I have no belief that any man of a liberal education, or common honesty, ever needed to have recourse to this idea in his mind, the better to restrain him from playing the knave. And if a saint had no other virtue than what was raised in him by the same object of reward and punishment, in a more distant state, I know not whose love or esteem he might gain

---

Spectator essays which I have seen mentioned by Hutcheson are by Addison. On the whole, Hutcheson thought well of his writings.

[65] *Hibernicus's Letters*, no. 59.

besides, but for my own part I should never think him worthy of mine.[66]

There are, then, a number of points of contact between Hutcheson and the ancients.

The role of moral philosophy. Hutcheson agrees with the ancients on the function of moral philosophy. It is not a pure inquiry; when properly conducted, it will affect people's lives positively. It will tend to improve relations with others and produce personal serenity and well-being.

Moral motivation. On the question whether the prospects of reward and punishment are a necessary motive, again raised in the passage from Shaftesbury just quoted, Hutcheson could find support for his view in many ancient writers. At the same time, Hutcheson does not altogether dispense with the view that the prospects of reward and punishment are necessary: they are necessary but only to motivate *some* people.[67] In Horace's formulation: they hate wrongdoing because they fear punishment (p. 80). For them, punishment is the *ultima ratio.*

This is an unstable position, but it seems that some of the ancients also equivocated on this matter. Plato introduces myths, but leaves the question of fact open. The problem is the one raised by the story of Gyges:[68] is it possible that, even in the long run, one *can* do wrong with impunity, that honesty is *not* the best policy? The ancient writers that Hutcheson primarily refers to were embarrassed by this question; so was he. The reason is simple. A positive answer offends our sense of justice, since those who have done evil should not be able to get away with it. A negative answer offends our sense of virtue, since it amounts to saying that it pays to be honest, which sounds mercenary.

Natural religion. There are similarities between Hutcheson and the ancients also on the relation between morality and religion. Many ancient philosophers had treated morality without assuming the close connection with religion that had come to be taken for granted subsequently.

---

[66] *Characteristics*, vol. I, pp. 84f.
[67] Viz. bad people. See *Reflections* ¶15.
[68] Plato, *The Republic*, 359d–361d.

Also, insofar as religion is at all relevant, natural religion – that is, religion based on natural reason alone without any special revelation – is enough. Hutcheson took particular care to develop at length the argument from design for God's existence.[69] His version of it relies, more heavily than validly, on alleged improbabilities.[70] These alleged improbabilities oblige us to infer purposiveness, and this purposiveness presupposes a divine mind. For Hutcheson, the natural functions inherent in things exist because of a divine designer and creator. From these natural functions we can read off what is good and bad relative to the kind of being in question, and then again we can read off the rules for right and wrong conduct. This is particularly emphasised in the *Lecture*.

In short: his theory of right and wrong conduct rests on a theory of natural inherent functions, which, in turn, cannot be conceived unless the world in which they exist is created by God. Materials for this eclectic synthesis of themes are furnished in ancient writers as, for example, in Plato, Aristotle, Cicero.

Rights. Another point of resemblance with the ancients is, negatively, the absence of any idea that a moral theory could be `rights-based'. This idea is as alien to Hutcheson as to the ancients. The rights-theories characteristic of Modern Natural Law Theory were unknown to the ancients; and although Hutcheson did develop a `natural jurisprudence', it was not supposed to cover the whole of moral theory, and his is in any case not a rights-theory properly so called: the concept of a right is analysed in terms of duties, and duties in turn are determined by the greatest-happiness principle.

Virtue-morality? In current debates among moral philosophers, the `return to the ancients' would call to mind some conception of a virtue-morality, in contrast to a conception of morality in which duties or rules are the key concepts.

It is not easy to give an adequate characterisation of the various distinctions that can be made under these broad headings, and a

---

[69] See e.g. *T1* section 5.
[70] `Of the enormous number of possibilities, just *this* one has been actualised – it cannot be due to mere chance!' ... etc. Curiously, even today arguments of this kind are very widely accepted. Also in Hutcheson's *Synopsis Metaphysicae*, 3, 1, 1-2, arguments *ex mundi fabrica* are presented with approval and a number of its proponents named: Plato, Xenophon, Cicero, Arrianus, Cudworth, Stillingfleet, Nieuwentijt, Ray, Pelling, Derham, Fénelon, Le Clerc, Nye.

discussion of this would here be out of place. We may note, however, that given such a contrast, Hutcheson can generally be placed on the side of virtue.[71]

It may, however, be useful to distinguish between *virtue-monism* and *virtue-pluralism*. Many of the ancients assumed that there are many virtues. On this important point, it might at first sight seem as if Hutcheson disagrees.

As for Hutcheson's own view, Leidhold draws attention to love in the Christian sense, agape, as the key to an understanding of Hutcheson's moral philosophy. Leidhold asserts that Hutcheson's basic position is that `all virtue flows from love towards persons'. This seems indeed to state unambiguously a virtue-monistic outlook. But the appearance is misleading. When quoted in full, Hutcheson's statement continues in a way that does *not* support this view: `all virtue flows from love toward persons, *or some other affection equally disinterested*'.[72] Here, there is an obvious suggestion that benevolence is *not* the only virtue. The same applies to the following statement:[73]

> If we could love, whenever we see it would be in our interest to love, love could be brib'd by a third person; and we could never love persons in distress, for then our love gives us pain. The same observation may be *extended to all the other affections from which virtue is suppos'd to flow.*

These statements obviously suggest a virtue-pluralism. But it must be conceded to Leidhold that there are other statements that clearly propose the simple view that actions and characters are considered virtuous insofar as they appear benevolent:

> the true original of moral ideas, viz. `This moral sense of excellence in every appearance or evidence of Benevolence.'[74]

---

71 A turn to a language of virtues in Scottish moral philosophy is diagnosed by Knud Haakonssen in `Natural Law and Moral Realism' in M.A. Stewart (ed.), *Studies in the Philosophy of the Scottish Enlightenment*, Oxford: Oxford University Press 1990, p. 72, and Hutcheson's moral theory is said to be basically a theory of virtue (p. 77). Haakonssen argues that this is a consequence of Hutcheson's opting for moral realism and his rejection of theological moral positivism.

72 *T2* (1st edn 1725), p. 137, section 2, ¶6 *ad fin.*; my italics. In *T2* (4th edn 1738), p. 157, section 2, ¶9, the word `Love' is replaced by `Good-Will'. Leidhold, *Ethik und Politik*, p. 14, p. 43, and *passim*.

73 *T2* (1st edn 1725), p. 142, section 2, ¶8; my italics.

74 *T2* (1st edn 1725), section 7 ¶1 p. 249. See also *T2*, sec. 3, and *Reflections* ¶5.

The standard interpretation is indeed that Hutcheson tried `to make the one concept of benevolence include the whole of virtue'.[75] But in fact there is an opposition between virtue-monism and virtue-pluralism which seems to have remained unresolved.

Curiously, there is a parallel in the way that Hutcheson himself wavers in his reading of Cumberland. He complains in the preface to the *Essay* and *Illustrations* that some `strange love of simplicity' has led Cumberland to take needless pains to reduce the laws of nature to one general practical proposition. He must have found Cumberland's theory unduly monistic: benevolence being the only virtue. But this complaint about Cumberland, in the first edition of *Inquiry into Beauty*,[76] was removed from subsequent editions. The reason may well have been that, on closer scrutiny, Cumberland's position is not unequivocally monistic. Alternatively, another possible reason is that Hutcheson's aversion to the simplicity of a monistic outlook had weakened.

One problem for virtue-monism is to show that justice and benevolence, which seem to be distinct, can be reduced to one. The usual approach is to explain justice in terms of benevolence. This question is relevant when assessing the argument against rights-theories[77] at the end of the *Reflections*, which concludes that a morality that confines itself to respect for people's rights would be servile or mercenary. The view that there is more to morality than rights has much to commend itself; but it could be said, against Hutcheson, that a person who is a strict observer of rights and justice, but uninterested in the rest of morality, may indeed be driven by a noble, disinterested, motive: simply an immediate respect for people's rights, a sense of justice. So a person who is only concerned about rights is not necessarily servile or mercenary.

There is, however, a possible rebuttal to this objection. The objection presupposed that there is a *distinct* virtuous motive of justice, but, it may be argued, in Hutcheson's moral theory there is no place for such a distinct motive, since, as far as relations with others are concerned, all morality can be reduced to benevolence. The sense of justice, the respect for people's rights, is then nothing

---

[75] David Daiches Raphael, `A New Light', in Damian Smyth (ed.), *Francis Hutcheson* [= Supplement to *Fortnight* no. 308], Belfast 1992, on p. 3, col. 3.

[76] *TI* (1st edn 1725), 3, 5 ad fin. On the seeming ambivalence towards Cumberland's ideas, see also p. 118.

[77] See p. 53.

but a form of benevolence. If that is granted, Hutcheson's challenge makes good sense. What should we think of a person whose benevolence is so limited that it only becomes operative in situations in which his non-performance is would be liable to permissible coercion? We should certainly have a low opinion of such a mentality.

If we grant the assumption that the sense of justice is a form of benevolence, Hutcheson's low opinion of those whose morality confines itself to a respect for rights has the merit of consistency. Whether we ought to grant Hutcheson the assumptions his argument needs is of course a different question. It is also an open question whether he consistently adhered to those assumptions in his ethical writings.

One might expect that when Hutcheson wrote his *System of Moral Philosophy* in the 1730s, he would have worked out a more definite position. In this work, he points to various powers and dispositions of which we approve. In the first instance we approve of the affections of the will that tend to the happiness of others, and to the moral perfection of the possessor, provided that the disposition flows from good-will (*System* 1, 4, 7). But that is not all. We also approve, without any reference to any good of others, of various affections and actions: innocent gratifications are one example. At a somewhat higher level, we approve of the pursuit of the ingenious arts and of knowledge, patience of labour, sagacity and spirit in business, etc., even if they are not exercised for the benefit of others, provided, of course, that it is not to their detriment.

At a higher level still, some dispositions and abilities, called moral dispositions, `distinct from both calm universal benevolence and the particular kind affections' (*System* 1, 4, 9) though `naturally connected with such affections', are immediately approved by our *moral* sense independently of any connection with a beneficent purpose or effect. The examples are fortitude, candour, openness, sincerity, and veracity.

Kind affections themselves are, however, more immediate objects of moral approbation, and the highest moral approbation is gained by the most extensive benevolence: the calm, stable, universal good-will to all (*System* 1, 4, 10). But not even this item in the ranking-list of virtues occupies the top place. The affection or disposition that heads the list is love of moral excellence, that is, love of good-will in people.

Hutcheson also has a reverse ranking-list of vices, mentioned here for the sake of illustration. In this list, the first item enumerates shortcomings that are not *moral* faults, and items 2-8 indicate increasing degrees of *moral* turpitude:

1 Imprudence, negligence, sloth, rashness, indolence; lack of taste.
2 Unjustified partiality: supporting a friend of insufficient merit to the detriment of the public good.
3 Weakness in the face of temptations or threats.
4 Sudden passionate motions of anger, resentment, and ill-will.
5 Injuries due to selfish passion and sensual appetite.
6 Injuries deliberately, calmly and selfishly designed.
7 Impiety.
8 Original malice; desire of the misery of others for itself, without any motive of interest. (Hutcheson doubts, however, whether the last is possible.)

Is Hutcheson, then, a virtue-monist or a virtue-pluralist? Hutcheson seems ambivalent. Benevolence is in some sense the principle of all *moral* virtue. On the other hand, there is clearly also a pluralistic tendency. The list of virtues is not confined to the moral, altruistic, ones, but includes all the affections and dispositions of which we approve without regard to our self-interest. Altruistic affections and dispositions are among these, but do not make up the whole list. The distinction that has to be worked out more sharply is that between altruistic dispositions, and those which are not self-interested.

Insofar as Hutcheson is a virtue-monist, he is closer to the Christian tradition, but also to the Stoics' very similar doctrine of universal benevolence as the one and only virtue. Insofar as Hutcheson is a virtue-pluralist, there is of course a similarity with Aristotle, whom he would have studied at school, and who also lists a plurality of virtues. It is probably this that led W.R. Scott to remark that 'It is worthy of note that Hutcheson has now [i.e. from 1730] fallen very greatly under the influence of Aristotle.'[78]

This statement is not correct with regard to the teleological assumptions in Aristotle (and in Plato, and also in the Stoics). These

---

[78] Scott, *Francis Hutcheson*, p. 212.

were always present in Hutcheson's philosophy. But it is true that Aristotle is mentioned more frequently after 1730 than before, as could be expected once the plurality of virtues is considered. Given the central theme of Hutcheson's theory, that we can decide to act, and that we can approve, on grounds other than self-interest, it would be possible for him to reflect that those other grounds need not all come under the heading of benevolence. A theory that incorporates that insight will easily have affinities with Aristotle's virtue-pluralism.

This kind of pluralism gives rise to a problem which Hutcheson would have found difficult to combine with his religious views. The problem is that the difference between the *moral* and the *non-moral* seems to fade away. It can be seen as spurious, or unimportant, or a mere matter of degree. This was precisely the view that Hume arrived at when he gave a more perfected form to Hutcheson's incipient virtue-pluralism in the *Enquiry Concerning the Principles of Morals*.

Early reactions to Hutcheson

Of the many early reactions, those to be presented below have been selected chiefly because they deal with Hutcheson's anti-egoist position. For reasons indicated in the preface, matters relating to his moral epistemology and ontology will be adverted to only in passing. Some of the information in the following survey may be new.

Orthodox theologians

The following statements by a historian of the Presbyterian Church in Ireland are very instructive[1]:

> Though the professor [i.e. Hutcheson] was a man of taste and genius, and though he deserves credit for checking that tendency to open licentiousness which characterised the philosophy of his age, his own spirit was decidedly anti-evangelical.

> His scheme throughout is so complimentary to human nature, as almost to supersede the necessity of an atonement and a Saviour.

> While the ethical system taught in Glasgow served to flatter the pride of human nature, it was also calculated to deceive men as to their state in the sight of God.

> The candidates of the ministerial office could scarcely have been exposed to the influence of a more insinuating, and, at the same time, a more dangerous teacher.

Also, Hutcheson is said to have held `very incorrect views of the way of salvation'. Another writer made the same point as follows:

---

[1] J. S. Reid, *History of the Presbyterian Church in Ireland*, vol. III. New edn, Belfast 1867, pp. 296, 297, 298, 305. Pp. 236ff. of this work were written by D.D. Killen on the basis of Reid's posthumous notes.

Though his theories were very beautiful, he taught a philosophy which sapped the foundations of evangelical religion, and
which was the more dangerous because of the glitter which
his beautiful speculations and eloquent Irish tongue threw
around it. With such professors [viz. John Simson, Hutcheson,
and Leechman] poisoning, at its fountainhead, the stream of
the ministry, it is not to be wondered at that the pulpits of the
Synod of Ulster began to give a very uncertain sound on the
great verities of the faith, and in some cases to ignore them
altogether.[2]

The statements just quoted are not contemporary, but it would
be difficult to find any that express more authentically the orthodox
outlook. At the time, there were many similar ones. The debate was
lively indeed, and the zeal of the evangelical party could yield
intemperate words and deeds. Less unpleasant and at times even
amusing was the anonymous contemporary satire `Ecclesiastical
Characteristics',[3] written by John Witherspoon (1723–94), who later
became President of Princeton College, and the only clergyman to
sign the American Declaration of Independence. He disapproved of
the high regard in which the writings of Aristotle, Marcus Aurelius,
Shaftesbury, and Hutcheson were held, and taunted the Moderates
with indifference to the doctrines of atonement, forgiveness, and
redemption. Hutcheson is the writer most frequently named or
alluded to.

Protestant theologians belonging to other churches also reacted
adversely. For instance, Siegmund Jacob Baumgarten (1706–57), an
eminent theologian in Halle, complained that by denying the
essential weakness and corruption of human nature after the Fall,
theories like Hutcheson's made revelation superfluous and gave
support to deism.[4]

---

2 T. Hamilton, *History of the Irish Presbyterian Church*, Edinburgh: T. & T. Clark 1887,
   p. 130. The author deplores with naive partiality the rising tide of error that
   resulted in the complete ascendancy of the `New Light' principles. One sign of the
   success of the moderate party is perhaps the fact that all the professors in Glasgow
   (except the mathematician Robert Simson) were on the subscription list for
   Hutcheson's posthumous *System of Moral Philosophy* (1755).
3 1st edn 1753. Now available in his *Selected Writings* (ed. Thomas Miller), Carbon-
   dale, Ill.: Southern Illinois University Press 1990.
4 J. A. Trinius, *Freydencker-Lexicon*, p. 326.

Prudentialists and hedonists

Many of the representatives of theological rational egoism remained unimpressed by the accusation of endorsing a purely mercenary account of morality, an accusation made by Shaftesbury and others and further argued for by Hutcheson.

George Berkeley

There was, as one might have expected, a reaction from Berkeley. But in the third dialogue of his *Alciphron* (1732), the target of his attack is Shaftesbury only. There is no passage that refers distinctively to Hutcheson.

This may seem surprising. The explanation is probably that this is an instance of a well-known phenomenon: the indifference of the centre to the periphery. On Berkeley's intellectual horizon, Hutcheson would have appeared as a writer of minor importance, a figure on the provincial periphery of contemporary culture. As a clergyman in the established church, soon to become a bishop, with access to the Court, where the Queen held him in high esteem, enjoying friendly contacts with the most eminent writers like Pope and Swift, Berkeley was not likely to assign much importance to the writings of a Presbyterian schoolmaster who had written in the spirit of Shaftesbury. To which can be added Berkeley's negative attitude to Lord Molesworth, Shaftesbury's friend, from whom Hutcheson had received encouragement and support. The hostility had been fanned by Molesworth's opposition to Berkeley's preferment.[5]

A number of other writers refer explicitly to Hutcheson. Among them are Gerschom Carmichael (1672–1729), Thomas Johnson (c1703–37), Daniel Waterland (1683–1740), John Clarke (1687–1734), Archibald Campbell (1691–1756), and John Gay (1699–1745). Some of their responses are simple reassertions of views that Hutcheson had argued against, but new arguments also began to emerge.

Gerschom Carmichael

Carmichael was professor of moral philosophy in Glasgow. He

---

5 See David Berman, `Dr Berkly's books', in Damian Smyth (ed.), *Francis Hutcheson* [= Supplement to *Fortnight* no. 308], Belfast 1992, p. 23.

died in 1729 and was succeeded by Hutcheson. In the preface to his *Synopsis Theologiae Naturalis*, dated 12 May 1729, he included a brief comment on the moral philosophy of some unnamed writers. That Hutcheson is the target of these remarks can hardly be doubted.[6]

Carmichael asserted that there is a universal motive for all human action, implanted in us by God. This motive ultimately determines all our volitions. Recent critics are wrong in condemning it as sordid self-love.

He agrees with a certain recent ingenious writer (certainly Hutcheson) that no reason suffices to determine our actions, unless there is an instinct which immediately determines our choice as soon as a certain quality is perceived in the objective situation. But, Carmichael objects, if more than one instinct is admitted, and thus different qualities in objects (and not only the one quality of serving the agent's self-interest to a certain degree) are capable of moving the will, there is no basis on which a person who follows one rather than another can be said to have acted better or worse. There is no longer any unique common criterion by means of which comparisons can be made. In particular, there can then be no ground for holding that morality should prevail over self-love, or vice versa. But if we admit that self-love is one universal motive, and indeed the only one, we can understand how it can serve as a basis on which we can be prompted to act morally by a demonstration that morality serves our self-interest best, all things considered.

Carmichael was also dismayed by the attempts to separate morality from religion, holding that a genuine moral philosophy must be based on natural theology. He alludes to the scruples that some people (among them obviously Hutcheson) have with regard to the doctrine of rewards and punishments in a future state, which, they think, is discredited because it reduces the moral interest to self-interest. His response is that there is no discredit to God or to morality in the fact that by natural necessity, due to God, all actions are motivated by self-interest, so that we are in this way impelled to seek our happiness in God.

Although brief, Carmichael's comment is of interest. He does not merely give a dogmatic reaffirmation of the common view, but points to the intractable problem that arises, both in theory and

---

[6] Gerschom Carmichael, *Synopsis Theologiae Naturalis*. Edinburgh: J. Paton 1729. The preface, pp. 9–12.

practice, regarding moral and non-moral motives, if neither can be reduced to the other or to a common basis.

Thomas Johnson

Johnson, already introduced above on p. 22, reasserted very clearly the standard view:

> he that reflects upon his having done an action which he thinks to be morally evil, will accuse himself, and be sorry for it, because he is conscious, that the breach of a moral duty will be attended with punishment. But when no such consequence is apprehended, there can be no such anxiety. What uneasiness can an atheist have in following any corrupt inclinations, provided he is but secure against halters, or disgrace, or other temporal inconvenience. Set these aside, and what uneasiness can there be, when the fear of God is out of the question. And so often a man can hope to prevent discovery, or can weather the disgrace or trouble, his virtue is at an end.[7]

Johnson also maintained that

> the only motive to action in general, or to any particular action, is, and necessarily must be, the prospect of procuring pleasure or avoiding pain, of some sort or other.[8]

Every agent, that is to say, is necessarily a pleasure-seeker or pain-avoider. Is there a hint here of a hedonism different from the the prudentialism previously encountered? On the whole, however, Johnson relies on the arguments of Locke, Pufendorf, and other representatives of the selfish school, and when rejecting the Stoics' non-mercenary view of virtue, he even ventures to assert that `Epicurus's notions were in that respect much wiser, and more philosophical than either Zeno's or Tully's'[9] – saying openly what

---

7 *Essay on Moral Obligation* (1731), p. 28f. J. Ferguson, *The Philosophy of Dr. Samuel Clarke and its Critics*, New York: Vantage Press 1974, p. 197, notes the close agreement between Johnson and Waterland and writes: `It is supposed that Waterland himself was partly the author of Johnson's work', but does not reveal by whom this has been supposed.

8 *Summary of Natural Religion*, Cambridge:Thurlbourn 1736, p. 43.

9 That is, than those of the Stoics. Johnson's remark is in sharp contrast to the high esteem that Cicero's works enjoyed in this period by most philosophical writers. That attitudes to Cicero could vary so is no doubt due to the eclectic quality of his

Pufendorf preferred to confine to a private letter (see p. 117 below).

Daniel Waterland

Daniel Waterland, a man of great learning and impressive scholarly achievement, was Master of Magdalene College, Cambridge, and became well known as a prolific controversialist.[10] In a sermon on self-love, it is said to actuate all our powers and faculties and to be the spring of all our movements. He argued further that

> there is no such thing as disinterested virtue [...] In opposition to the doctrine here laid down, some fanciful men have pretended[11] that any view to our own interest and happiness, is mercenary, and takes off from the merit of piety and virtue; leaving it less worthy of esteem: as if it were not sufficient for perfect love to cast off fear, but it must cast off hope too. Virtue, they say, must be entirely disinterested, separate not only from all low and sordid views of temporal things, but from all views whatever, all prospect of advantage, and chosen for its own sake only. But these gentlemen mistake the maxim of the old philosophers, from whom they seem to have borrowed their notion, attending more to the sound of words, than to the truth of things. The meaning is no more than this, that true virtue is not, cannot be founded on any low temporal regards; neither ought it to be forsaken, however unserviceable it may sometimes prove to our worldly interests or pleasures. True and solid virtue is indeed disinterested, in respect of any mean and sinister views, but not entirely and absolutely so. Those who pretend to follow virtue for virtue's sake, yet are used to heighten and magnify the delight and pleasure attending it. They plead that it is agreeable to nature, as food is to the appetite; as beauty, order, and symmetry to the eye, or to the mind. That is, it carries temporal pleasure and satisfaction along with it; and it is for the sake of that pleasure, they embrace and follow it. And what else is this, but chusing virtue upon a principle of self-love, self-love pursuing a

---

writings. Among his many admirers was Samuel Clarke, who wrote: 'Cicero, the greatest and best philosopher that Rome, or perhaps any other Nation, ever produced.' (*A Discourse Concerning ... Obligations*, p. 222.)

[10] Waterland is styled *disputeur de profession* in *Bibliothèque Raisonnée* 14 (1735) 135, with reference to an attack of his on Barbeyrac in *Bibliothèque Britannique*.

[11] *pretended*: claimed.

present satisfaction, making temporal good its end?[12]

Waterland refers to Hebrews 11, in order to reinforce his argument against the views represented by Shaftesbury and Hutcheson. There can be little doubt that they are among the 'fanciful men' to whom he refers.

There are, in fact, two different lines of argument in Waterland. One is that only a fool would be virtuous unless there was a prospect of reward.[13] The other is that one's benevolence or beneficence is selfish as soon as one is happy to help others. This argument began to reappear regularly in the debate; it has remained topical, and will be further discussed below.

His views obviously differed markedly from Hutcheson's. It would be a matter of some surprise if, as has been alleged, he recommended Hutcheson to his students. In fact, he did not. For the details, see appendix 11 on p. 155.

John Clarke

John Clarke[14] was at the time Master of the Public Grammar-school in Hull, and a successful author of Latin textbooks for school use. He had entered into theological controversy in 1725, coming out against Wollaston, and soon after he returned to the fray, writing against Samuel Clarke and Hutcheson:

there neither is, nor can be, any other Principle of human

---

12 Sermon on self-love, probably written in the 1720s (no. III in *Sermons on Several Important Subjects*, pp. 29–46 on pp. 33 and 35. The heading reads in full: 'The Nature and Kinds of Self-Love explained and distinguished: and the Boundaries of an innocent and culpable Self-Love, limited and ascertained. 2 Tim. III 1, 2: This know also, that in the last Days perilous Times shall come: For Men shall be Lovers of their Own Selves.' Also in Waterland's *Works* (1st edn 1823, vol. IX; 3rd edn 1856, vol. V) and, slightly edited, in [Anon.] *The English Preacher*, vol. I.

13 '... in this life, undoubtedly, virtue, in any high degree of perfection, is present self-denial and cannot be made *rational*, that is, cannot be *virtue* (for virtue and folly are not the same thing), without taking into consideration *future* prospects', *Christianity Vindicated against Infidelity*, part I (1731). In *Works* (3rd edn 1856) vol. IV, p. 54.

14 Not to be confused with John Clarke, Dean of Salisbury, author of *Enquiry into the Cause & Origin of evil* (1720), nor with John Clarke, younger brother of Samuel Clarke, Fellow of Corpus Christi College in Cambridge, who took on the posthumous defence of Samuel's theories. Also to be distinguished from Joseph Clarke (d. 1749) who wrote in support of and edited the sermons of Daniel Waterland, Samuel Clarke's main opponent.

Conduct than Self-Love, or a regard to Interest in this Life or a future.

. . . it appears to the last degree evident, that Self-Love, or a regard to Interest either present or future, of this Life or another, is the sole Principle of Human Conduct, which it seems impossible for Mankind to act in Contradiction to.

He also argued that injustice can be rewarding on single occasions, were it not for the fact that God has disposed otherwise, and this is why the rules should always be followed, and that Socrates had been virtuous for the sake of reward in a future state.[15] Clarke also had another kind of argument, used also by Archibald Campbell, which will be further discussed below.

Two kinds of theory can be discerned in the statements quoted so far. Initially there is a view of motivation which can be called *prudentialist egoism*: it is assumed that only considerations of self-interest can move a person to action. It is then argued that it is in the self-interest of every person to be moral.

When challenged, prudentialist egoism is often defended by arguments that actually support not it, but rather support another theory, one which may be called *hedonistic egoism*.[16]

Prudentialist egoism is the view that *the prospect of benefit to the agent* is a universal motive of action. Hedonistic egoism is the view that nothing can move an agent to action except the prospect of pleasure for the agent, produced by the satisfaction of a desire. What moves an agent is, it is claimed, necessarily the prospect of pleasure for the agent, no matter what it is that is desired. On *this* standpoint, anti-egoism is not simply starry-eyed optimism, but is turned into a conceptual impossibility, a logical absurdity. Anti-egoism is seen as a doctrine which assumes that an action can occur although there is nothing that can bring it about: like an effect without a cause.

Prudentialist egoism can be understood as a general statement, claiming to be based on solid empirical evidence. If challenged by

---

15 John Clarke, *Foundation of Morality*, York: Thomas Gent [1726] n.d., pp. 15, 27, 36; pp. 65ff.

16 The distinction between prudentialist and hedonistic egoism is explained with commendable clarity by Gregory S. Kavka in terms of a distinction between psychological and tautological egoism in his *Hobbesian Moral and Political Theory*, Princeton N.J.: Princeton University Press 1986, ch. 2, section 2.

contrary evidence, its defenders tend to shift their ground and adopt hedonistic egoism, which has the merit of being empirically unassailable: even the altruist, no matter how complete the absence of so-called ulterior motives of self-interest, seeks necessarily his own pleasure. It is a point expounded at greater length by John Clarke. His most important objection to Hutcheson is this: benevolence is an inclination, the satisfaction of which *pleases* the benevolent agent. So the benevolent agent is as selfish as the selfish agent: in every action, the agent seeks to please himself.

An anonymous defender

It will be of interest to pause to consider some statements of a writer who quickly sprang to Hutcheson's defence. The anonymous pamphlet[17] was designed to show that John Clarke `had carried the principle of self-love much too far, and that his heavy charge against the author of Beauty and Virtue could with more reason, be retorted upon himself'. The author of the pamphlet considers that Hutcheson `writes with uncommon ingenuity and greatly entertains the reader: but he does not sufficiently build *Virtue* upon *Reason* to please my taste fully'. A certain uneasiness is also expressed because Hutcheson `appears to pay but a low Regard to the Christian motives, taken from rewards and punishments'. In these two respects, the writer agrees with Samuel Clarke rather than with Hutcheson.

Still, the writer argues strongly in defence of Hutcheson against the egoistic theory of John Clarke. One of Clarke's arguments, that self-love is a principle common to all mankind, is rejected on the ground that even if this is so, it simply does not follow that benevolence is *founded* on self-love, since there could be two common principles, neither reducible to the other. Again, to Clarke's most important argument, from hedonistic egoism, the anonymous author's reply is that pleasure is the *result* or *consequence* of the affection working towards its object, but that there is no need to admit that every such affection is self-interested. This is a point that was also made by Butler at about the same time.

Returning now from the unknown defender, it can be noted that

---

17 [Anon.] *A Letter to Mr. John Clarke ...*, London 1727.

Hutcheson himself did not respond immediately, but two years later, in the preface to *Essay* and *Illustrations*[18], he mentioned John Clarke by name, described his objections as the most ingenious that he had so far seen in print, set out the reasons why he had preferred not to respond directly in a separate reply, and expressed the hope that the book, particularly the first section of *Essay*, would adequately answer Clarke's objections. In the preface to the third edition 1742, this passage is somewhat revised, and Clarke is no longer mentioned by name.

At this point, the 'death-bed argument', already mentioned, should be considered again. This important argument seems to be absent from the first two editions of *Inquiry*. Its first appearance seems to be in *Essay* and then in later editions of *Inquiry* and in the *Lecture*.[19] The reason is no doubt that it was an argument developed in response to the two-headed challenge from prudentialist and hedonistic egoism, and designed to apply to both. It tells strongly against prudentialist egoism. But that is not all. The argument also blocks the attempt to defend egoism by a switch to its hedonistic version, an attempt which might take this form: there is indeed a tendency to benevolence. But this is only because there is a natural tendency for everyone to seek his own pleasure. Now, seeing another person doing well can produce pleasure in an observer, and the prospect of another person doing well is the prospect of a future situation in which pleasure is produced in the observer. It follows, then, that even in benevolent action we seek our own pleasure, and our benevolent desires and actions have in view some pleasure that we expect to experience.

Hutcheson's death-bed argument can be used against this: what if we had no such expectation? What if we were faced with total imminent annihilation? We would not, Hutcheson argues, be indifferent to another person's happiness. But according to the egoistic theory we would have to be indifferent, since in the example all selfish considerations, all prospect of future advantage, all prospect of an experience of pleasure are ruled out. This refutes the egoistic theory.

---

18 *T3&T4* (1st edn 1728, and again in 2nd edn 1730).
19 *T3* (1st edn 1728) section 1, Art. IV, pp. 22–25; *T2* (3rd edn 1729 2, 5, p. 147; 4th edn 1738 2, 5, p. 148), and in the *Lecture*, ¶27.

Archibald Campbell

Whilst the writers named so far were not of the Presbyterian persuasion, Campbell in contrast, was a minister in the Church of Scotland, and became a professor at St Andrews. Like Hutcheson, he opposed the conservative Evangelical tendency and sympathised with the Moderate wing of the church.

Campbell's orthodoxy was questionable, at least from the conservative point of view.[20] He did not, however, show any caution in declaring where he stood. In the preface to his *Enquiry into the Original of Moral Virtue*,[21] he defiantly declared for the heterodox John Simson, who had also been Hutcheson's teacher, and who had been suspended from teaching in 1729, convicted, after many years of hearings and deliberations, of heterodoxy. Campbell wrote:

> I stand greatly obliged to the pious and learned Professor Simson, whose scholar I was for some years; and I am proud of being called his friend. And since it here falls in my way, I will take notice of one particular, which, I dare say, will bring no small credit to my book. My worthy and learned friend, the Reverend Professor Simson, Professor of Divinity in the University of Glasgow, did very carefully give several readings to this book when in ms. he corrected some things in it.

So far, it would seem that Campbell and Hutcheson are on the same side: against the orthodox party. They had both studied under Simson, at the same time.[22] Both have title-page announcements indicating their design to refute the author of the *Fable of the Bees* (Mandeville). Indeed, Campbell states explicitly (p. xvii) that, although their principles differ, Hutcheson and he are on the same side (against Hobbes, Mandeville, and other notorious writers).But against Hutcheson, Campbell reasserted the primacy of self-love, relying, like John Clarke, on the defensive fall-back position of hedonistic egoism.

---

[20] Charges of heterodoxy, in the event unsuccessful, were brought at various times against Campbell, Hutcheson, and Leechman.

[21] Edinburgh 1733, p. xii. For additional information on this work, see appendix 12 on p. 156.

[22] It seems that Campbell commenced his theological studies in Glasgow 1712 and Hutcheson the year after. See *Munimenta almae universitatis Glasguensis*, Vol III. Glasgow [Maitland Club] 1854, pp. 252f. Campbell seems later to have continued his studies in Edinburgh. Cf. *DNB*. On Simson, see also p. 110 below.

In the preface, Campbell explains that although he espouses self-love as the principle of all action, he is unhappy to be seen as a disciple of Epicurus and is concerned that `the ingenious author of the *Enquiry'* (Hutcheson) should express himself in the manner he does; Campbell does not complain of any scurrilous treatment or any personal reflections on Hutcheson's part: `he is of too polite and refined a taste, to prostitute himself to so unmanly a practice. I am only sorry, he would have the world to think of us, that we are no better than the disciples of Epicurus.' In the body of the work, Campbell then deals at length with Hutcheson's arguments against egoism. It seems that he consistently assumes that whenever we delight in something (e.g. another person's good fortune) or delight in doing something (e.g. endeavouring to promote another person's welfare) we (tautologically) take pleasure in it and therefore (here is the rub!) our motive is self-interested.

Campbell also quotes copiously from ancient thinkers, especially Socrates (as he appears in Plato and Xenophon). His purpose is to show that among the ancients, psychological egoism was widely embraced, and not only by the Epicureans. A return to the ancients, so strongly recommended by Hutcheson, would not lead away from psychological egoism. This point, which had also been made by John Clarke, does not, of course, tell against Hutcheson. He never claimed to be in agreement with *everything* that the ancients wrote.

John Gay

John Gay (1699–1745) argued that we all, by nature, inevitably and invariably seek self-gratification. But he gave the argument a new twist, by not denying that there is a motive of benevolence. But, he maintained, it has its origin in self-love. We discover early in life the pleasure of being approved, favoured, and loved by others, and desire this. We discover also that the method of obtaining this pleasure and satisfying this desire is by promoting the welfare of others. Thus, a habit of beneficence develops, and we forget its origin, and it becomes, at least in some people, a second nature.

The analogy is with a miser, who initially wants money for the sake of the pleasure it brings, but then develops a habit of hoarding and values the possession of money as an end, and not as a means only. Similarly a benevolent person initially wants to be beneficent for the sake of the pleasure it produces for himself (when others react approvingly) but then develops a habit of beneficence and values doing good to others as an end, and not as a means only.

In this sense, benevolence can be reduced to self-interest. Yet, it is doubtful whether Gay's view is contrary to Hutcheson's. Gay discusses the causal origin of benevolence, Hutcheson the motives of beneficence.[23] Nevertheless, the causal theory proposed by Gay helped psychological egoism to retain a semblance of plausibility, and gave it a new lease of life.

Other early comments on Hutcheson

The doctrines of man's natural corruption and man's inevitable egoism, had their defenders. But there were those whose opinions came closer to Hutcheson's. A full review is of course out of place, but it may be of interest to note a few early responses.

John Balguy and Gilbert Burnet

One of the earliest discussions of Hutcheson's ideas was that of John Balguy (1681–1748), a country clergyman. His view of the dangers of mercenary motives will be mentioned in the section on La Roche below. He had no quarrel with benevolism:

> That the Author of Nature has planted in our minds benevolent affections towards others, cannot be denied without contradicting experience, and falsifying our own perceptions. Whoever carefully reflects on what passes within his own breast, may soon be convinced of this truth[24] ...

but remained unconvinced by the theory of a moral sense. He defended a version of ethical rationalism, and argued against Hutcheson's theory of a moral sense, noting that morality would become something `arbitrary and positive' not only if it was identified with divine commands, but also, by parity of reasoning, if it was identified with instinct. That is, Hutcheson had correctly seen the problem with theological moral positivism, but had overlooked

---

[23] A very clear and helpful account of the difference between this Causal Egoism and other egoistic theories is given by Kavka (see note 16 on p. 72 above).

[24] *The Foundation of Moral Goodness*, pp. 7f.

the very similar problem with his own theory.[25]

The same applies to the questions raised by Gilbert Burnet (d. 1726).[26] He also argued in favour of a rationalist account which could avoid both the objections to egoism and the difficulties in the theory of a moral sense.

Henry Grove

Other writers were even more emphatic in their anti-egoist stance. Henry Grove (1684–1738), a Presbyterian minister, who was in charge of a dissenting academy in Taunton in Somerset, followed Hutcheson closely in his own major text. On the subject of charity, or the love of others, as opposed to self-love, he wrote:

> Some have thought (as particularly Mr. Hobbes, who herein, as well as in many other of his opinions, was a follower of the Epicureans), that the love of others, however disinterested it may sometimes appear, is only selflove in disguise.[27]

and in the following section Grove gives what is in effect a resumé of Hutcheson's arguments from `matters of fact': we feel spontaneous pity for those in distress; we take immediate delight in the joy of others; we have feelings, independently of self-interest, towards persons and events in distant ages and nations, etc.

Some early reviews

Other reactions to Hutcheson appeared in periodicals. It will be useful to record them here, since they have attracted little or no attention in the secondary literature.

To be noted only for the record is the review of the second edition of the *Inquiry* in the Leipzig *Acta Eruditorum* (1727), pp. 349–356. In conformity with the original practice of the early journals of the works of the learned, the review is an abstract only, without any discussion or evaluation. Special attention is given to

---

[25] See also the lucid account on pp. 319–24 in Mendel F. Cohen, `Obligation and Human Nature in Hume's Philosophy', *Philosophical Quarterly* 40 (1990).

[26] In a correspondence with Hutcheson in the columns of *The London Journal*. See the bibliography, p. 175 under *Letters between the Late Mr. Gilbert Burnet ...*

[27] Henry Grove, *System of Moral Philosophy*, London: J. Waugh 1749, 2, 8, 17f. See appendix 4 on p. 149.

the attempt to introduce arithmetic in moral reasoning.

Philopatris

A few weeks after its publication, Hutcheson's *Inquiry* received a very favourable `puff` in *The London Journal* no. 296, 27 March 1725. It consisted mainly of quotations, with a few brief words of praise by the signature Philopatris, and need not detain us here.[28]

Michel de La Roche

Michel (Michael) de La Roche (d. 1742)[29] reviewed the *Inquiry* in his monthly magazine *New Memoirs of Literature* 1 (1725) 51–7, by giving fairly long extracts, interspersed with positive comments. He later found opportunities to mention Hutcheson again, and it is clear that the rejection of a mercenary view of morality seems to have had a particular appeal for him. Thus, in a later issue, La Roche mentioned Hutcheson favourably, when giving a summary of the anonymous *A Letter to a Deist ...*[30] Although its author, John Balguy, emerged as a critic of Shaftesbury and Hutcheson in other writings, there are in this *Letter* important points of agreement or at least compatibility: virtue is essentially disinterested and merely self-serving conduct cannot be virtuous.

But even if self-interest can never enter into the nature and constitution of virtue, yet, why may it not be allowed to *accompany* her? There would be no inconsistency in this. Why

---

28 This review is reprinted together with the correspondence between Burnet and Hutcheson in *Letters*. For a discussion concerning the identity of Philopatris, and Hutcheson's contact with *The London Journal*, see appendix 16, pp. 159–67.

29 Margaret Thomas notes, in `Michel de La Roche: a Huguenot critic of Calvin`, *Studies on Voltaire and the Eighteenth Century* 238 (1985) 97–195, his `persistent advocacy of toleration and freedom of thought`. His rejection of Calvinism came to clear expression through his book on Michael Servetus, executed for heresy in Geneva in 1543. Even when La Roche wanted to consult primary sources, almost two centuries after the event, access to the relevant archives in Geneva was refused (!). There is a contemporary comment on him in *The London Journal* no. 378, 22 October 1726 that `he is more interested in Religion and Politics than Wit and Politeness`. Among other literary activities of his can be noted his participation in translating Bayle's dictionary into English, and the Leibniz–Clarke correspondence into French.

30 [John Balguy], *A Letter to a Deist ...* , London: J.Pemberton, 1726. La Roche's review is in *New Memoirs of Literature* 4 (1726) 48–51.

should one's past or future conduct have to be less virtuous, less disinterested, if one were to be told that it was actually going to be rewarded?

La Roche concludes his review as follows:

> When I consider that Men are generally very selfish, I am of opinion that disinterested virtue can never be too much recommended to them. I shall always admire these two verses, which the author of this letter doubtless approves as well as I:
>
> > Oderunt peccare boni virtutis amore;
> > Oderunt peccare mali formidine poenae,³¹
>
> I shall never trust a man, who has no other motive to abstain from evil, but the fear of hell-torments. But I shall trust a man, who practices virtue, because Reason (and consequently the Supreme Being) teaches him that he ought to do so.
>
> The author of the *Enquiry into the original* [sic] *Ideas of Beauty and Virtue* is called in this letter an *excellent writer*. I am well pleased with that encomium.

La Roche returned to this theme the following year, in an editorial comment to `A Letter written from Copenhagen ...'³² The letter describes `two savages from Greenland', that were brought over for a visit (one of them `a married man, and indeed he has a melancholy look'). The end of the letter is rendered as follows:

> They affirm that there is no religion among them, nor any knowledge of the Deity ... They abhor adultery, and though they are dispersed in the country, without any kind of policy,³³ or government, yet 'tis affirmed that they observe among themselves the rules of equity.

On this, La Roche comments:

---

³¹ Good people hate wrongdoing because they love virtue; bad people hate wrongdoing because they fear punishment. The well-known lines are a variant, probably mediaeval, of lines 52–3 in the quotation from Horace used by Hutcheson in *Reflections* ¶2.

³² *New Memoirs of Literature* 3 (1726) 177–9, in a piece headed `A Letter written from Copenhagen. October 31. 1724. Taken from the Bibliotheque Germanique ...' (i.e. from *Bibliothèque Germanique* 9 (1725) 206–8).

³³ *policy*: civil administration.

This last passage, and what has been said of the Californians above pag. 90 and 91,[34] show that Men have naturally a sense of Virtue, as it has been proved by the author of an Inquiry into the Original of our Ideas of Beauty and Virtue; one of the most honest and beneficial books that have been published in our days; a book that deserves to be read once in a year. I have given some account of it in the first volume of this Journal, Art. VII.[35]

Journal de Trévoux

Not all reviews were so warm in their welcome. In contrast, there is the more reserved reaction from the other side of the religious divide. The reviewer in *Journal de Trévoux*,[36] December 1726 seems, on the whole, to be more pleased with Hutcheson's theory of beauty than with his theory of virtue (which is also given much less space in the review). Hutcheson's attack on 'universal egoism' is mentioned with approval, but his attack on theological moral positivism is mentioned without comment, and there is probably an element of sarcasm in the observation that it would be unsuitable to present the algebraic treatment of moral science to the readers, as it has not yet sufficiently established itself in France.[37] In the concluding words of this long review, the reviewer mentions La Roche's favourable review, but is critical towards it and disapproves of his enthusiastic praise:

Besides, the Literary Memoirs of London have already spoken

---

34 In extracts from George Shelvocke's *Voyage round the World 1719–1722*, London 1726, in which these Indians' way of life is described as being simple, peaceful, virtuous, and harmonious, without discord or contention, so that nothing could be added to their happiness but the true knowledge of God.

35 I first came across this piece through a reference in *Neue Zeitungen von gelehrten Sachen*, 18.12.1727, p.1009. This illustrates interestingly how news was diffused in the Republic of Letters: from Copenhagen and then in turn to Amsterdam, London, and Leipzig. The German editor has used the English version and included the concluding editorial remark, except that he mentions Hutcheson by name, without comment but with obvious approval.

36 Its name was actually *Mémoires pour l'Histoire des Sciences & des Beaux Arts*. It was founded in 1701 and until 1762 edited chiefly by Jesuits attached to the College of Louis-le-Grand in Paris. See e.g. Cyril B. O'Keefe, S.J., *Contemporary Reactions to the Enlightenment (1728–1762)*. Geneva: Slatkine 1974.

37 'La science des moeurs par l'Algebre, n'est pas encore assez établie en France pour la proposer à nos lecteurs.'

of this work, and the journalist made his extracts like those who are happy to limit themselves to selecting quotations from a book in a way that will make others accept their own false idea of the work as a whole. The work certainly deserves high praise in some respects, [but] the plan is superior to the execution. [Although] the terminology and turns of phrase are in a pure and lucid style, the content remains veiled in almost impenetrable darkness, at least as regards morals and conduct.[38]

Bibliothèque Angloise

The reviewer in *Bibliothèque Angloise*,[39] which was edited by Armand de La Chapelle (1676–1746), was only moderately impressed. He commented mainly on Hutcheson's theory of beauty, denied that much support for this theory beyond some generalities could be found in the ancients, and maintained that in fact the theory was quite modern; it was not, however, original with Hutcheson, but its essential elements were to be found in Crousaz's *Traité du Beau* [1st edn 1715; 2nd edn 1724], of which an English translation was going to be published.[40]

---

[38] `Au reste, les Mémoires Litteraires de Londres ont déjà parlé de cet Ouvrage: & le Journaliste a fait cet Extrait sur le modèle de ceux qui se contentent de reciter quelques morceaux d'un Livre, par lesquels ils puissent faire prendre, à l'égard de tout l'Ouvrage, l'idée fausse qu'ils en ont conçuë. Cet ouvrage mérite, sans doute, de grandes loüanges à plusieurs égards; le projet est au-dessus de l'execution: avec un style pur et clair pour le tour & pour les termes, les choses demeurent dans une obscurité presque impénétrable, en matieres néanmoins de Morale & de conduite.'

[39] For the review, Hutcheson's reply, and the editor's comments, see *Bibliothèque Angloise ou Histoire Litteraire de la Grande Bretagne* 13 (1725) 280–2; 509-18. There is a very informative discussion, and a translation of Hutcheson's reply, in David R. Raynor, `Hutcheson's defence Against a Charge of Plagiarism', *Eighteenth-Century Ireland* 2 (1987) 177–181. For a discussion of the authorship of the review, see appendix 13, pp. 157 f.

[40] No such translation is mentioned in *BLC, NUC,* or *Bibliotheca Britannica.* J.-P. Crousaz (1663–1750), enjoyed a good reputation among the Huguenots in the Netherlands. The imposition of doctrinal restraints in Lausanne made him move from a chair there to one in Groningen in the mid-1720s, following Barbeyrac's earlier example and with his assistance, but he did not remain there for long. A century later, his reputation had declined. Victor Cousin (see p. 38) described his *Traité du Beau* as *un ouvrage insipide et ennuyeux,* and considered Hutcheson's to be the first modern treatise on aesthetics: a view apparently shared by Monroe Beardsley, who does not even mention Crousaz in his historical survey in the *Encyclopedia of Philosophy.*

In a letter to the editor, Hutcheson firmly rejected the implied accusation of having made unjustified claims to originality.

Bibliothèque Ancienne et Moderne

When Hutcheson first wrote to protest against the unfavourable review in *Bibliothèque Angloise* he mistakenly believed that it was edited by Le Clerc, an error that he would hardly have made if at the time of writing his letter he had already seen *Bibliothèque Ancienne et Moderne*, which has Le Clerc's name on the title-page.[41] Le Clerc's own review did not please Hutcheson either. He made a brief but acerbic reference to it in the preface to *Essay* and *Illustrations* (1st edn 1728 and 2nd edn 1730), subsequently omitted from the preface to the 3rd edn (1742). His dissatisfaction was caused by Le Clerc's remarks, but the explicit complaint is against the abstract given by Le Clerc `especially [...] that of the last section of the *Inquiry*, [which shows] either that I don't understand his French, or he my English, or that he has never read more than the titles of some of the sections.'

Le Clerc had also noted, though only in passing, the similarity between Crousaz and Hutcheson in proposing a principle of uniformity in variety as the criterion of beauty.

Like the reviewer in *Journal de Trévoux*, he did not care much for the attempt to introduce mathematics into moral reasoning, and rejects it rather sharply. His main objection in relation to the *Inquiry into Virtue*, however, is against the idea of a moral sense, a direct perception of moral good and evil, which he regards as an unnecessary hypothesis. It is obvious, he argues, that some of our moral ideas were introduced by revelation and remained even after the Fall, with varying degrees of clarity depending on the level of enlightenment in a society, whilst others arise from the perceived necessities of human society. On the whole, Le Clerc's preferred explanation is that we learn what is morally good and evil by instruction, which has its origin in divine revelation in ancient times, and that consequently there is no need to assume a special moral sense. He also expresses concern that the theory could be put to bad use by fanatics: if the difference between good and evil is a

---

41 The review is in *Bibliothèque Ancienne et Moderne* vol. 24 (1725) 421–37 and continued in vol. 26 (1726) 102–15.

matter of taste, feeling, emotion only, then there is no place for reasoned judgement, and irrational passions will hold sway.

Early reactions to Hutcheson: a summary

To conclude this section, a summary overview of early reactions to Hutcheson is in order.

Political aspects received little attention, chiefly because comparatively little is said about political matters in his early writings. We have seen, however, that a reviewer like Philopatris discerned and praised the moderate Whig political stance of Hutcheson.

Hutcheson's *theory of beauty* attracted interest, not least on the continent, where some early reviewers expressed doubts about its claim to novelty.

In matters of *religion* many writers emphatically rejected Hutcheson's moderate theological views in preference to the more orthodox ones. The focus of contention was theological anthropology: especially on the question whether human nature is thoroughly corrupt, sinful, and selfish. Hutcheson's more optimistic view did, however, have considerable appeal.

In *moral philosophy*, the attempt to introduce arithmetical reasoning in morals did not meet with a favourable response, and Hutcheson later abandoned it. In moral psychology, the anti-egoist theory of motivation is of course central; although it was resisted in a number of early responses, it also came to be widely accepted. At the level of meta-ethics, especially moral epistemology, the theory of a moral sense was of major significance: it came under debate immediately, and was soon to be regarded, by Reid, Hume, Smith, and Kant, as a theory which deserved serious consideration. If little has been said about the moral sense in this introduction, it is because little has been said about it in the two texts.

Hutcheson and present-day ethics

In the post-war period academic philosophers took an interest in Hume's moral philosophy primarily because of his critique of rationalism and his subjectivism, which could be interpreted as a proto-non-cognitivism. It is in this perspective that Hume is above all the author of one single paragraph,[1] the one in which Hume first observes that all the common systems of morality use *is*-statements at the outset, and *ought*-statements at the end, and then asks how the latter can be conclusions from the former. This has served as an important source of inspiration for many philosophers in the present century, who have advocated is–ought and fact–value dualisms. These dualisms are to the effect that statements of the former kind cannot alone imply statements of the latter kind. For instance, factual statements alone cannot imply a value-statement.[2] To this has often been adjoined the additional assumption that only statements of the first kind can be true or have some kind of objectivity, and that value-statements are in an important sense subjective. Hutcheson was read in the same spirit as Hume was read. For instance, Peach comments in the very instructive introduction to his edition of *Illustrations* that `it is in this controversy [with rationalism] that Hutcheson probably has the greatest interest for the present-day reader'. Furthermore, Hutcheson was seen, like Hume, as a precursor of modern emotivist theories of ethics, and according to Peach, `[Hutcheson] has a theory of the meaning of moral judgements that is thoroughly noncognitive'.[3] This has, however, been keenly disputed by David F. Norton and others.

---

[1] *Treatise* 3, 1, 1, the last paragraph.

[2] It is this *dualism* that has been a centre of lively philosophical controversy; that there is a *distinction* between the two concepts, fact and value, is of course uncontroversial.

[3] Peach, `Editor's Introduction' p. 78. Roy A. Sorensen, `Vagueness Implies Non-Cognitivism', *American Philosophical Quarterly* 27 (1990) 1–14, similarly asserts in

To approach the Scottish philosophers from this angle was quite
natural, given the predominant direction of interest within recent
moral philosophy, summed up in this statement:

> The central problem in moral philosophy is that commonly
> known as the *is–ought* problem. How is what *is* the case
> related to what *ought* to be the case – statements of fact to
> moral judgements?[4]

The relevance and interest of the moral philosophers of the Scottish Enlightenment for the present day was taken to be due to their
inquiries in the areas of moral ontology and epistemology. More
recently, however, another point of view has emerged.

In their time, philosophers like Shaftesbury, Hutcheson and
Hume, dissatisfied with the prevailing moral outlook and moral
theories, found it worth their while to turn to the ancients.
Approached in this spirit, it is no longer the `is–ought' paragraph
that first and foremost makes Hume an interesting moral philosopher, but the fact that he is the author of *Enquiry Concerning the
Principles of Morals,* the substance of which is a review and analysis
of the various virtues, copiously illustrated with examples from the
ancient moralists and historians. It is, incidentally, the work that he
himself described as incomparably his best.

In our time, a sense of dissatisfaction, similar to the one that
came to expression in the eighteenth century, has developed over
the past few decades, both with prevailing modes of moral thinking
in our culture and with much of our moral philosophy. And again,
as in the eighteenth century, there is a tendency, most conspicu-
ously in the form of `neo-Aristotelianism', to develop a better
approach by turning to the writers of classical antiquity.

To illustrate this, one can point to the similarity between
Hutcheson's complaint against those whose moral concern is
centred on rights, and Mary Midgley's statement:

> Rawls does not demand that we toe a line which would make
> certain important moral views impossible . . . he simply leaves
> them out of his discussion. This move ought in principle to be

---

endnote 3 that Hutcheson and Hume (like Ayer, Carnap, and many others)
represent moral non-cognitivism.

[4] These are the first lines of the editor's introduction in W.D. Hudson (ed.), *The
Is–Ought Question,* London: Macmillan 1969.

harmless. But when it is combined with an intense concentration of discussion on contractual justice, and a corresponding neglect of compassion and humanity, it inevitably suggests that the excluded phenomena are relatively unimportant.[5]

As in Hutcheson, the complaint is against treating what is only one part of a moral theory as if it were the whole.

Another obvious point of similarity is the revival of the view that not all moral concerns are other-regarding. All dispositions and character traits, including self-regarding ones, which are required for the full 'flourishing' of the person are counted as virtues.

It could be said, of course, that self-regarding moral concerns were never forgotten. In Kant and in the Kantian tradition, duties to oneself are part of the system. There is, however, an important difference. The duties to oneself are, for Kant, those actions which a person, to use a colloquialism, *owes* to himself. In contrast, the self-regarding virtues favoured by present-day 'neo-Aristotelians' relate to what a person *needs* in order to flourish.

The attempts, then and now, to cope with a moral and intellectual crisis show many parallel features. This adds present-day relevance to the intrinsically worthwhile study of the eighteenth-century moral philosophers.

---

[5] 'Duties concerning Islands' in R. Elliot and A. Gare (eds.), *Environmental Philosophy*, St. Lucia, Queensland: University of Queensland Press, at p. 171.

The texts

The text

REFLECTIONS ON THE COMMON SYSTEMS
OF MORALITY

An overview

This essay is a preview to the *Inquiry*. It was originally published in *The London Journal* with the signature Philanthropos.[1]

Being virtually unknown, it has not been much discussed. Many of those who have studied Hutcheson's life and work have been unaware of the existence of this text. This applies to the editor of the *Collected Works*, where it is not included, and to others before him, e.g. Fowler, Scott, and Jessop.[2] There is now, however, an excellent exposition by James Moore of Hutcheson's thought, with an interesting discussion in which this essay is given due attention.[3]

Hutcheson begins by quoting a passage from Horace; this, and his general approach, would place him close to Shaftesbury in the minds of well-informed readers. He then formulates his challenge: the 'systems of morality' do not seem to succeed in what they are supposed to do: to make people *feel* better and *be* better.

In paragraph 5, Hutcheson explains how he will conduct his discussion. He takes for granted that there are two major questions dealt with in the 'systems of morality'. One concerns *motivation*: why are people moral? Why should I be moral? The other concerns the precepts of morality: what actions are *right*? The first of these is

---

[1] The signature Philanthropos was used again by Hutcheson in the correspondence with Gilbert Burnet in *The London Journal* 1725 (see *Letters* in the bibliography).

[2] A. O. Aldridge ('A Preview of Hutcheson's ethics', *Modern Language Notes* 46 (1946) 153–161) identified it although, as noted by Turco, 'La prima Inquiry ...' (1968) but overlooked by Leidhold, *Ethik und Politik* (1985), p. 40, n. 27, he had been anticipated by Kaye, who mentions it in his edition of Mandeville's *Fable of the Bees*, vol. II (1924), p. 345, footnote, and p. 420.

[3] James Moore, 'The Two Systems of Francis Hutcheson' in Stewart (ed.), *Studies*, pp. 37–59.

dealt with in paragraphs 6-15 and the second in paragraphs 16-21.[4]

The text divides, accordingly, into three main parts. The first is introductory and articulates Hutcheson's view of the task of moral philosophy. The next two deal in turn with moral motivation and moral precepts. The table sums up this basic structure:

Introductory	¶¶1–5
Moral motivation	¶¶6–15
Moral precepts	¶¶16–21

Moral motivation

Hutcheson states that all virtue consists in benevolent affections: in love of God and love of one's neighbour.[5] This part of his paper has four subdivisions:

¶6   the motivation for virtue cannot be self-interested

¶¶7–8   a critique of the current theory of a religious basis
            for moral motivation

¶9   motivation relating to love of God

¶¶10–15   motivation relating to love of one's neighbour.

Paragraph 6. The motivation for virtue cannot be self-interested. In the present context, the emphasis is particularly on the fact that considerations of interest cannot give rise to the virtue that moralists want to inculcate. Such virtue consists in love of God and our neighbour, and cannot arise from considerations of private advantage.

Paragraphs 7-8. `Our moralists', Hutcheson complains, err badly on this matter. They make self-interest the only possible motive of good conduct. In addition to this, Hutcheson accuses Pufendorf of arguing from the usefulness of a belief in God to its truth. Hutcheson rejects this and points out that we can neither hold a belief sincerely nor feel genuine affection merely on the ground that doing so would serve our interests.

A brief comment on this may be in order. Hutcheson is probably

---

[4] Aldridge calls ¶¶10–15 the second half of the paper and describes ¶¶16–21 as concluding remarks. This description can easily mislead, even though it is true that the second *instalment* began with ¶10.

[5] See, however, the discussion on pp. 60 ff. above.

stretching a point. Pufendorf certainly held that without a belief in God there can be no fear of God, that without a fear of God there is no such thing as a conscience, and that without a conscience, human society would be impossible.[6] But it is doubtful whether he uses this as an argument for God's existence.

Paragraph 9. The alternative view is that God must be seen not as a strict master and severe dispenser of justice, but as a benevolent father.

Paragraphs 10-15. From the divine nature Hutcheson turns to human nature. In conformity with what had virtually become a literary convention, Hobbes is singled out for criticism. This had been a popular activity amongst writers ever since the publication of *De cive* (1642) and *Leviathan* (1651). There can be little doubt, however, that as was argued earlier,[7] Hutcheson's main target was certain theories prevalent among orthodox theologians.[8]

Hutcheson entirely rejects the description of human nature as being thoroughly selfish or malicious. He complains that the bright side of human nature is much neglected. In paragraph 11 he urges that there are in human nature many kind affections, that pure spite, disinterested malice, detestable wickedness are extremely rare, and that when we go wrong it is largely due to weakness or excessive zeal for some worthwhile end. Most vices, he suggests, are nothing but virtues taken too far. Many of these considerations reappear in the *Lecture*.

Having sketched this more engaging view of human nature, Hutcheson asks what a person whose actions were motivated in the way proposed by the criticised theory would be like. We would not have a high opinion of a person who regulates his conduct entirely by an account-statement of his profits and losses in this world or the next. And the idea of *dulce et decorum est pro patria mori* would not even make sense.[9]

Morally desirable attitudes in political and social contexts are discussed in paragraph 13. They cannot develop on the basis of the mercenary outlook under attack. With a better understanding of

---

[6] See e.g. *De officio*, 1, 4, 9.

[7] See pp. 36ff.

[8] Were Samuel Clarke and Wollaston foremost among those whom Hutcheson had in mind? This has been suggested, although neither of them was very orthodox. On this, see appendix 14 at p. 158. On Hobbes's egoism, see appendix 9 on p. 153.

[9] Horace, *Odes*, iii, 2. See p. 20 note 31 above.

human nature, love of country would be strengthened. That a better theory would lead to a better practice is stressed again in #14 which concerns dealings between individuals. Once more, it is not mercenary consideration that move us:

> The poor creatures we meet in the streets seem to know the avenues to the humane breast better than our philosophers: They never tell us we shall be damned if we don't relieve them. The old cant,'God will reward you', is of no great force: 'A wife and many small children', when we know they speak truth, has much more influence.

An obvious illustration to choose, given the conditions in Ireland at the time. `In every road the ragged ensigns of poverty are displayed.'[10]

In the concluding paragraph 15 of this section, Hutcheson concedes that there is a place for rewards and punishments, to keep the worst kinds of people in check. `But there must be much more to form a truly great and good man.'

The precepts of morality

So far, the question was: why should one do the right thing? In the second part of the *Reflections*, paragraphs 16-21, another question is raised: What is the right thing to do?

Hutcheson does not discuss wherein the rightness of conduct consists. This conceptual question is not raised. He addresses directly the substantive question: what kind of conduct is right? This is discussed in terms of the three types of duties.[11]

Paragraph 16. Duties to God are briefly mentioned. Hutcheson complains that the moralists bypass them, but here he does likewise.

Paragraphs 17-19. The duties to ourselves get most of the space in this second part of the *Reflections*. It is under this heading that we find counsel, inspired, it would seem, by Marcus Aurelius and like-minded sages, on how to cope with adversity and achieve peace of mind. Hutcheson complains that this part of ethics was poorly treated by the scholastics, and subsequently neglected.

---

[10] Editor's introduction, *The Works of George Berkeley*, vol. VI, p. vi.
[11] See pp. 47f.

Paragraphs 20-21. In the final paragraphs duties to others are discussed. As discussed earlier, these would become the whole of
morality, once we relegate duties to God to theology, and duties to
ourselves to psychology. Again, the complaint is against the tendency unduly to narrow the scope of morality: `our later moralists'
concentrate exclusively on rights and on perfect external duties,[12]
like the `civilians', (i.e. legal writers).

In this first publication of Hutcheson we have, then, the beginning of a comprehensively argued campaign against the predominant systems of morals. In his view,

> they were *false*, in that they misrepresented the facts;
>
> they were morally *bad*, in that they encouraged a servile and
> mercenary mentality;
>
> they were *harmful* in that they induced despondency in those
> who took morality seriously and cynicism in those who did
> not.

He expected the alternative outlook, advocated by Shaftesbury and
developed by himself, to have the opposite, beneficial, effects in all
three respects.

Editorial remarks

The text of the *Reflections* presented here reproduces a photographic
copy, supplied by The British Library, of a microfilm with the
press-mark Burney Papers vol. 205B, of *The London Journal*, nos. 277
and 278.

The original spelling and punctuation has been reproduced,
except that apostrophes in verbs and pronouns have been elimi-
nated, and the use of italics and capitals modernised.

The numbering of paragraphs has been introduced in order to
facilitate reference to the text.

---

[12] See p. 51.

The text

To the Author of the London Journal.

SIR,

I send you the inclosed paper, containing some reflections on our common systems[1] of morality, that if you like the specimen you may communicate it to the publick; and at the same time let your readers know, that they may shortly expect *An Essay upon the Foundations of Morality, according to the Principles of the Ancients*, in a book, entitled, *An Enquiry into the Original of our Ideas of* Beauty *and* Virtue. I am

SIR, Your, &c.

PHILANTHROPOS.

2. *Nec furtum feci, nec fugi, si mihi dicat*
Servus: habes pretium; loris, non ureris, aio.
Non hominem occidi: non pasces in cruce corvos.
Sum bonus et frugi: renuit, negat atque Sabellus.
Cautus enim metuit foveam lupus, accipiterque
Suspectos laqueos, & opertum Milvius[2] hamum.
Oderunt peccare boni virtutis amore;
Tu nihil admittas[3] in te formidine poenae:
Sit spes fallendi, miscebis sacra profanis.[4]

Hor. Lib.1 Epist. 16.

3. A very small acquaintance in the world may probably let us see, that we are not always to expect the greatest honour or virtue

---

[1] *systems*: theories, sets of principles; treatises.
[2] This should read: *miluus* (a fish).
[3] This should read: *admittes*.
[4] `If a slave were to say to me, "I never stole or ran away"; my reply would be: "you have your reward, you are not flogged." "I never killed anyone." "You will not hang on a cross to feed the crows." "I am good and honest". Our Sabine neighbour shakes his head emphatically. For the wolf is wary and dreads the pit, the hawk the suspect snare, the pike the covered hook. The good hate vice because they love virtue, but you [i.e. the slave] will avoid crime only for fear of punishment. You are prepared to commit sacrilege if you believe that you can get away with it.'(F.R. Fairclough, (ed.), Loeb Classical Library, verses 46–54, with minor changes.)

from those who have been most conversant in our modern schemes of morals. Nay, on the contrary, we may often find many, who have, with great attention and penetration, employed themselves in these studies, as capable of a cruel, or an ungrateful action, as any other persons: We shall often see them as backward to any thing that is generous, kind, compassionate; as careless of the interest of their country; as sparing of any expence, and as averse to undergo any danger for its defence, as those who have never made the law of nature[5] their study: Nay, we shall often find them plentifully stored with nice[6] distinctions, to evade their duty when it grows troublesome, and with subtile defences of some base practices, in which many an undisciplined[7] mind would scorn to have been concerned.

4. Nor shall we observe any singular advantages arising from their studies, in the conduct of themselves, or in the state of their minds. We may often find them sour and morose in their deportment, either in their families, or among their acquaintances; they shall be easily put out of humour by every trifling accident; soon dejected with common calamities, and insolent upon any prosperous change of fortune. Are all the efforts of humane wisdom, in an age which we think wonderfully improved, so entirely ineffectual in that affair, which is of the greatest importance to the happiness of mankind? Shall we lay it all upon a natural corruption in us, growing stronger, the more opposition it meets with? Or may we not rather suspect, that there must be some mistakes in the leading principles of the science; some wrong steps taken in our instruction, which make it so ineffectual for the end it professes to pursue?

5. All virtue is allowed to consist in affections of love toward the Deity, and our fellow creatures, and in actions suitable to these affections. Hence we may conclude, 1st, `That whatever scheme of principles shall be most effectual to excite these affections, the same must be the truest foundation of all virtue: And, 2dly, Whatever rules of conduct shall lead us into a course of action acceptable to the Deity, and most beneficial to mankind, they must be the true

---

5 The allusion is to Grotius and Pufendorf, and other writers influenced by them. See pp. 51f.
6 *nice*: fine, subtle.
7 *undisciplined*: untrained, uninstructed.

precepts of morality.' We shall enquire into these two Heads more distinctly.

6. Our affections toward rational agents seem generally incapable of being engaged by any considerations of interest. Interest may engage us to external good offices, or to dissimulation of love, but the only thing which can really excite either love, or any other affection, toward rational agents, must be an apprehension of such moral qualifications, or abilities, as are, by the frame of our nature, apt to move such affections in us. How ridiculous would it be to attempt, by all the rewards or threatenings in the world, to make one love a person, whom he apprehended to be cruel, selfish, morose or ungrateful; or to make us hate a person, whom we imagine kind, friendly and good natured? Some qualities of mind necessarily raise love in every considering spectator, and their contraries hatred; and where these qualities don't appear, we in vain attempt to purchase either love or hatred, or expect to threaten men into either of them. And this is the reason of what a very ingenious writer[8] justly[9] observes, viz. that mens [*sic*] practices are very little influenced by their principles. The principles he means, are those which move men to virtue from considerations of interest.

7. Now let us observe how our moralists inculcate these great foundations of all virtue, the love of God and of our neighbour. One of the great authors of morality (Puffendorf) reasons thus, as one would be led to imagine, from the chief argument he pursues: `All our worldly happiness depends upon society, which cannot be preserved without sociable dispositions in men toward each other, and a strict observation of any rules adapted to promote the good of society. Nothing is looked upon as more effectual for this end, than the belief of a Deity, the witness and judge of human actions; and therefore, as we expect to promote our civil interest, we should believe in a Deity, and worship him with love and reverence.'[10] As to the belief of a Deity, that author does indeed suggest other arguments for it than this, that it is necessary to support society, therefore it is true. And by suggesting other grounds and motives to love him, in different places of his works, he seemed sensible of

---

[8] Pierre Bayle. See pp. 43f.
[9] *justly*: correctly.
[10] See *De officio*, 1, 4, 2.

the deficiency of his grand argument, for, it is certain, that views of worldly interest are as unfit to beget love and reverence in our hearts, as to form opinions or belief in our understandings,[11] however they may procure obsequiousness in our outward deportment, and dissimulation of our opinions.

8. The greater part of moralists are indeed ashamed of this scheme; but how do they mend it? 'They first give us rational arguments for the existence and power of the Deity, and his government of the universe: He is represented as fond of glory, jealous of honour, sudden in resentment of affronts, and resolute in punishing every transgression of his laws: His natural laws are whatever conclusions he has made us capable of drawing from the constitution of nature, concerning the tendency of our actions to the publick good.' The better sort of our latter moralists always attempt to prove 'his good intentions toward the happiness of mankind; and hence infer, that if we co-operate with his intentions, we may expect his favour; and if we counter-act them, we must feel the severest effects of his displeasure'. Now it must be owned, that writers on this last scheme do really suggest one good motive to religion and virtue, by representing the Deity as good; but upon this they dwell no longer than is necessary to finish a metaphysical argument; they hurry over their premises, being impatient till they arrive at this conclusion, that the Deity will interest his power for the good of mankind, that thus they may get into their favourite topicks of bribes and terrors, to compel men to love God and one another, in order to obtain the pleasures of heaven, and avoid eternal damnation. But what kind of love can be excited by such motives? In humane affairs we should certainly suspect whatever was procured merely by such means, to be little better than hypocrisy.

9. With how much more ease and pleasure would an ingenuous mind be led, by the very frame of its nature, to love the Deity, were he represented 'as the universal Father of all, with a boundless goodness consulting the interests of all in the most regular and impartial manner; and that of each individual, as far as it is consistent with the good of the whole. Did we set before mens view, as far as we can, the wise order of nature, so artfully adapted to make

---

11 In the original, this comma is incorrectly placed after 'however'.

men happy: Did we let them see what variety of pleasures God has made us capable of enjoying by our senses, by our understandings, by our generous instincts toward friendships, societies, families: Did they apprehend the necessity of subjecting human nature to the friendly admonitions of sensible pain and compassion, to excite us to preserve our selves, and those who are dear to us; nay, to preserve the most indifferent persons in the world: Could we enlarge mens views beyond themselves, and make them consider the whole families of heaven and earth, which are supported by the indulgent care of this universal parent; we should find little need of other sort of arguments to engage an unprejudiced mind to love a being of such extensive goodness.'[12]

10. As to our fellow-creatures, it is much more difficult to give a tolerably engaging representation of them. Every body is furnished with a thousand observations about their wickedness and corruption; so that to offer any thing in their behalf, may make a man pass for one utterly unacquainted with the world. And yet without giving better representations of them, than our systems of morality do, we may bid farewel to all esteem of, or complacence[13] in, mankind: for tho' a strong humanity of temper may entertain compassion and good wishes toward such an abandoned crew, yet these wishes must be very joyless, despondent, and weak, if men are really as bad as they are represented. Many of our moralists, after Mr. Hobbs, are generally very eloquent on this head. `They tell us, that men are to each other what wolves are to sheep; that they are all injurious, proud, selfish, treacherous, covetous, lustful, revengeful: Nay, the avoiding the mischiefs to be feared from each other, is the very ground of their combinations into society, and the sole motive in this life of any external good offices which they are to perform.' We scarce ever hear any thing from them of the bright side of humane nature. They never talk of any kind instincts to associate; of natural affections, of compassion, of love of company, a sense of gratitude, a determination to honour and love the authors of any good offices toward any part of mankind, as well as of those toward our selves; and of a natural delight men take in being

---

[12] This is the end of the first instalment. There is an editorial line: `To be concluded in our next.' The second instalment, in *The London Journal* no. 278, 21 November 1724, is headed `The Conclusion of the former Paper'.

[13] *complacence*: tranquil pleasure or satisfaction.

esteemed and honoured by others for good actions: which yet all
may be observed to prevail exceedingly in humane life.

11. Could we lay aside the prepossessions of our systems a little,
and some of their axioms*, (better suited to an omniscient being,
than to poor mortals,) we should find, `That every action is amiable
and virtuous, as far as it evidences a study[15] of the good of others,
and a real delight in their happiness: That innocent self-love, and
the actions flowing from it, are indifferent: And that nothing is
detestably wicked, but either a direct study and intention of the
misery of others, without any further view; or else such an entire
extinction of the kind affections, as makes us wholly indifferent and
careless how pernicious our selfish pursuits may be to others.' In
this light it would appear indeed, that there are many weaknesses
in humane nature: We should find self-love apt to grow too strong
by bad habits, and overcoming the kind affections in their more
remote attachments; we should find too much rashness in receiving
bad notions, concerning those whose interests are opposite to our
own, as if they were men so opposite to the publick good, that it
were a good deed to suppress them. But for this goodly effect we
are often indebted to education, and to many a grave lesson which
nature would never have taught us. We should find men sudden
and keen in forming their parties and cabals, and so fond of them,
that they overlook the inhumanity towards others which may
appear in the means used to promote the interests of the espoused
faction. And yet notwithstanding all this, we shall find one of the
greatest springs of their actions to be love toward others: We shall
find strong natural affections, friendships, national love, gratitude;
scarce any footsteps of disinterested malice, or study of mischief,
where there is no opposition of interests; a strong delight in being
honoured by others for kind actions; a tender compassion towards
any grievous distress; a determination to love and admire every
thing which is good-natured and kind in others, and to be highly

---

* [Hutcheson's note:] *Bonum ex integra causa: et malum ex quolibet defectu* (The good
is brought about by an uncorrupted cause; evil springs from some flaw). Apparently a commonplace in the textbooks on metaphysics. I have not found the
source for this, but there are very similar statements in St Augustine, e.g. *mali
causa non est bonum, sed defectus in bono* (`it is not the good, but a lack of it, that is
gives rise to evil').

[15] *study*: solicitous endeavour.

delighted in reflecting on such actions of their own: And on the other hand, a like determination to abhor every thing cruel or unkind in others, and to sink into shame upon having done such actions themselves. We shall see a creature, to whom mutual love and society with its fellows is its chief delight, and as necessary as the air it breathes; and the universal hatred of its fellows, or the want of all kind affections toward others in it self, is a state worse than death. In short, we shall see in humane nature very few objects of absolute hatred, many objects of high esteem and love, and most of all of a mixture of love and pity. Their intention, even when their actions are justly blameable, is scarce ever malicious, unless upon some sudden transitory passion, which is frequently innocent, but most commonly honourable or kind, however imperfectly they judge of the means to execute it.

12. As to the method these moralists take to make us love our neighbours, I doubt much if ever the hopes or terrors of laws would have produced those noble dispositions, of which we have had many instances in patriots, friends and acquaintances. With what an ungainly aire would a good office appear from one, who professed, that he did not do it out of love to us, but for his own interest in civil life, or to avoid damnation! How fruitful should we find humane nature in distinctions and subterfuges, to avoid any laborious, expensive, or perilous services to their country? Were interest the only spring of such actions, a selfish temper, before it would act, would state an account with virtue, to compare her debt and credit, and be determined to action or omission, according as the ballance favoured her or not. A superstitious temper might be terrifyed by religion, to submit to the hard terms of a generous or publick-spirited action, to avoid damnation, and procure heaven to itself; but upon motives of interest, we should never find a man who could entertain such a thought as *Dulce & decorum est pro patria mori*.[16]

13. Were men once possessed with just[17] notions of humane nature; had they lively sentiments of the natural affections and kind passions, which it is not only capable of, but actually influenced by,

---

[16] It is agreeable and fitting to die for one's country. Horace, *Odes*, iii, 2. Cf. the references to this on pp. 20, 21, 22.

[17] *just*: correct.

in the greatest part of its actions; did men reflect, that almost every mortal has his own dear relations, friends, acquaintances; did we consider all the good-natured, kind solicitudes which they have for each other; did we see the vast importance of laws, constitutions, rights and privileges; and how necessary they are to preserve such vast multitudes as form any state in a tolerable degree of happiness, and in any capacity to execute their kind intentions mutually with any security: did men understand the distress, the dejection of spirit, the diffidence[18] in all kind attempts, and the uncertainty of every possession under a tyrant; these thoughts would rouse men into another kind of love to their country, and resolution in its defence, than the mere considerations of terror either in this world or in the next.

14. Again, in the more private offices of virtue, it is generally compassion to visible distress, assisted by gratitude to God and our Redeemer, which moves the religious to charity; and the bulk of mankind are most powerfully moved by some apparent virtuous dispositions in the miserable object along with the distress. The poor creatures we meet in the streets, seem to know the avenues to the humane breast better than our philosophers: They never tell us we shall be damned if we don't relieve them. The old cant,[19] God will reward you, is of no great force: A wife and many small children, when we know they speak truth, has much more influence. A visible distress, a shame to be troublesome, an ingenuous modesty, with an aversion to discover their straits, if we imagine them sincere, do seldom fail of success. We see then that gratitude, compassion, and the appearance of virtuous dispositions, do move us most effectually: And how little many of our moralists employ of their labours, in giving us such representations or motives, every one sees who is not a stranger to their writings.

15. What is here said does no way imply, that the considerations of rewards and punishments are useless: They are the only, or best means of recovering a temper wholly vitiated, and of altering a corrupted taste of life; of restraining the selfish passions when too

---

[18] *diffidence*: distrust, suspicion.

[19] *cant*: stock phrase. It is possible, however, that the intended sense is rather 'sudden Exclamations, Whinings, unusual Tones'. This is the definition given by Steele in *The Spectator* no. 147 (ed. Bond, vol. 2, p. 80).

strong, and of turning them to the side of virtue; and of rousing us to attention and consideration, that we may not be led into wrong measures of good from partial views, or too strong attachments to parties. But still there must be much more to form a truly great and good man.

16. The second subject, was to consider the rules of conduct laid down by moralists as to particular duties of life. As for our duty to the Deity, we are recommended to other instructors: The moralists treat this subject very superficially.

17. As to our duties to our selves, they give us many directions to restrain our passions. 'We are told that they hurry us into violations of laws, and expose us to their penalties; that many of these passions are immediately uneasy and tormenting, even in their own nature.' These are no doubt just conclusions from reason and experience. But then a passion is not always flexible by reasons of interest. A man in deep sorrow will not be immediately easy, upon your demonstrating that his sorrow can be of no advantage to him, but is certainly pernicious. Anger, jealousy, fear, and most other passions, are not suppressed by proving that we are the worse for them. The only way to remove them, is to give just ideas of their objects. Shew to a sorrowful, dejected mind, that its state may still be happy: let it see that its loss is repairable, or that it has still an opportunity of valuable enjoyments in life: If it mourns the loss of a friend, let it see that death is no great evil; and let other friendships and kind affections be raised, and this will more easily remove the sorrow. Let the wrathful man see that the resented actions have been only the effects of inadvertency or weakness, or, at worst, of strong self-love; and not of deliberate malice, or a design to affront; and he will find few occasions for his passion, when he's convinced that he has not to do with devils, who delight in mischief, but with good-natured, tho' weak and fallible men. Let the coward see, that the prolonging life which must soon end, is but a sorry purchase, when made by the loss of liberty, friendship, honour and esteem. The covetous and ambitious must surely feel the uneasiness of their passions, and yet they still continue slaves to them, till once you convince them, that the enjoyments of the highest stations and fortunes, are very little above those which may be obtained in very moderate circumstances. Unless just representations be given of the

objects of our passions, all external arguments will be but rowing against the stream; an endless labour, while the passions themselves do not take a more reasonable turn, upon juster apprehensions of the affairs about which they are employed.

18. The school-men in their morals, by their debates about the *Summum Bonum* [the highest good], would make one expect just representations of all the objects which sollicit our affections; but they flew so high, immediately to the beatifick vision and fruition, and so lightly passed over, with some trite common-place remarks, all ordinary human affairs, that one must be well advanced in a visionary temper to be profited by them. They seldom mention the delights of humanity, good nature, kindness, mutual love, friendships, societies of virtuous persons. They scarce ever spend a word upon the earthly subjects of laborious diligence in some honest employment; which yet we see to be the ordinary step, by which we mount into a capacity of doing offices.[20] And hence it is, that we find more virtuous actions in the life of one diligent good-natured trader, than in a whole sect of such speculative pretenders to wisdom.

19. The later moralists, observing the trifling of the school-men, have very much left out of their systems, all enquiries into happiness, and speak only of the external advantages of peace and wealth in the societies where we live. But this is, no doubt, a great omission, since amidst peace and wealth, there may be sullenness, discontent, fretfulness, and all the miseries of poverty.

20. As to our duty toward others, our later moralists hurry over all other things till they come to the doctrine of rights, and proper injuries; and like the civilians,[21] whose only business it is to teach how far refractory or knavish men should be compelled by force, they spend all their reasonings upon perfect or external[22] rights. We never hear a generous sentiment from them any further. 'Some borrowed goods, for instance, perish by an accident, which would not have befallen them with the proprietor. This accident is no way chargeable upon any negligence in the borrower. Who shall bear

---

20 *doing offices*: showing kindness, doing favours, to a person.
21 *civilian*: an expert on civil law, a jurisprudentialist.
22 The three varieties of rights: perfect, imperfect, and external, are explained in the last section of T2. See also p. 52.

the loss? A generous lender would think with himself, Am I far wealthier than the borrower? I can more easily bear the loss. The borrower, in like case of superior wealth, would reason the same way. If their wealth was equal, each would bear his share; or an honest neighbour, if the loan was gratuitous, would scorn to let any man repent of his having done him a kindness.' But thoughts of this kind never come into the heads of many of these moralists. Mankind are, with them, all resty[23] villains: Our only inquiry is, which side will it be most convenient to compel? This question is indeed very necessary too, because there are bad men who need compulsion to their duty. But may not better sentiments prevail with a great many? All men are not incorrigible villains. There are still a great many who can be moved with sentiments of honour and humanity.

21. Should we run over other matters of right, we shall find them treated in the same manner. Seldom ever a generous, or manly sentiment. We only see how far in many cases the civil peace requires that we should force men to action: And we see, at the same time, how far we may play the villain with impunity, when we can evade their great foundation of virtue, viz. the force of a penalty. In short, according to the motto prefixed to this essay, `The avoiding the prison or the gallows, appears a sufficient reward for the virtue which many of our systems seem to inspire.'

PHILANTHROPOS.

---

[23] *resty*: unruly.

INAUGURAL LECTURE ON THE SOCIAL NATURE OF MAN

An overview

There is a contemporary report of the occasion of Hutcheson's inaugural lecture by Robert Wodrow (1679–1734), a minister and indefatigable chronicler.[1]

> *November*. Upon the 3rd of this month Mr. Francis Hutcheson was publickly admitted, and had his inaugural discourse. It's in print, and I need say no more of it. He had not time, I knou, to form it, and it's upon a very safe generall subject. I knou he communicat it to Mr. M'Laurin and Mr. Anderson,[2] and som little amendments were made upon it, of no great importance. He delivered it very fast and lou, being a modest man, and it was not well understood. His character and carriage seems prudent and cautious, and that will be the best vidimus[3] of him.

Neither then, nor subsequently, has there been much comment on or discussion of this lecture. One reason is that it was published in Latin, at a time when the lively and fruitful British debate on moral philosophy was predominantly conducted in the vernacular. Also, it would have had a limited circulation, being published in Glasgow, and many of the arguments do of course have counter-

---

[1] Robert Wodrow, *Analecta or Materials for a History of Remarkable Providences*, vol. IV, ed. M[atthew] L[eisman], Edinburgh [Maitland Club] 1843, p. 186. The editor gives 30th as the date. My suspicion about the date was confirmed by M.A. Stewart, who kindly informed me of the result of his close inspection of the original manuscript in the National Library of Scotland.

[2] John MacLaurin (1693–1754), in Glasgow from 1723, was a well-regarded preacher and theologian; William Anderson was professor of ecclesiastical history at Glasgow from 1721 until his death 1752.

[3] *vidimus*: inspection, examination.

parts in other writings by Hutcheson.

It has, however, been observed recently that in this lecture Hutcheson argues more carefully and in greater detail than in his subsequent compend, that is, the Latin and English versions of his *Short Introduction to Moral Philosophy*, and the posthumously published *System of Moral Philosophy*.[4] Hutcheson himself expressed dissatisfaction with his later works, on the ground that in his position at Glasgow he did not find sufficient time and opportunity to devote himself to extended periods of concentrated reflection and writing. The lecture can therefore be regarded an important and quite authoritative statement of Hutcheson's position.[5]

As for the quality of Hutcheson's Latin, McCosh considered it good, Leechman praised Hutcheson's `spirit and purity of style, seldom to be met with in modern Latin compositions', and Hume commented favourably on the language of the Latin *Compend*.[6] Latin was used because this was an academic oration held on a solemn occasion. In ordinary teaching, Hutcheson was one of those who pioneered the use of the vernacular.

The structure of the text

The lecture has the following structure:

1. Introduction (¶¶1–6)
   (i) Introductory courtesies (¶¶1–3)
   (ii) Choice of topic for the lecture (¶¶4–6)

---

[4] `Es ist unverständlich, warum Hutcheson seine Antrittsvorlesung, in der er sorgfältiger und ausführlicher argumentiert, weder in das "System" noch in die "Short Introduction" eingearbeitet hat. Hier wird deutlich, daß diese späten Schriften in sehr unfertigem Zustand publiziert wurden, und daß die Unzufriedenheit sehr berechtigt war, die Hutcheson selbst zu diesen Werken geäussert hatte.' Leidhold, *Ethik und Politik*, p. 224, note 47. I wish to thank Knud Haakonssen for first having drawn my attention to Leidhold, and also for having in many other ways been generously helpful to my inquiries in this area.

[5] G. de Crescenzo, *Francis Hutcheson e il suo tempo*, Turin: Taylor 1968, devotes a chapter to this lecture. More recently, it has received due attention in Moore, `The Two Systems', in Stewart (ed.), *Studies*.

[6] J. McCosh, *The Scottish Philosophy*, London 1875, p. 59. In a letter dated 10 January 1743, Hume wrote to Hutcheson: `I am surprised that you should have been so diffident about your Latin. I have not wrote any, in that language, these many years, and cannot pretend to judge of particular words and phrases. But the turn of the whole seems to me very pure, and even easy and elegant.'

2. Discussion of man's social nature (¶¶7–38)
   (i) What does it mean to say that something is *natural* generally? (¶¶7–10)
   (ii) What does it mean to say that something is *natural to man*? (¶¶11–12)
   (iii) Is *social life* natural to man? (¶¶13–38)
   > 13–17: The concept of *social life* analysed more closely: discussion of the concept of a state of nature.
   > 18–20: Elaboration and proper formulation of the question: Is social life natural to man? The prudentialist and benevolist alternatives.
   > 21: The prudentialist answer.
   > 22–27: Rejection of the prudentialist answer, with arguments supporting benevolism.
   > 28–37: Objections to benevolism, with replies.
   > 38: Restatement of the main thesis.

3. Concluding exhortation to the young students (¶39).

The survey that follows will briefly present the main content, with added background information on certain points, and references to parallel places in other writings of Hutcheson.

1. Introduction (paragraphs 1–6)

Hutcheson begins by elaborating on his pleasant memories of his student days, which fell in the period 1710–17, expresses his pleasure at being able to return again to the land of his ancestors (who had emigrated from Scotland to Ulster, where Hutcheson was born and raised), and his gratitude to the university for inviting him to the chair. He mentions how in his student days he discovered the joys of classical studies, and his delight in other branches of learning: theology or recent philosophy and science. Only classical authors are mentioned by name, not modern ones. The difference is interesting.

When Scott remarks that

> it is not without significance, that in his Inaugural Lecture ... he enlarges rather upon his recollection of classical than of philosophical works

he wishes to imply that Hutcheson had been taught philosophy of a

Cartesian kind by Gerschom Carmichael (1672–1729), but had since developed philosophically in a different direction, although he did not wish to bring it up on this occasion.[7]

There are some difficulties with Scott's remark. The conflict between pro- and anti-Cartesians was not of any great moment in Glasgow at this time. Moreover, there is no evidence that Hutcheson had been a student in Carmichael's class. This does not, however, preclude the possibility that he may have attended classes given by Carmichael, who had taught at Glasgow since 1694, and whose annotated edition of Pufendorf's *De officio* Hutcheson was later to mention with great approval in the prefaces to the Latin and English versions of the Compend. It is known that he studied natural philosophy 1710–11 under James Loudon before going on to divinity after a break of one year.[8]

What is true, however, is that on this occasion, it would be appropriate not to make any reference to certain matters. His theological studies had been `under the direction of the reverend and learned Professor John Simson'.[9] But it would have been less than tactful to lay stress on that fact. Simson was, to put it mildly, under a cloud. He had been charged in 1715 with teaching Arminianism. A report on this in 1717 acquitted him with a warning

> not to attribute too much to natural reason and the power of corrupt nature to the disparagement of revelation and efficacious free grace.

But in 1724 he was charged again, with having taught Arianism following Samuel Clarke's *Scripture Doctrine of Divinity*, a book that had created quite a stir in England. At the end of proceedings, the General Assembly of the Church of Scotland suspended Simson from teaching in 1729, although he was not deprived of his chair or his emoluments.[10]

---

[7] Scott, *Francis Hutcheson*, p. 14.

[8] Hutcheson enrolled for the session 1710–11, and began his four-year course in theology 1712–13. Dr M. A. Stewart, to whom I am much obliged for information kindly supplied on these matters, suggests that Hutcheson may have devoted the intervening year to a study of Greek and Latin authors under the professors of Greek (i.e. Alexander Dunlop) and Humanity (i.e. Andrew Ross).

[9] William Leechman, in the Preface to Hutcheson's *System*, p. iii. Note Archibald Campbell's similar remark about Simson, p. 75 above.

[10] H.C. Burleigh, *A Church History of Scotland*, London: Oxford University Press 1960, pp. 287, 290.

The fact that Hutcheson mentioned theology only in passing, although this had, after all, been his main study in Glasgow, is explained by natural caution and his wish not to create embarrassment. To bring it up would inevitably have involved an allusion to matters of great controversy, and to do so on this public occasion would have been indelicate. The reason he mentions classical works is that he genuinely took a great delight in them.[11] As for philosophical works, he does refer, although not by name, both to works in natural philosophy, i. e. the scientific works of writers such as Boyle and Newton, and to works which even today would be regarded as philosophical. His favourite philosophers in his favourite branch of philosophy, that branch which deals with beauty and virtue, were, among the moderns, Shaftesbury, and among the ancients Aristotle, Cicero, and Marcus Aurelius, and some of their ideas are mentioned in paragraph 4.

Usually, inaugural lectures would explain the value of the discipline to be professed. Hutcheson adverts to this briefly, but explains that this has been done so often before, that he now prefers to deviate from the standard convention.[12]

2. Discussion of the social nature of man (paragraphs 7–38)

This is the main question of the lecture. Hutcheson begins, as a competent philosopher would, by analysing the question. Its meaning is discussed in paragraphs 7–12, which deal in general with the concept of human nature.

The concept of what is *natural* for things belonging to a certain kind is illustrated in paragraphs 7–10. Hutcheson adopts the view that we can, by observation, establish the natural ends or purposes,

---

[11] Not only this lecture, but also the four treatises, refer extensively to classical poets and philosophers. The names mentioned most frequently in the four treatises taken together are Horace (14 times), followed by Shaftesbury (8), Epicurus and his followers (7), Cicero (6), and Malebranche (6 times, but only in T3 and T4). This is according to my own count. None of the original editions has an index, nor is there one in any of the modern facsimile reprints.

[12] Typical titles were Gerhard Noodt's (1647–1725) at Franeker, on the utility and indispensability of jurisprudence in the widest sense, comprising the law of nature and nations, as a source of civil law, Barbeyrac's at Lausanne in 1711, on the worth and usefulness of his subjects, history and law, and William Forbes's at Glasgow in 1714, on the worth and usefulness of civil law, and on its nature, history, and authority. A study of the conventions governing the inaugural academic lecture might prove rewarding.

common to all things of a given kind. This teleology, this doctrine of final causes, can of course be traced back to Aristotle.

The claim that, we can *observe* the end or design of our frame can also be found in the introduction to *Essay*.[13]

Next, in paragraphs 11 and 12, Hutcheson explains what is *natural to man* in terms of innate abilities and appetites. Ancient thought is again present: he mentions the threefold division of desires which goes back to Epicurus.

We now come to the main body of the lecture, with its subdivisions. The main question is whether social life is natural to man.

Paragraphs 13–17. First of all, the concept of man's natural state is discussed.

When the state of nature is compared with civil society in this section, two distinct questions are raised. First, What are human beings like by nature, considered individually? Secondly, How will they interact?[14] The discussion of both questions is conducted on the assumption that the individuals, whose nature is in question, have not already been exposed to the influence of civil society.

When Hutcheson deals with these two questions, he introduces an important Stoic ingredient, insisting that man's natural condition is one in which there is a natural hierarchy, so that one faculty of the soul has a natural authority.[15] He also urges that 'We ought to judge nature from her intention or perfect state',[16] against Hobbes's unattractive description of that condition, and against Pufendorf, who, following Hobbes, explicitly states in *ING* 2, 2, 1 that the state of nature he wishes to discuss is not the best or most proper condition, but the condition in which men would be in the absence of or in abstraction from various human inventions and institutions. Hutcheson makes his point with some flourish: where Hobbes, in chapter 13 of the *Leviathan*, had five characteristics of the life of man in the state of nature, the famous 'solitary, poor, nasty, brutish, and short', and in *De cive* 10, 1 has nine (used by Pufendorf in *OHC* 2, 1,

---

[13] (1st edn 1728) p. xvii.

[14] These two questions are clearly distinguished also in Pufendorf's major work *ING* 2, 2, 1, and in his *De officio* 2, 1, 4-5.

[15] It has been suggested that it was due to Butler's influence that he adopted this Stoic idea, but some commentators argue that it is adumbrated in the *Inquiry*, prior to the publication of Butler's *Sermons*.

[16] See the quotations from Aristotle and Cicero in footnote on p. 47.

9 *ad fin.*): `dominion of passions, war, fear, poverty, slovenliness, solitude, barbarism, ignorance, cruelty', Hutcheson, at the end of paragraph 13, has fourteen! He regrets that Pufendorf allowed himself to be influenced by Hobbes.

A few comments on the debate on this question and on some of the writers mentioned by Hutcheson may be called for. It was not merely a matter of speculative conjectural history. The debate had strong political overtones. The Hobbesian view could be taken to favour tyranny: the anti-Hobbesian anarchy.

Pufendorf's view of man's natural condition can be gathered from *De officio* 2, 1, 9, where the comparison between the natural and civil states reflects very unfavourably on the former. His view does indeed come very close to that of Hobbes, and, as just mentioned, the last part of the comparison is taken verbatim from Hobbes's *De cive* 10, 1.[17]

Most writers utterly rejected the Hobbesian view. Richard Cumberland (1632–1718), mentioned in paragraph 14, whose *De legibus naturae* was published in 1672, was one of them. The two main aims of this work were to refute Hobbes and to develop a moral theory from one single principle of benevolence.

Among others who disagreed with Hobbes and Pufendorf, were Titius and Barbeyrac, also mentioned in paragraph 14. Gottlieb Gerhard Titius (1661–1714) was a professor of law in Leipzig and Rostock. He wrote a comprehensive commentary on Pufendorf's *De officio*, first published separately (1703) but later (1709, 1715, etc.) together with Pufendorf's text. Jean Barbeyrac (1674–1744), who at the age of eleven escaped religious persecution in France, became a professor first in Lausanne (1711–17) and then in Groningen (1717–44). As a translator (into French) and commentator of the major works of Grotius, Pufendorf, and Cumberland, his significance in the history of moral philosophy is very great. In his copious notes, Barbeyrac very frequently referred to Titius's comments on various points in Pufendorf.

These two writers adopted a view much closer to that advanced by Locke in the *Second Treatise of Government* (1st edn 1690), which had been translated into French. Titius suggested that peaceful social life was possible even without a government, and that the

---

17 As noted by many commentators, e.g. by Immanuel Weber in his edition of *De officio*, Frankfurt (1st edn 1700) 1719.

shortcomings of such a condition could be far less serious than those of an oppressive ruler.[18] These sentiments were echoed by Hutcheson, who wrote, e.g., `But we must not hence conclude, as some have rashly done, that the very worst sort of polity is better than the best condition of anarchy.'[19] So the claim that he was the first to break with a whole tradition according to which `anarchy' is worse than any political condition cannot be sustained.[20]

Carmichael, who published an annotated edition of Pufendorf's *De officio*,[21] an edition highly regarded by Hutcheson,[22] refers very frequently to Titius and Barbeyrac.[23] But on this question his comment was:

> Pufendorf has borrowed the concluding part of this paragraph from Hobbes, perhaps without being sufficiently careful, and he has been criticised on this point by Titius and Barbeyrac. Yet, for my part I hesitate to adopt their rather severe criticisms; and I have little doubt that the condition of the members of a civil society, as long as it is not governed in a patently unjust manner (I would not venture to go further than that), is greatly to be preferred to the condition of individual men or individual families, living in a state of natural liberty in relation to one another. At the same time it should not be denied that by those statements of Hobbes that Pufendorf has repeated here, the worst aspect of the state of nature is compared with the condition of civil society as it ought to be, not as it actually is in this corrupted condition of mankind.[24]

---

18 In his observations nos. 460 and 461 on Pufendorf's *De officio* 2, 1, 9, Titius insists with considerable vehemence that people suffering from oppression under a government may be far worse off than they would be even in a Hobbesian state of nature. His points are adopted and developed by Barbeyrac in the notes to Pufendorf's *ING* 2, 2, 2 *ad fin*.

19 *System*, 3, 4, 3, p. 218. Similarly 3, 4, 5, p. 222.

20 Leidhold seems to have erred on this point, when he writes, `Hutcheson scheint in der gesamten Tradition der erste gewesen zu sein, der [...] in Erwägung zieht, daß "Anarchie" nicht in jedem Fall ein schlechterer Zustand ist als irgendein Zustand politischer Ordnung.' Leidhold, *Ethik und Politik*, p. 215f.

21 Like Weber, Titius, Barbeyrac, Thomas Johnson, Otto, and many others.

22 It is praised in the preface of Hutcheson's Compend (1742; 1747).

23 He is said to have conducted in later years `a considerable correspondence with Barbyrack and other learned men abroad'. Wodrow, *Analecta*, vol. IV, p. 95. My efforts to find this correspondence have so far been unsuccessful.

24 `Quae sequuntur ad finem hujus # ex Hobbio desumpsit Auctor, forté nimis secure; eo certé nomine Cl. Viris Titio & Barbeyracio jamdudum dedit poenas.

Hutcheson's primary concern is obviously to reject views proposed by Hobbes, who is mentioned by name more than once, and quoted towards the end. This tells against a suggestion by de Crescenzo that in this lecture the anti-egoist argument is much more directed against Mandeville than against Hobbes.[25]

But Hutcheson also has to deal with some theological views, and refers in paragraph 15 explicitly to the Protestant theologians, arguing that their doctrines of original sin and man's natural corruption, properly understood, are not in conflict with his own theory of man's natural sociality, which allows for the 'possibility of genuine natural benevolence. He was of course eager to present his views in a manner that would not arouse controversy with those who suspected his orthodoxy. Wodrow's impression that he seemed prudent and cautious was not mistaken. For an interesting confirmation, see appendix 17 on p. 167.

Pufendorf had in his time been at the centre of a resounding and long-lasting controversy with orthodox Protestant theologians in Leipzig, Lund, and elsewhere.[26] It was in the early decades of the eighteenth century, in Scotland, not unusual for charges of heterodoxy to be brought before presbyteries, synods, or assemblies. The tone of the public controversies relating to such charges cannot be described as refined, and was not relished by Hutcheson.

In paragraphs 16 and 17 Hutcheson develops his view that the natural state is most desirable. It is, however, a state which for the most part does not actually obtain; it is only potentially present. The condition that Hobbes and like-minded writers call natural is not properly so called. Less misleadingly, that condition can be described as uncultivated or uncivilised.

Horum quidem ego severiores censuras nolim temeré meas facere; multo minus dubitare quin Status Civium, sub Imperio non plane nequiter administrato (amplius quid affirmare non audeo) longe sit praeferendus conditioni singulorum Hominum, vel etiam singularum familiarum, in libertate invicem naturali degentium: dissimulari interim non oportet Hobbianis istis verbis, ab Auctore hic adoptatis, pessimam status naturalis faciem, conferri cum Statu Civili, qualis hic esse debet, magis quam, in hac Hominum pravitate, usquam est.' Pufendorf, *De officio* (ed. Carmichael) Edinburgh 1724: editor's note to 2, 1, 9, pp. 318f.

25 De Crescenzo, *Francis Hutcheson*, p. 179.

26 As indicated in the name of his *Eris Scandica*. There is an excellent survey and descriptive bibliography in F. Palladini, *Discussioni seicentesche su Samuel Pufendorf.* [Bologna:] Il Mulino 1978.

Paragraphs 18-20. After the preliminary conceptual analysis, the next step is to formulate more precisely the question: is social life natural to man? The upshot of Hutcheson's argument is that we can distinguish two conditions: one with civil authority, the other without. In either condition, there can be social life. The question whether social life is natural to man, can then be understood to refer to social life without civil authority, or with civil authority. The lecture only deals with the first, as Hutcheson observes at the end of the lecture, where he promises to return to the second on some other occasion.

The next paragraphs, 19-20, make it clear that sociality is distinct from gregariousness. Hutcheson believed that there is an immediate desire for company, and explains that there is something like hunger, thirst, and sexual appetite in the desire for society, or the company of our fellow creatures. Absence of company produces an uneasy fretfulness, sullenness, and discontent – though we may not be clearly aware of the reason for the uneasiness.[27] Sociality, now under discussion, is, however, something else. It is the disposition to help others and not to harm them, the tendency to engage in mutual aid and to abstain from injury. The question is whether this tendency is inherent in human nature, or whether it develops only insofar as there is a prospect of benefit to the agent. The terms *benevolism* and *prudentialism* will occasionally be used in the following to designate these alternatives.

Paragraph 21. In this paragraph the prudentialist answers are presented. Hutcheson sees an affinity between Pufendorf's views and those of Epicurus and Hobbes. He also takes Cumberland's view to be similar to Pufendorf's.

It seems worth while to digress for a closer look at this.

That Pufendorf and Hobbes have much in common is quite clear. Pufendorf actually uses Hobbes's very words when describing man's natural condition.

There is also an affinity between Pufendorf and Epicurus.[28] At

---

27 *T3* 4, 2 (1st edn 1728, pp. 90f.)
28 Two interesting articles on the Epicurean presence in Hobbes and Pufendorf are A. Pacchi, `Hobbes e l'epicureismo', *Rivista Critica di Storia della Filosofia* 33 (1978) and F. Palladini, `Lucrezio in Pufendorf', *La Cultura* 19 (1981).

least in private, Pufendorf had no wish to deny this. In a letter to Thomasius,[29] he wrote:

> Without any doubt, the ethics of Epicurus is better than that of Aristotle. But the name of Epicurus is so odious among the idiots that one must be afraid that Bileam's ass would ascend all the pulpits and preach, if one said anything good about Epicurus.[30]

There is certainly a prudentialist Epicurean–Hobbesian tendency in Pufendorf. He maintained that self-love, weakness and an inclination to harm others were three salient features of the natural human condition. The precepts that have to be followed for the sake or self-preservation include, importantly, those of non-injury and mutual aid, that is, sociality. Sociality, again, is a necessary condition for our happiness. It is these precepts that constitute natural law. Moreover, since God wills our happiness, he wills that we be social, so the precepts of natural law are also his commands. The whole argument is clearly prudentialist. Sociality is to be valued as a necessary means to an end.

This has of course been observed by most commentators. To take just one voice, Nyblæus finds that Pufendorf understands the social instinct, ascribed by Grotius to human nature, as the *means* to secure satisfaction of one's desire for self-preservation.[31]

But there are also statements in Pufendorf that point in a different, benevolist, direction, and it has been argued that Pufendorf is inconsistent since he also takes man's social tendency to exist independently of prudential considerations. Spitz, for instance, writes:[32]

> Pufendorf takes care to indicate that the sociability which defines the state of nature does not result solely from the fact that everyone understands it to be in his self-interest to associate with others, but also – and perhaps chiefly – from an abstract and general benevolence towards human beings as such.[33]

---

29 Christian Thomasius (1655–1728) taught first in Leipzig and from 1690 in Halle. He is often described as the founder of the German Enlightenment.

30 Letter dated 17 July 1688, in E. Gigas (ed.), *Briefe Samuel Pufendorfs an Christian Thomasius (1687-1693)*, Munich & Leipzig: Oldenbourg 1897.

31 [Nyblæus, Axel] *Om Puffendorfs plats ...* , Lund 1868, p. 41.

32 Spitz, `Le concept d'état de nature', pp. 439f.

33 `Pufendorf prend bien soin de marquer que la sociabilité qui définit l'état de

It is not a recent discovery that some statements in Pufendorf point away from prudentialism. Already Carmichael mentions in his annotations to *De officio* that Titius has accused Pufendorf of subordinating sociality under self-love, but leaves open the question whether the accusation is justified, and argues that in either case it has to be agreed that social life is necessary for the preservation and well-being of mankind.[34] Hutcheson was familiar with Carmichael's comments on Pufendorf and thought well of them, as noted above on p. 110, though on this point he maintained, like Titius, that the main thrust of Pufendorf's theory remains along the lines of Epicurus and Hobbes.

With contrary interpretations of Pufendorf's view of the natural state still being debated, the last word has not been said, but I shall abstain from proposing it here. There is, arguably, some inconsistency between some of his statements, especially if his later writings on the subject are also taken into account, as has been been done in the recent works by M. Seidler and F. Palladini.[35]

As regards Cumberland's view, Hutcheson initially[36] maintained that it agrees with Pufendorf's, and does so again in paragraph 21 of the *Lecture* . But there is also a different slant, more favourable to Cumberland.[37]

If there is some wavering in the treatment of Cumberland, the reason may well be that that Hutcheson, who, as we learn from Leechman's account, had been treated by Lord Carteret (1690–1763; Lord-Lieutenant of Ireland from late 1724 until 1730) `with the most distinguishing marks of familiarity and esteem',[38] had some contact

---

nature, ne résulte pas seulement du fait que chacun comprend que son intérêt lui commande de s'associer avec les autres, mais aussi – et peut-être surtout – d'une bienveillance abstraite et générale pour les membres du genre humain en tant que tels.' The same point had been made earlier by Hans Welzel, *Die Naturrechtslehre Samuel Pufendorfs*, Berlin: de Gruyter 1958, p. 46.

[34] In Carmichael's annotation to *De officio*, part 1, ch. 3; at p. 47 in his 1718 edition.

[35] See the editorial introduction to Samuel Pufendorf, *On the Natural State of Men* (ed. M. Seidler) and F. Palladini, *Samuel Pufendorf, discepolo di Hobbes. Per una reinterpretazione del giusnaturalismo moderno.* Bologna: Il Mulino 1990. These excellent works are of great value also because of their extensive coverage of the relevant primary sources and secondary literature.

[36] *T2* 2, 1, 4: 1st edn 1725 p. 115; 2nd edn 1726 p. 125; 3rd edn 1729 p. 115; 4th edn 1738 p. 119.

[37] In paragraph 23. The apparent differences between the references to Cumberland have also been noted by de Crescenzo, *Francis Hutcheson*, p. 177.

[38] On Carteret's positive interest, see Scott, *Francis Hutcheson*, and the dedication of the second and following editions of *Inquiry*.

with Carteret's chaplain John Maxwell, who at that time was translating Cumberland's *De legibus naturae*, [39] and that such a contact, or the translated work itself, led him to reconsider his earlier view.[40] But it should be noted that Cumberland's own position was far from unambiguous: in some places in his unwieldy work his position seems to be egoistic, in others anti-egoistic, and this could explain at least in part why Hutcheson's comments on him vary.[41]

That public spirit can *in part* be motivated by self-interest is not denied by Hutcheson:

> To represent these motives of self-interest to engage men to publicly useful actions, is certainly the most necessary point in morals. This has been so well done by the ancient moralists, by Dr. Cumberland, Pufendorf, Grotius, Shaftesbury;[42] ...

> Cumberland and Puffendorf show that benevolence and social conduct are the most probable ways to secure to each individual happiness in this life ... so that all obstacles to our moral sense and our kind affections, from false views of interest, may be removed.[43]

His objection is against those who adopt the prudentialist view, and take self-interest to be the *only* basis.

Paragraphs 22–27. In this section, Hutcheson raises a series of objections against prudentialism. As already observed, they all appeal to commonly known facts, and do not rely on ontological or epistemological principles.

First, in paragraphs 22 and 23, he draws attention to our immediate desire for the pleasures of praise and honour and to the way

---

[39] The translation was published in 1727. The translator was for a long time Prebendary of Connor. He is to be distinguished from John Maxwell, a Presbyterian minister who succeeded Hutcheson's father.

[40] Hutcheson's name does not appear in the list of subscribers, but that of his brother, with whom he had cordial relations, does. In any case, printed subscription lists were not always complete, and there were ways for non-subscribers to acquire copies.

[41] De Crescenzo, *Francis Hutcheson*, p. 362, points to the ambivalence in Cumberland, who attacks Hobbes's egoism but at the same time concedes too much to it. In the end, he argues, Cumberland succumbs to the theory of psychological egoism, despite his efforts to overcome it.

[42] T4, 4, 1: 1st edn 1728 p. 277; 3rd edn 1742 p. 282.

[43] In the Letter to Gilbert Burnet of 19 June 1725. *Letters* (1735), p. 27; *Illustrations*, ed. B. Peach (1971), p. 214.

in which our joy in the discovery of truths increases if it is shared
with others; he also reminds us that sharing enhances virtually all
pleasures. In this context, Shaftesbury is mentioned, and again
Hutcheson tactfully tries not to cause offence: he mentions
Shaftesbury with great approval, but does add a word of caution,
making it clear that he does not necessarily agree with all of his
theological views. It was important for him to temper his praise in
order to reduce the apprehensions of the orthodox.[44]

The next two paragraphs (24–25) give examples of direct general
benevolence and examples of direct particular benevolence. They
are counter-examples, designed to refute the prudentialist account,
and to urge the view that there is in human beings immediate
altruistic motivation.[45] The following paragraph (26) argues by a
further appeal to introspective observation and reflection that, in
addition to our immediate tendency to *act* benevolently, we also
have an immediate tendency to *approve* of benevolence.

Of particular significance is the discussion in paragraph 27 of
the attitude of a man facing the indubitable prospect of divinely
ordained imminent annihilation, which was mentioned above at
p. 74. It is designed to tell against hedonistic, as well as
prudentialist egoism.

> There are, therefore, in man benevolent affections, which are
> immediately and often exclusively directed towards the
> happiness of others.

Paragraphs 28–37. Hutcheson next considers a series of objections to
his view. The first major objection is this: human beings have both
social and anti-social tendencies. Why should the first be regarded
as more natural than the second?

In reply, Hutcheson first dismisses the suggestion that anti-social
tendencies arise from the corrupting influence of civil society – a
view which was to gain lasting popularity when it was later

---

[44] In the same vein is the warning added in the introduction to the second and
subsequent editions of *T1&T2* at p. xix against some who have misused
Shaftesbury to give vent to their prejudices against Christianity. Cf. p. 37.

[45] Many similar examples appear in other writings. For instance, our attitudes to
characters and events in distant ages and nations are also mentioned in *T2* 1, 2:
1st edn 1725 p. 111, 2nd edn 1726 p. 121f; 4th edn 1738 p. 115; in *T4* 1st edn 1728
p. 209, in *Short Introduction* 1, 1, 10, and further examples of direct benevolence,
general and particular, are given in the last subsections of *T2* section 2: see e.g. *T2*
1st edn 1725 2, 10, p. 147, expanded in *T2* 4th edn 1738 2, 11, pp. 163f.

proposed in earnest by Rousseau. He finds this answer insufficient.

He also asserts, with an appeal to the teachings of the Stoics, that there is a natural hierarchy in the human mind. So that even if in one sense the social and anti-social tendencies are equally innate, the former have a natural authority: they are born to rule, the latter to serve.

A further argument, designed to show that good-will and ill-will are not equally `natural', is this. There is an asymmetry between the two. The former has a certain priority. There is, so to speak, a *general* presumption in favour of good-will. It does not require any particular fact of cooperation, friendship, or well-doing. In contrast, ill-will presupposes some *particular* fact of competition, hostility, wrongdoing, or the like.

Another objection is that the tendencies claimed to be natural are actually the products of education and indoctrination (paragraph 32). This suggestion has of course a Hobbesian and Mandevillean flavour. In response, Hutcheson argues that education can only mould, not create. No amount of aesthetic education can make a person perceive anything as beautiful unless he has a sense of beauty, and the same applies, *mutatis mutandis*, to morality (paragraph 33).[46]

This is followed by a further objection to Hutcheson's benevolism, based on Locke's rejection of innate ideas. On this point, Locke had many followers. But Hutcheson retorts that the rejection of innate ideas has been taken too far. For one thing, the objections against innate benevolence would tell equally against innate self-love. Again, he bases much of his argument in paragraph 34, as in other places in this text, on the ancient doctrine of natural teleology.[47]

The next two objections, in the following paragraph, can be found almost verbatim in Hobbes's *De cive* 1, 2 and 2, 1. The first of them is that if there was natural benevolence towards other human beings, then, since they are all human beings equally, they would be equally liked, which is not the case. Hutcheson replies that it could be argued, by parity of reasoning, that if material bodies have

---

[46] These points are also in *T1* sect. 7 (*inter alia*, the colour cannot be a blind person's reason for favouring a garment), and in *T2* 1, 7.

[47] Similar warnings against excessive fear of innate ideas can be found in the preface to *T1&T2* (1st edn 1725 p. vii; 2nd edn 1726 p. xivf.; 4th edn 1738 p. xiv); in *T1* 6, 8; and in *T3* 1st edn 1728 6, 3 p. 198 (see item 8).

weight, then, since they are all equally material bodies, they would have equal weight. The second objection is that whenever people associate for business or pleasure, they seek only their own gain or glory. In reply, he appeals to a series of reminders of common observations of social contexts and interaction.

Hutcheson goes on to make two further pertinent points. Many so-called selfish acts are actually for the sake of one's family, kindred, country, or even for a political party.[48] Such acts often involve sacrifices and to call them selfish is rather far-fetched. And, finally, it is not selfishness to prefer pleasant to unpleasant company (paragraphs 36 and 37). This point is also made elsewhere:

> To alledge that our[49] chusing persons of knowledge, courtesy, and good-nature for our intimates, and our avoiding the ignorant, the morose, or selfish, argues all our intimacies to arise from selfish views, is plainly unjust.[50]

Paragraph 38   Hutcheson concludes that social life in a condition under no civil authority is natural to man. A discussion of social life under civil authority is postponed for another occasion. He assures his audience that the road of virtue is most agreeable.

3. Peroration, exhortation to the young students (paragraph 39)

In the concluding paragraph, Hutcheson extends his best wishes to the young students in the audience and exhorts them to pursue knowledge and virtue.

Editorial remarks

The first edition of the inaugural lecture was published in 1730. It is photoreprinted in reduced size in vol. VII of the *Collected Works* (Hildesheim: Olms 1971). The second edition, typographically vastly superior to the first, was published 1756. The text of the title-pages runs as follows.

---

[48] The reference to party zeal reappears e.g. in *System*, 1, 5, 4, p. 88.

[49] *System*, ibid., where Hutcheson has a footnote which reads: `Hobbes, Bayle, Mandeville, in many places, after Rochefoucault.'

[50] *unjust*: incorrect.

Francisci Hutcheson Profess. Glasgoviensis De naturali hominum Socialitate Oratio Inauguralis. [Device]. Glasgoviae. Typis Academicis M.DCC.XXX. Pp. (i) + 1–24.

De naturali hominum socialitate. Auctore Francisco Hutcheson LL.D. Philosophiae professor in academia glasguensi. Glasguae: In aedibus academicis excudebant Rodbertus et Andreas Foulis MDCCLVI. Title-page + pp. 1–39.

In the second edition, the printer's device and the dedication to the colleagues are omitted. The errata listed in the first edition have been corrected.

Paragraph-numbering has been introduced into the translation in order to facilitate reference to the text. A few paragraphs have been divided here: thus 7 and 8, 32 and 33, and 38 and 39 each correspond to one paragraph in the original.

The quotation marks and the italics in the original Latin text have been preserved. As for the quotation marks, it seems that they are not only used to indicate that the clause is taken verbatim from some author.

The title of this lecture admits of different translations. The most literal would be `... on the natural sociality of human beings', closely followed by `... on man's natural sociality'. For stylistic reasons, I have, however, preferred the present title `... on the social nature of man'. For the history of the word `sociality', see appendix 15 at p. 158.

The translation of the *Lecture* began life as a draft of my own, but owes its present publishable form to Colin Mayrhofer of the Department of Classics, The Australian National University, who also identified the classical poetry quoted in the text. I am most grateful to him for his expert and most generous assistance. In this final version, the translation has also benefited from extensive comments, based on a very detailed review, which I had the good fortune to receive from Michael Seidler, of Western Kentucky University, for whose help I remain deeply grateful.

The text

Francis Hutcheson
Professor in Glasgow

Inaugural lecture on the social nature of man

[Emblem representing the College arms][1]
Glasgow. The university printer. 1730.

Gratefully delivered and dedicated to the eminent and
distinguished professors of the College of Glasgow:

Neil Campbell, Principal and Professor primarius of Divinity

John Simson, Professor of Divinity

John Loudoun, Professor of Philosophy

Alexander Dunlop, Professor of Greek

Andrew Rosse, Professor of Humanity

Charles Morthland, Professor of Oriental Languages

Robert Simson, Professor of Mathematics

William Forbes, Professor of Civil Law

John Johnston, Doctor and Professor of Medicine

Robert Dick, Professor of Philosophy

Thomas Brisbane, Doctor of Medicine and Professor of Anatomy
and Botany

William Anderson, Professor of Ecclesiastical History[2]

---

[1] David Murray, *Memories of the Old College of Glasgow*, Glasgow 1927, p. 96, deplores
this example of how popular heraldry had degenerated at the time.

[2] The order of precedence is: principal, professor of divinity, and then the others in
order of seniority. (*Munimenta*, vol. II, p. 580).

1. After six years devoted to the study of humane letters and philosophy in this University, private considerations and duties removed me from this most beloved place to Ireland, where I became involved in very strenuous and unpleasant tasks and found very little time for intellectual improvement or literary pursuits. It was therefore with great joy that I learned, thirteen years later, that this University,[3] my alma mater, was restoring her former alumnus to liberty and that the distinguished moderators and professors of the University, who had once been to me *in loco parentis*, had invited me to be their colleague. Mindful of my ancestry, it seemed all the less painful to me to leave my dearly beloved native soil to

seek my ancient mother
from whom my lineage sprang[4]

since I ardently longed to regain Scotland, this venerable country, the parent of brave and learned men, a land not enfeebled by the spirit of the times, and, although ancient, of undiminished fertility.[5]

2. To recognise with a sense of joy, as I now do, those very places, buildings, gardens, fields, and riverbanks[6] where I once roamed carefree, joyful and happy – that I had expected. But it was above all this University, the learned and serious lectures given in this auditorium and the private tutorials given by the professors, that came before my mind. It is indeed with the greatest delight that I see again the places where I absorbed the first elements of the search for truth, where I tasted to the full the immortal sublimities of Vergil and Homer, the delights, tasteful charm, elegant wit, the jest and humour in Xenophon, Horace, Aristophanes and Terence, and likewise the abundant elegance and scope of Cicero's writings in all branches of philosophy, as well as the copious polemical fervour in his pleadings.[7] This is also where I first inquired into the nature and foundation of virtue, and tried to explore the eternal relations of numbers and shapes on which the prodigious fabric of

---

[3] *academia*: the terms 'university' and 'college' were used interchangeably.
[4] After Virgil's *Aeneid* 3, 95.
[5] '...rev'rend with Age, but not impaired by Years'. Thus James Arbuckle, Hutcheson's friend, in *Glotta, A Poem*, Glasgow: William Duncan 1721, p. 12.
[6] More pleasant then than now, McCosh wrote in 1875 in *The Scottish Philosophy*, p. 51.
[7] *patrociniis*. McCosh mistakenly reads this as if Hutcheson enjoyed studying the (Church) Fathers, but the word does not connote patristics.

our world rests; and indeed the nature, the power, the wisdom and the benevolence of the eternal Deity himself, who governs all things by his power, mind, and counsel; and this is where all the things mentioned were implanted and took a firmer root in the mind after repeated examination in polite but amicable conversation, and in lively but respectful exchanges with fellow students when we walked in the College gardens or in the suburban fields that are washed by the gentle flow of river Clyde.[8] Recalling all this, the departure for Scotland became for me a sweet, agreeable, and joyful prospect.

3. This alone, however, was and remains for me a matter for anxiety: that I might be unworthy of membership in this circle of most learned and worthy men by whose votes I have been invited into the body of professors, and that I might disgrace their most honourable opinion of me by being found unequal to the task. Even now I am fearful of this, but I shall gratefully admit that if I have any ability, well knowing how slight it is, or if a method and a discipline to teach true philosophy has resulted from my study and training in the most excellent subjects of study, to which I have been constantly devoted, then this University would seem to have the right to claim from me the fruits of all this, having first introduced me to these studies and guided me along the way in which they ought to pursued. Having been formed thanks to her instruction, I have received all that might enable me to be of benefit to the students; and since the University is now demanding this from me, I overcame my fear of coming here to teach, not wishing dishonourably to withhold what I might have to contribute.

4. It is customary, gentlemen of the audience, for men of learning to deliver a public discourse on taking office, and normally about the origin, development, worth, and usefulness of their discipline. I would also have said something of that kind, had not many learned men already virtually exhausted the subject. So on this occasion it has seemed to me preferable to attempt a closer consideration of human nature and to inquire whether there are in our nature the seeds of almost all virtues or, in other words, motives to virtue of every kind. This was clearly the view of the best ancient writers, who described virtue as life according to the best and most perfect

---

[8] *Glotta* in Latin, celebrated in Arbuckle's poem.

nature. There would hardly have been any need to dwell on the value or usefulness of moral science, since undeniably almost everything in life that is becoming, amiable, or lovely, springs from morality, and the same applies to whatever a man does that is agreeable or useful to his country, companions, friends, or himself. These things do not depend on bodily strength, health, nor on wealth or power: because by means of such many flourish who are odious, harsh, base, or peevish, and who ought to blush before friends and companions, nay even before themselves. And if lawyers have done excellent work on easements, the law concerning dividing walls and eaves,[9] if physicians have distinguished themselves with treatises on bodily secretions, then it is certainly not an unworthy task for a man of learning to investigate human conduct, the control of one's affections and passions, the direction of one's life as a whole, and the best and most perfect education of speech and action.

5. When we now go on to consider human nature, we will not deal with the whole theory, which would take us too far, but only with those aspects of the human mind which make us sociable. And even if most recent writers[10] have declared this sociality to be the source of almost every duty, they nevertheless do not seem to have sufficiently explained, in general, what things are properly called natural to man, nor, more specifically, what this sociality of ours is, nor, finally, which parts of our nature render us fit for and inclined towards society, be it civil society or a society not subject to human authority. And as long as these things are not sufficiently explained, a whole host of cavils and follies are being produced by some clever writers, who seem to vaunt and glory in giving a very bad and repugnant misrepresentation of human nature.

6. So I shall first inquire into what kinds of things can rightly be called natural to man as far as morality is concerned, and then, to what extent society, be it civil society or society under no human authority, can be counted among things natural.

*** *** ***

---

[9] There is a section dealing with precisely these topics in the *Institutes* of Justinian.
[10] Among them Grotius and Pufendorf.

7. In any inquiry into what is *natural* for a given kind of thing or into what occurs *naturally*, it seems that we ought to note first that anyone who has knowledge of some natural thing or some artifact, and of all its parts, can easily discern to what end that naturally or artificially designed contrivance or structure is destined. We should also note that he can easily distinguish that which occurs fortuitously or by external force to this being from that which occurs within it according to its own nature and for a determinate purpose. But this can be understood in two ways.

8. First, if the structure under consideration is whole and perfect, the observer sees all that is accomplished by this mechanism and he then correctly infers that it was constituted for the sake of achieving these things. After all, nobody who observes the integrated structure of a natural or man-made thing has any doubts about the ends for which each of them is suited; nobody doubts, that is, that eyes are intended for seeing, teeth for chewing, houses for dwelling, ships for sailing. Secondly, even if the structure is not altogether complete but has been flawed or impaired by some accident, but if all the parts, albeit damaged, remain, deteriorated and disjoint as they may be, the experienced observer of these things will still be able to discern the end for which they were intended, the prior natural constitution of the parts and, finally, the purpose and the use of them all. Indeed, who will fail to recognise, when looking at a house, even if it be in ruins, that it was intended for habitation so that mortals would have protection from the harm caused by the elements. Furthermore, who can fail to distinguish those things which happen in accordance with the nature or constitution of the structure in question from those events which occur because of some fault or decay? In a building, for instance, we may see cracks, broken roofs, leakage of rain, as a result of which the inhabitants, afflicted by the cold, contract diseases; and sometimes we also see a building collapse into ruins and unfortunate people, taken by surprise, buried in the rubble. But who would infer from this that it happened by design or that the builder had constructed traps against human lives; everyone knows that it is due to accident, negligence, or faults attributable to defects in the building materials: indeed, we infer properly only that the builder was unable or for some reason unwilling to make the structure more lasting, but

this does not make any difference to the judgement about the purpose and proper use of his work.

9. Furthermore, once the proper use of a contrivance is established, then, even if some things at first sight may seem contrary to that end, the overall purpose of the structure ought not immediately to be doubted, until a more complete inquiry has been made as to whether those parts which seemed contrary to the overall end contribute to that end in some other way or are necessary for it; or on the other hand whether there may be other parts of the contrivance which offer a remedy to or are capable of hindering the parts that appear to be bad. Thus, in a building, window-openings could seem designed to permit the entry of storm and tempest, until we take note of the glass which can easily slide closed, admitting all the light and heat but excluding inclement weather. But I am perhaps belabouring the obvious.

10. Therefore one would hardly call something natural just because it happens frequently to any nature in some way or other; not even if it happens to each and all, as long as no contrivance of that nature appears naturally fitted for bringing it about. Since, however, I wish to avoid verbal disputes, I shall, in order to bring out the distinction, only call these things imperfectly natural;[11] that is, they occur because God, who has made all things, did not wish these things to be more solid or durable. And although God, by his most wise counsel, willed our nature to be weak, all our innate tendencies, which oppose this weakness, show that it is not the end of our duties and even less the purpose set by nature for our actions.

11. Accordingly, I should call natural to man, first, that for which God has given our nature not only suitable powers for its accomplishment, but also a natural appetite. For it is hardly possible to conceive of any other device in an active being that separates natural states and actions from their opposites, than an appetite implanted by nature, especially if there is another equally innate sense conjoined with this appetite, which makes the actions or the results sought pleasing and agreeable. But since man is a living being endowed with intelligence, knowledge, memory, reason, and

---

[11] Hutcheson writes: *naturalia ex infirmitate.*

foresight, capable of considering not only what occurs presently, but also its causes and effects, he does not only seek those things for which nature has directly implanted an appetite, or which by themselves arouse pleasure, but also things of any other kind which are necessary for obtaining those which gratify any of the senses. Consequently many things are said to be sought naturally, although they do not directly give any pleasure, provided only that they are seen to be useful, as means by which something agreeable can be obtained. Therefore, things natural are rightly divided into those which are sought primarily and for themselves, and those which we seek for the sake of other things; into primary and secondary things natural.

12. There are, besides, many other natural things which belong to one of the kinds mentioned, that is, we seek them for themselves or for the sake of something else, and yet the appetite for them is not so strong that it cannot be impeded or defeated by other equally natural appetites. In this way there are many who are disposed to cultivate music, geometry, poetry, and other arts for their own sake, but who also have other appetites so much more powerful and pressing as to conquer and subdue the former. Similarly, avarice is often overcome by sloth or self-indulgence. Contrariwise, there are natural appetites so violent and supported by natural impulses so powerful that there is no way of overcoming them. Appetites of the former kind I should call natural but not necessary, those of the latter both natural and necessary,[12] and examples of such, in almost every mortal species, would be the appetite for nourishment, the love of offspring, and the like.

13. This, I believe, sufficiently explains the natural appetites. In addition, it should be noted that the expression 'state of nature' suffers from an even greater ambiguity. I shall not dwell on the highly objectionable abuse of these words which occurs when the state of nature is not only contrasted with civil society but when it is also imagined to exclude everything that is produced by human powers, application, and ingenuity, as well as all exercise not only of man's natural powers, but even of many natural appetites; and

---

[12] An allusion to an ancient division of the appetites, originally ascribed to Epicurus. See Cicero, *Tusculan Disputations* 5, 33, and Diogenes Laertius 10, 127 (Letter to Menoeceus).

when man in this natural state is imagined – heaven forbid – to be a naked, mute, wretched, solitary, filthy, uncouth, ignorant, repulsive, cowardly, petulant, rapacious, and unsocial brute which neither loves nor is loved by anyone.

> Great father of the gods, let this be the way
> in which you decide to punish cruel tyrants ![13]

14. I shall not dwell on this abuse of words, which is a slander on human nature, an impiety against our heavenly Father, and a matter of ridicule in philosophy. It was on this account that in recent times not only Hobbes but even Pufendorf were castigated by such distinguished men as Titius, Barbeyrac, Cumberland, Carmichael, but above all by the elegant Lord Shaftesbury.

15. If we are to care at all about our use of words, the 'state of nature' ought to denote either that condition to which men are for the most part brought through the exercise of all the natural appetites and powers, or else that most perfect condition to which men can rise by the most sagacious use of all their powers and faculties, a use that seems to be enjoined by the innate desire for the greatest happiness and by whatever benevolent and kind[14] affections that may be natural to man. Accordingly, the natural state will signify either the ordinary condition of man, or the most perfect condition that can be attained by means of the powers implanted in human nature. But it is certainly this most perfect state that has a better claim to be called natural. Granted that certain parts of our nature and certain appetites draw us into many vices in this fallen state; yet, when we consider the entire structure of human nature, no matter how perturbed or corrupted it may have become, as well as its several parts; and above all the public and benevolent affections, and again that moral sense that we also call natural conscience, we also see clearly that the vices do not belong to our nature; and we discern those parts that ought to restrain and govern the lower appetites. Therefore, however much the force and power of this sense or conscience may have been reduced, so as often to be incapable of ruling over the lower impulses, it is nevertheless seen to be fit to rule by its very nature and it is in fact *tò*

---

[13] Persius, *Satires* III 35–36.
[14] In the present translation, 'kind' is standardly used for *communis*.

hegemonikón, the ruling principle, to which, in the uncorrupted state of our nature, everything was subjected and rightly so.[15] But the true structure of our nature and the true condition of our nature that God instituted cannot indeed be restored until conscience, reinstated on her throne, shows her dominion over the bodily appetites. The Protestant theologians agree with all this in their teaching and show most correctly what was the original contrivance and structure of our nature. But even if they, in their popular sermons,[16] sometimes call our fallen and corrupt state natural, in order to distinguish it from a state brought about by divine grace, they do not thereby deny that the original structure of our nature was destined by divine art and design for everything seemly, virtuous, and excellent,[17] and admit that clear signs of this design and art are preserved even in the ruins of this structure.

16. Since we therefore may rightly call that state of mankind *natural* which is most cultivated, the question still remains what the contrary state, prior to all culture, should be called. It should properly be called an *uncultivated* state (insofar as such a condition, which can only be temporary, deserves to be called a state at all),[18] in which the natural powers have not yet been exercised. In respect of inanimate things, or [animate] beings without a mind,[19] a natural and uncultivated state is, indeed, rightly contrasted with a state cultivated by human art. But among men, the natural state is perhaps aptly distinguished from an adventitious state in which men may find themselves, not due to the exercise of their natural powers or appetites, but rather to external force, cunning schemes, exceptional and dire indigence, or, finally, some clever and ingenious scheme which outwits the generality of people. Indeed, an animal endowed with reason, which constantly desires to learn and

---

15 Allusion to Stoic doctrine. Cf. e.g. Cicero, *On the Nature of the Gods,* 2, 29.
16 Popular sermons would of course require less analytical precision than sermons which were in effect lectures in theology or philosophy.
17 An echo of Phil. 4:8?
18 Similarly in the Compend 2, 4, 1. According to Aristotle a *state* differs from a *condition* by being more stable and durable (*Categories* ch. 8, 8b26). Similarly also Shaftesbury, *The Moralists* 2, 4 (*Characteristics,* vol. II, p. 78): 'Nor could we properly call that a state which could not stand or endure for the least time.' Again, Hume writes: 'Whether such a condition of human nature could ever exist, or if it did, could continue so long as to merit the appellation of a state, may justly be doubted.' *Enquiry ... of Morals,* 3, 1, p.190.
19 I.e. plants, trees, etc.

whose mind is capable of acquiring and exercising new arts, does not in the least abandon the state natural to itself, but does truly follow its own nature with God as a father and guide, when it devises and learns various arts and, being aware of mutual affection, seeks or offers assistance and when, on a basis of mutual trust, it endeavours to maintain itself and mankind safe and sound.

17. Since we are, then, arguing that political writers should abandon their use of this expression (*state of nature*), it may be asked what that state should be called that is contrasted with civil society.[20] Now, their own axiom,[21] i.e. *that any right vested in a ruler removes original liberty*, makes it plain enough that the state which stands in contrast to civil society should be called a *state of freedom, subject to no human authority*. It could, however, seem as if we were dwelling too long on these verbal questions, were it not for the fact that behind them there are matters of great importance.

18. I come now to the main topic that I had proposed to deal with in this lecture, that is, in what sense social life, be it in a state of entire freedom or under civil authority, is natural to man, and shall first deal with social life in a state of freedom.[22]

19. Were it not for the error of certain writers in this matter, it would hardly have been necessary to remark that no philosopher has taken our natural sociality to signify that men seek human company for its own sake, or that it gives man immediate pleasure to mingle in a crowd. Something like that is sought, perhaps because of some instinct, immediately and by itself, by other animals who live in herds, although, for all we can see, they do not engage in common undertakings as a group or decide by deliberate intention jointly to defend themselves against dangers. I doubt that men seek this kind of congregation for its own sake, no matter how frequently they assemble for other reasons: they may come together for mutual help and support, for joint undertakings or commercial ventures, or again a person may, out of kindness, wish to be supportive or to benefit others, or may shrewdly design to gain a

---

[20] *status civilis*: in the standard idiom, reinforced by Locke's *Second Treatise of Government*, the contrast is between 'state of nature' and 'civil society', and here this usage is for the most part adopted.

[21] The quoted sentence is one that all the major writers would agree on.

[22] The second topic is reserved for another occasion. Cf. ¶38.

good reputation, honour, power, or pleasure for himself. It is in this, of course, that writers on morality situate man's natural sociability, teaching that `man, if all the constituents and faculties of his nature are considered, is born with the propensity and the aptitude to lead his life without harming others, to render mutual assistance, and to protect and preserve other men; and he is therefore equally born fit to have what is clearly subsidiary to these things'. And I doubt whether anyone either has or could have denied this, not even Hobbes himself, who teaches that it will be seen on easy reflection that living peacefully and harming nobody is to everyone's greatest advantage.

20. There is, however, a full-blown dispute about the sense in which this social life can be said to be natural to man. The question is this. Does all that benevolence toward the general public, which is concerned with the protection and welfare of whole nations, spring from everyone's poverty, weakness, and need; namely, that there be those through whom everyone can obtain what he needs, so that, by giving and receiving what is due, everyone can receive from another what he is unable to obtain by himself? Or does benevolence rather arise by nature, and do we have a natural inclination to beneficence, not for the sake of favours, and without any thought of how much advantage may be gained from it?

21. Pufendorf, and most recent writers, advocate the doctrine once proposed by the Epicureans, that is, that self-love alone, or everyone's search for his own pleasure or advantage, is the spring of all actions, and they refer to this source all affections of the mind, including even the seemingly most benevolent ones. They do, however, maintain that social life is natural to man on the ground that the nature of man and of external things is such that in order to avoid human ills and attain the external pleasures or advantages which human life is capable of, we need, almost without exception, the help of others, so that without the company and assistance of others, we would not be able to live, let alone live well. Further, they say that men's skill and mental and physical powers are such that they can greatly help or hinder others by means of them. From this it can easily be gathered that for each and all it is above all useful to choose a mode of life whereby they obtain help and material support from others, and whereby others are least provoked to do

them harm. This requires that we abstain from harming others and that we help them to the extent of our powers and as far as our circumstances permit. Therefore, it is agreed, a life of this kind will be of the greatest advantage to everyone. And this, precisely, is social life. Indeed, Pufendorf rises to a higher level, maintaining that it is easy for man to know God and the duty that he requires from us; and the constitution of this nature of ours, beings who seek happiness, provides clear signs of this duty since this happiness cannot be gained without social life. From this it is obvious that God has made us for social life and that all the duties of this life are laid down by divine law and sanctioned by rewards and punishments, and that all contrary conduct prohibited. And, according to this view of Pufendorf's, even if social life apparently is not immediately and in itself natural to man, still it is rightly considered to be natural to man in a secondary sense, and certainly indispensable. This whole doctrine has been abundantly elucidated by the eminent Richard Cumberland who has also added many profound thoughts. These writers have indeed shown, correctly, clearly and copiously, that social life is natural in a secondary sense: such is our natural helplessness and so hard is it to avail ourselves of external things, that the human condition would be truly miserable without social life, but with it the human condition can become safe, agreeable, joyful, and altogether desirable.

22. Pufendorf's doctrine is without doubt correct, but he has left out of account many considerations that are very important in the present context. If one did not look deeper into the matter, one would infer that men were driven into society only for the sake of external advantage, and for fear of external evils, but in opposition to their natural turn of mind and to all natural affections and appetites, in the same way that most people are compelled by fear of hunger, thirst, and cold to endure heavy toil to which they are naturally averse. But there are without doubt many appetites immediately implanted by nature, which are not directed towards physical pleasure or advantage but towards certain higher things which in themselves depend on associating with others. These higher pleasures do not affect the external senses, and there is no conceivable way in which they can be pursued outside society. Among these are pre-eminently the pleasures of praise and honour. God has given us a mind and a sense by which we can discern something

beautiful, becoming, and honourable in intentions, words, and deeds, be they our own or those of others. Hence, we bestow praise and favours on those who deserve well of mankind accordingly, and such is the character of all men that hardly anything provides a man with more joy than the praise and honour that he may receive, even if he expects no further reward. Again, there is great pleasure in the pure search for truth, but by a wonderful arrangement of nature this pleasure is vastly enhanced if there is someone else with whom to share one's discoveries. And on this point I call upon – as the most suitable judges – the blessed minds, those noble hearts who

> brought the distant stars to our vision
> and subdued the heavens to their intellect.[23]

23. There are, indeed, few pleasures or none, not even physical ones, which the company of others does not for the most part considerably increase, by some wonderful natural contagiousness. Every happy or joyful state of the mind carries with it the urge for communication to others and sharing with them. Whatever is agreeable, pleasant, cheerful, witty, or humorous will hardly ever, indeed never, fail to spring up and burst forth from the human heart, endeavouring to unfold itself amongst others. Nothing gives man greater joy than sharing his joy with others.[24] For this reason, even if we were to suppose that everyone seeks his own pleasure or advantage, nevertheless, such is the nature of most pleasures and of the greatest ones, of such a kind are most of our desires, that they induce us to seek social life for its own sake almost without any reasoning, and make the offices of social life in themselves joyful and agreeable. The ancients seem clearly to have seen all this, and it was certainly not overlooked by the excellent Richard Cumberland. But it was the excellent Lord Shaftesbury, a man combining nobility of mind with that of birth, who gave the best and most elegant account of this matter, although in other respects he is liable to censure from the theologians. And for my part I can assuredly not think of any objection to this.

---

[23] Ovid, *Fasti*, 305–6.
[24] That sharing enhances enjoyment: also in *Short Introduction* 1, 1, 9. It is a piece of ancient wisdom, and can be found e.g. in the sixth of Seneca's *Letters to Lucilius*.

24. Their doctrine is even more elevated. It is not only because of some pleasure or advantage to oneself that human nature is sociable, in this secondary sense; but human nature is also in itself, directly and in a primary sense benevolent, kind and sociable, even in the absence of any calculation of advantage or pleasure to oneself. They explain this more fully as follows. They maintain that there are implanted by nature in man many kind and benevolent affections and passions which, both immediately and in the longer view, have regard to the happiness of others, and that the structure of the human mind is such that when things of a certain kind appear before it, particular affections will arise by the guidance of nature alone without any artifice or deliberation and indeed without any prior decree of the will. It is in this manner that when hope for some private pleasure or advantage is kindled, there arises a desire for it, mostly to be explained by self-love; and public and kindly affections are aroused in the very same way when other persons or the good or bad fortunes of others come in view, although there is no question of private advantage. For instance, the appearance of a sentient being painfully tormented produces pity and a very strong desire to remove the pain. Likewise, the appearance of a happy, cheerful, and joyful being produces a kind and social joy, and the continuance of that state is desired for its own sake. Nor is this concern for the situation of others to be seen only when they are present and perceived by our external senses (in which case our mental perturbations or passions are perhaps more vehement), but whenever we calmly imagine other persons, or whenever by reading history or travellers' reports, or by watching a stage performance, we receive a certain view of human nature, even in very distant countries or ages where no advantage of ours is involved, we have a strong interest and concern for the fortunes of all virtuous individuals and societies. And we recoil with the utmost horror from the great evils that can befall man, from wretched slavery, the outrageous devastations of conquerors, the cruelty of tyrants, and it is with great fervour that we join the prayer of the ancient chorus:

> May good fortune abandon the proud
> and return to those in distress.[25]

---

[25] Horace, *Ars Poetica* 201. Translated by C. Passage as 'let it [the chorus] pray to the gods for Fortune's return to the wretched and present retreat from the haughty'.

25. But truly this general kinship of human nature and that universal affection which extends, although rather weakly, to all mankind, does not have to be invoked when explaining our sociality. For there are many closer bonds between men by means of which some become much dearer to us than others. The appetite for procreation is common to all living beings and so is the special concern for the offspring; but in this search for a union men have regard not only to the things that beasts also look for, but they seek a spouse of good character, endowed with many virtues, and above all a mild, friendly, and kind disposition. The offspring is cherished with the tenderest benevolence and concern. From this arises also love between siblings and love of kindred, always evident where it has not been disrupted by injury, emulation, or conflicts of interest. In turn, most of those to whom we are not related by ties of blood commend themselves to our more special love and benevolence by habit, by acquaintance, by exchange of favours, and by fellowship in matters of gravity or levity; with nothing creating a closer bond than virtue itself. From this arise relations of friendship and companionships that everyone seeks for himself, but often, in addition to this, there remains a benevolent concern for the welfare of friends, companions, and neighbours that is independent of any advantage.

26. These writers[26] further postulate a sense, natural to man, of what is right and becoming. It is because of this sense that we seek to honour all kindness, loyalty, mildness, and friendliness and therefore also embrace with much greater willingness and love those who possess these virtues. And where among ourselves or those who are beholden to us by closer bonds of affection a favour is bestowed, there is an effusion of gratitude, a most tender love towards benefactors, and a desire to return the favour. And besides, since there can be nothing more desirable for persons with a noble mind than a good conscience, honour, and uprightness, benevolence diffuses and spreads itself as widely as possible, and we do not call to account, in a petty and mean spirit, such external damage as may be imputed to friendship or beneficence, but make little of it when clearly the intention was right and virtuous. Hereby the kind disposition of the mind acquires new strength and is

---

[26] Those mentioned in ¶23 *ad fin.*

reinforced by practice; the effort to deserve well of others by performing all honest offices is further encouraged. Those who enjoy these benefits, indeed all who observe them, give praise and thanks, and desire to give an equal return; hence, these humane and beneficial offices, in themselves most agreeable, are almost always followed by the greatest benefit for everyone, although this is rarely contemplated in the course of action.

27. I shall perhaps set out more fully in another place the arguments which prove this more attractive description of human nature to be closer to the truth. Here I should only want to point out that any man has only to look within and examine himself to see and feel whether he does not regard many persons as dear to him in themselves, apart from all advantage, for instance, his children, parents, friends, kindred, and fellow citizens. Does he not find in himself any concern for the condition of others, especially good people, on reading, say, a tragedy or a history, where there can be no thought of his own advantage? What if God were to say to this man: `You are about to perish shortly. You will experience no pain or fear. Your mind will not survive your body. I am all-powerful and such is my will. Know that in the meantime anything you request to happen to others, even if it is with your last breath, I shall accomplish for you, but nobody will be grateful to you or return any good no matter how much good that they receive by means of your prayer; and nobody will revile or execrate you for any evils that you have prayed for. Nor will you afterwards experience any joy or sorrow over the fate of others, since, once you have become nothing you will experience nothing. Under these conditions, would everything of human concern be altogether alien and indifferent to you? I shall make your offspring, your friends, your fellow citizens, as happy or miserable as you care to ask. They will flourish by virtue, health, friendships, wealth, and honour; or they will be in a state of wretchedness due to vice, disease, hatred, envy, poverty, dishonour, shame and slavery.' Now, is there any human being to whom all this would be a matter of indifference? Who would not at the moment of death desire for everyone dear to him the same things, and pray for them with as much fervour and firmness as he would on any other occasion, although in this case all consideration of advantage to himself is eliminated? There are,

therefore, in man benevolent affections, which are immediately and often exclusively directed towards the happiness of others.

28. But again somebody will perhaps ask why a social life, that is, being benevolent to others and causing them no harm, is said to be more natural to man than a life of plunder, strife, savagery, and brutishness, given that there seems to be a large number of natural desires, such as self-love, anger, and vindictiveness, which often incite men to injure one another? How many vile and execrable things are not done because of lust or greed! How much struggle is there not for riches, and battles for intellectual pre-eminence, giving rise to so much arrogance and injustice? How numerous and serious would be the insults proferred unless people were restrained from doing injury by the civil power! Now, all these vices spring from natural appetites, so should they not then be called natural?

29. In order to break the force of this objection, it has been observed very rightly by many learned men that most of the secondary affections and desires of the mind that above all have an unsettling influence on human life, and for which there was hardly any place in the state of liberty, are either entirely introduced through civil society or [at least] greatly increase in importance in civil society. Among them are avarice, ambition, and certain evil, oppressive, and power-hungry religions. These evils arise from the coming together in civil society and therefore the remedies are to be sought from the civil power. But I shall not dwell on this answer, which perhaps will not be to everybody's satisfaction. It may instead be preferable to address the person who proposes such arguments as follows: suppose that men were made by God for the social life that we are talking about, would you not admit that it would have been at the same time altogether necessary that they also be endowed with all the desires for private advantage, and even with anger, by God himself, who creates them for social life? So from the fact that these latter desires are innate we must not infer that men are not by nature fit for social life. But, someone might say, is not then the structure of our nature absurd and in conflict with itself? Are we born equally fit for virtue and for vice? Far be it from us to ascribe such a pointless creation to God! We certainly have keen appetites craving for private pleasure and advantage; we have equally, as I hope to have demonstrated sufficiently, more virtuous affections,

which render us sociable; there often arises a struggle between the
two, desire urging one thing, reason another. But anyone who has
looked closely at himself, and examined himself thoroughly will
find a certain part of his nature to be a fit remedy for these evils and
well suited to bring peace between these competing affections.
Certainly *Pronoia*,[27] that Divine Providence, which we often call
nature, has not been ungenerous in her care for us. For God has
given us reason and a keenness of judgement which easily discerns
that it is by means of a life in society and in friendship that we can
most effectively procure and retain all pleasures, including the private and sensuous ones. Reason also teaches that the enjoyment of
modest and restrained pleasures is most advantageous and most
agreeable to us and does not produce an unsettling effect on human
society. Conversely, there is no reason to believe that any man
needs for the sake of an agreeable and secure life to hoard unlim-
ited stores of goods or to indulge in continuous exquisite sensual
pleasures, in the obtaining of which others are harmed or morally
proper action is neglected. This does not require any lengthy or
laborious deduction. God has given us a sense of what is becoming
and beautiful; conjoined with it is a sense of shame, by which all
the more lowly pleasures are restrained. Likewise, He has given us
the keen incentives of praise. All this leads to a kind and social life,
and gives rise to virtuous actions which benefit others and which
are most useful and most pleasant to the agent. There also arises
that self-love of our nature which, although innate, is in no manner
in conflict with our public and benevolent affections.

30. I should think that it is also of prime importance to note that in
order to attract someone's good-will, it is not necessarily required
that we first vie with him in performing good offices. We certainly
favour any blameless person even if we do not owe him thanks for
any service. We favour even very distant nations and deplore their
calamities, even if we have only heard of them. But in contrast, in
order for any anger or ill-will to be aroused there must be some
opposition of interest, some rivalry or insult, or some idea of a prior
injury or act of violence. And this seems to show that benevolence

---

[27] A term much used by the Stoics. See Cicero, *On the Nature of the Gods*, 2, 58. It
occurs frequently in Marcus Aurelius, whose *Meditations* were very highly
esteemed by Hutcheson and translated by him in collaboration with his friend
and colleague James Moor (1708–79).

is immediately and in itself natural, whilst ill-will arises only secondarily and often only by chance or through ignorance.

31. The structure of our nature must not be held responsible for any of that slackness and idleness in the control of our passions and affections which besets the human mind, nor for any of that excessive inclination towards sensual pleasures which throws all things in turmoil. It is of course true that our nature is fallen, weak, and corrupted in many respects. But who does not easily perceive the order natural to the human mind? Who is ignorant of which parts are by nature fit to rule, no matter how much they may be deflected from fulfilling that role? Does anyone think that natural conscience, that sense of what is beautiful and becoming, every honourable affection and even that power of the mind that we call reason, are only handmaids to those desires that are commonly said to be merely sensual, and only pander to pleasure? On the contrary, we discern without any doubt that this conscience and sense of virtue, which has human reason as its permanent counsellor, is destined by nature to govern, and that the bodily appetites are born to serve.

32. Those who hold the opposite view are wonderfully clever in their ways and transform themselves in thousands of ways like Proteus,[28] in order escape these conclusions. All the social affections, they say, are due to the daily attentions of parents and teachers. They make much of education and statecraft, which, they say, explains this actual human sociality and those affections which either seem or actually are kind.[29] Having been moulded by long practice and by fear of punishment to an outward show of friendliness, politeness, and easy manners, we think of these habits as natural in the same way that common people regard their native language as natural. And it does indeed seem that we must concede

---

28 A minor sea-god, able to assume different shapes. If pinned down so as to be in his true shape, he will give truthful answers. Hutcheson makes the same complaint in *T2* 1, 4 (1st edn 1725), p. 114: `Some Moralists ... will rather twist Self-Love into a thousand Shapes, than allow any other Principle of Approbation than Interest.'

29 `Man is made fit for Society not by Nature, but by Education' according to the English version of Hobbes's *De cive*, (*Philosophicall Rudiments Concerning Government and Society*, 1st edn 1651) ed. H. Warrender, Oxford: Oxford University Press 1983, ch. 1, section 2, p. 44. Mandeville similarly stressed the role and importance of education.

to our opponents that these external offices and civilised manners can result from respect for the law and the efforts of those in authority; everyone's thought of his own interest can be relevant to this extent and can have that effect. But is it really possible that hope for advantage, education or custom can induce new inner affections and new senses contrary to one's natural constitution? Instruction may cause us to take the true to be false, and we may, because of false preconceptions, come to regard useless things as useful. Indeed, perhaps even the bodily organs themselves will be changed by long use so that things formerly unpleasant would be rendered pleasant. Moreover, it often happens to us prior to a difficult trial that we regard it as unwelcome but have the contrary view after the event. Indeed, in these matters,

> Is there anything pleasing or offending which you believe
> to be immutable?[30]

33. But all these things occur in accordance with the very senses antecedently implanted in us by nature; no new senses or affections come into being. Nor do these things come before the mind under an appearance different from those for the perception of which nature has implanted suitable senses. By what artifice or what effort, I ask, could anyone commend garments or furnishings to a blind person by referring to the beautiful colour?[31] And even more, how could anyone make a thing or event appear desirable to a being who only pursues his own pleasure or advantage and who does not distinguish good from bad in any other way, unless it was by reference to his own pleasure or advantage? But we do find that men judge most acts to be virtuous, praiseworthy, beautiful, and becoming, even when no advantage of their own is involved; likewise, we find a solicitous concern for others and a great willingness to help them even though all appearance of private advantage has been entirely removed.

34. For some reason or other, ever since the celebrated Locke and other writers seemed to have sufficiently demonstrated that no ideas, no knowledge [*notitia*], and no theoretical or practical

---

[30] Horace, *Epistolae*, 2, 1, 101, in *Opera*, ed. Wickham and Garrod. In C. Passage's translation, the number is 2, 1, 107 and reads, 'Is there, however, a good thing or evil not subject to change?'

[31] Similarly in *T1*, section 7.

judgements present in the mind (these were in their view the only kinds of things that could be called innate) have their origin there, a great number of very distinguished and honourable men have almost completely avoided all inquiry into natural ideas, knowledge [*notitiis*], and judgements, as well as the natural sense by which various kinds of things are perceived. But as far as I recall, the ancients said that all ideas, apprehensions, and judgements which we form of things under the guidance of nature – no matter at what time – or which are universally and, as it were, necessarily received by no matter which natural faculties of ours, are innate. And it would certainly be much more useful to inquire into these natural judgements, perceptions, and appearances of things that nature presents, than to dwell on what may or may not be observed in that animalcule which ultimately develops into a human being, or in some very few unfortunates born in some barren corner of the earth, who eke out a rough and brutish life, without any of the skills and conditions of life proper to human beings. What would be the point of telling a shipwright who seeks building materials for the royal navy about the puny shoots which spring forth from an acorn in a year or two, but which lack appropriate size, hardness, strength, and firmness, or of informing him about oak-bushes that spring up in infertile soil or cling to stony fissures in broken rocks? For there are indeed many powers natural to all kinds of things, many senses and appetites in animals, many natural structures that are not at all apparent from the outset. Some, indeed, will never come to light, if there is no appropriate occasion, or if some condition, required by nature, remains unfulfilled. Who has ever observed any desire for a mate at such embryonic stages? And yet, what is more natural to every kind of animal than conjunction for the sake of procreation? Who will find anger unless there appears to be some injury, or love unless something appears lovable? We perceive a huge, craggy rock, on a mountainside, in a threatening overhang over a precipice, and yet remaining in its place. Will anyone deny that it has weight? If the support is removed and the continuing force of adhesion ceases, a headlong tumbling down will be observed. They should therefore cease objecting that there are no innate ideas, and that affections and desires cannot be conceived without prior ideas. For this would equally tend to show that the private[32] affections and desires are not natural either, inasmuch as not even ideas of private pleasure or advantage are innate, in the sense in which recent writers call something innate.

35. Others raise the further objection that if men were desirous of each other, then, being equally men, they would be equally desired.[33] But this is like denying that some bonds of nature can be closer than others. Yet they persist, arguing that in all human company everyone seeks his own advantage, pleasure or glory. When meeting in the market-place for the sake of commerce, everyone works for his own profit; when gathered for purposes of recreation everyone seeks to get the others to laugh with him in order to assert his own superiority over those whom he ridicules; or he reviles those who are absent, or boasts about himself and his possessions. And when the conversation turns to more serious matters almost everyone, considering himself superior in wisdom, seeks glory and intellectual domination, all of which results in quarrels and hatreds. Those with less self-confidence nevertheless wish to learn something from which they can later derive glory.[34] The answer that ought to be given to all this is obvious: Men of virtue, distinction, wit, and kindness often get together without expecting profit or glory, and without attempting to boast of themselves or to ridicule or revile others. And when they discuss more serious matters in friendly conversation, all express their opinions freely, pleasantly, and considerately, without striving for glory or intellectual superiority. And even if we were to admit that it is rather rare that men come together without the hope of some private advantage, what can our opponents make of it? Who ever denied that private affections were implanted in man by nature? What if we were to grant them this as well, that private affections are quite often stronger than the public and kind ones? Will they infer from this that there are no truly benevolent affections? One might equally infer that most bodies are weightless from the fact that some of them are heavier than others. But further, if several ends can be simultane-

---

[32] Here, as elsewhere, `private' means self-interested, selfish.

[33] Hobbes, *De cive* ch. 1, section 2, p. 42: `For if by nature one Man should Love another (that is) as a Man, there could no reason be return'd why every Man should not equally Love every Man as being equally Man'

[34] These points are also made by Hobbes in *De cive* 2, 1.

ously pursued by one course of action, this will be used by some to argue that we have no regard for each other. But very rarely does it seem likely that men would come together to form a private association or a civil society if they completely lacked any kind or social affections. If indeed benevolence, and with it the trusting, unsuspecting expectation of reciprocity of benevolence, which almost always accompanies a kind character, were foreign to human nature, then those ambitious men who usually vie for political power, would not find the people so easy and tractable as to entrust their persons and all their fortunes to their good faith.

36. Finally – and this is above all something that needs to be noted – when men are said to seek their own profit or advantage, they are undoubtedly for the most part acting for the sake of offspring or kindred, impelled by benevolent motives and the most tender love. And by far the greater part of all care and concern in human life is claimed by parental affection[35] and the devotion to family, friends, and country: how great and how continuing is not the concern that springs from these affections! How much zeal for a party is there not in a state, even among those who do not presume even tacitly to aspire to distinctions, public office, or sinecures! They readily favour the party which seems to them more honest and more useful to the state, without any thought of private advantage.

37. But our opponents persevere: if human society were not sought for the sake of advantage or pleasure, why do we seek the company of those who are learned, elegant, affable, gentle, generous, powerful, and respected, from which we may derive something advantageous, pleasant or indeed virtuous; whilst we avoid those who are ignorant, gloomy, bad-tempered, boastful, ungenerous, and disreputable? As if we were capable of being benevolent, or kindly or sociably disposed exclusively to those whom we wish to have as our intimate companions! As if, indeed, it were asserted that the only desire implanted in the mind is the desire for society; or that there was nothing disagreeable or offending in the manners of some men which would make us reluctant to have them as our

---

[35] Frequently mentioned by Hutcheson. See e.g. *T*3 2, 6, (1st edn 1728) p. 52. Parental affection as a natural instinct was a recurrent topic in most writers on natural religion and morality, e.g. by Cicero in *On the Nature of the Gods*, 2, 47–52, and by Addison in *The Spectator*, nos. 120 and 121.

companions; or again, that there were no natural or acquired virtues in others, which would make some of them more suited than others for friendship and for a happier lifelong association.

38. I hope, therefore, to have sufficiently confirmed my initial statement that social life, in a condition under no civil authority, is in itself natural to man; on some other occasion perhaps I shall speak about the probable causes and origin of civil society. From what has been said, however, the benevolence towards mankind of the Deity, whom we should always gratefully worship and admire, is obvious from man's very constitution; since the most beneficent Father of all has, with so much skill and care, with such wise counsel, provided and equipped us for all that is excellent and virtuous, and indeed joyful and agreeable. And when we urge men to lead an upright, harmless, virtuous, temperate, friendly, and beneficent life, let it not be thought that this is a demand for something gloomy, toilsome, disagreeable, and sorrowful, which one would naturally find repugnant. There is, in the end, no other road to that which we by nature seek above all, that is, safety, peace, happiness, indeed a pure pleasure undisturbed by remorse or secret guilt.

39. Cultivate virtue, therefore, my dear young friends, you who are the hope of the present age and who will, I hope, adorn the future with your achievements; follow nature and God as your guide, engage in honourable pursuits, and acquire a foundation for all kinds of useful knowledge, later to be applied temperately, modestly, courageously, and honestly in all kinds of service for the benefit of your country and mankind. You should no less hope for and aspire to that most agreeable sense of a good conscience, dignity, esteem, and deserved good reputation, and the sublimest pleasures of life.

THE END

Appendices

Appendix 1 *The quotation from Bayle's dictionary*

'Remarquez bien, s'il vous plaît, qu'en parlant des bonnes moeurs de quelques athées, je ne leur ai point attribué de veritables vertus. Leur sobriété, leur chastété, leur probité, leur mépris pour les richesses, leur zêle du bien public, leur inclination à rendre de bons offices à leur prochain, ne procedoient pas de l'amour de Dieu, & ne tendoient pas à l'honorer & à le glorifier. Ils en étoient eux-mêmes la source & le but; l'amour propre en était la base, le terme, toute l'analyse. Ce n'étoient que les pechez éclatants, splendida peccata, commes Saint Augustin l'a dit de toutes les belles action des Païens.' Pierre Bayle, *Dictionnaire Historique et Critique*, 2nd edn 1702, 'Eclaircissement sur les athées', p. 3137, ¶7. The English quotation is from *The Dictionary Historical and Critical of Mr Peter Bayle* (transl. P. Desmaizeaux et al.) 2nd edn, London 1734–38. In the translation of selections from this work edited by R. Popkin (Indianapolis: Bobbs-Merrill 1965) the above passage is rendered as follows: 'Please notice carefully that in speaking of the good morals of some atheists, I have not attributed any real virtues to them. Their sobriety, their chastity, their probity, their contempt for riches, their zeal for the public good, their inclination to be helpful to their neighbor were not the effect of the love of God and tended neither to honor nor to glorify him. They themselves were the source and end of all this. Self-love was the basis, the boundaries, and the cause of it. These were only glittering sins, *splendida peccata*, as St Augustine has said of all the fine actions of the pagans.'

Pierre Bayle (1647–1706) had to leave his native France because of the religious persecution that raged during the years around the revocation of the Edict of Nantes 1685, and settled in Rotterdam. He was a prolific writer with a prodigious memory. He started the first literary-cultural magazine, *Nouvelles de la République des Lettres*, wrote single-handed a monumental historical and critical dictionary, and a number of books, mainly concerning controversial points of religion. He attacked religious persecution and intolerance with immense erudition and brilliant eloquence. During his stay in the Netherlands he had friendly contacts with many distinguished men in the world of learning, among them Locke and Shaftesbury. He

148

became embroiled in theological controversy with both Roman Catholic and Protestant writers, since his own theological views seemed highly suspect to both kinds of opponents. Many aspects of his literary activities, including his spirited plea for toleration, have led later historians to praise him as the father of the Enlightenment.

Appendix 2 *Bayle's reputation*

The problem was discussed at length in J. F. Buddeus, *Theses theologicae de atheismi et superstitione* (1st edn 1716), ed. H. Buurt, Utrecht 1737, pp. 114–118. Buddeus lists (in a page-long sentence!) a large number of reasons for suspicion and finds that even if they are not sufficient for a conviction, they create a strong presumption of guilt, and he maintains that it is beyond doubt that Bayle's selection of topics and manner of writing are eminently suited to promoting the cause of atheism and probably so intended. One sign of the ambiguous reputation of Bayle is that he was regularly mentioned together with other writers of doubtful reputation among the *bien-pensants*: the title-page of *Aretelogia* is just one example, and in his *System* (written in the mid-1730s) Hutcheson likewise placed Bayle in the suspect company of Hobbes, Mandeville, and La Rochefoucauld (see note 49 on p. 122). There is a comprehensive account of the early reception of Bayle in Rétat, *Le Dictionnaire de Bayle*. In the current debate, two main interpretations remain opposed. For Paul Hazard and many others, Bayle in subtle ways shows up the *irrationality* of religious belief, in support of a free-thinking position. This view is rejected by Elisabeth Labrousse, who reads Bayle's arguments as establishing the *non-rationality* of religious belief, as a basis for a fideist acceptance of Christian doctrine.

Appendix 3 *A terminological point*

Self-love was the term regularly used at the time, with *benevolence* as its antonym. There were also alternative turns of phrase, for instance in terms of the contrast between *private* and *public*. In Maxwell's translation of Cumberland (1727) we read at 3, 2, 2: `A *private* good is that which profits one, *public*, which is of advantage to *many*.' *Desire for private happiness* was used as a synonym of *self-love*. The same contrast was also expressed in the opposition between *selfish* and *kind* affections. *Selfishness* and *sociableness* were understood as opposites (Shaftesbury, *Characteristics*, vol. I, p. 77). It was through Auguste Comte, a century later, that *altruisme* was coined and the present-day sense of *egoism* gained currency. In English, *altruism* was introduced by G. Lewes in the early 1850s and became fully naturalised through the writings of Herbert Spencer.

Appendix 4 *The contrasting of rationality and sociality*

Henry Grove (1684–1738), Presbyterian minister, head of an academy at Taunton in Somerset, rose in defence of benevolence against the egoistic theories in Epicurus, Hobbes, etc. Among his writings are four essays in *The Spectator*.

According to the traditional view (Aristotle, Grotius), man is essentially a rational and social animal. Grove alludes to this view, but then goes on to associate rationality with self-love and sociality with benevolence. Neither of these two principal tendencies in human nature can be reduced to the other. His essay in *The Spectator* no. 588; 1 September 1714, is headed by a motto from Cicero's *De Natura Deorum* (On the nature of the gods) and refers, for purposes of refutation, to the Epicurean view that goodness and benevolence is based on weakness. The essay begins as follows (my italics):

> Man may be considered in two views, as a *reasonable*, and as a *sociable* being; capable of becoming himself either happy or miserable, and of contributing to the happiness or misery of his fellow-creatures. Suitably to this double capacity, the Contriver of human nature hath wisely furnished it with two principles of action, *self-love* and *benevolence*; designed one of them to render man wakeful to his personal interest, the other to dispose him for giving his utmost assistance to all engag'd in the same pursuit.

It is curious to see this early identification of rationality with pursuit of self-interest.

Appendix 5   *A note on* 'The Whole Duty of Man'

A brief comment on this may prevent possible confusions. The title given to the English translation of Pufendorf's *De officio hominis et civis* was *The Whole Duty of Man According to the Law of Nature* (transl. Andrew Tooke, 1st edn 1691, 5th edn 1735). It was no doubt chosen because of its allusion to the title of another book, *The Whole Duty of Man*, a very popular and widely read work of moral and religious edification, reliably attributed to Richard Allestree, an Oxford theologian. Most sources have 1659 as the year of publication, but according to John Spurr in his *The Restoration Church of England 1646–1689* (1991) it was 1658. Spurr discusses the content at some length in a very informative chapter. Elsewhere (at p. 230) he also remarks that it 'reached a saturation of the market equal to that of modern bestsellers.' BLC has about fifty different entries (translations not included) up to 1740. It was about this work that there was an important court case concerning infringement of copyright in 1735 (according to *The Oxford Companion to English Literature*, 5th edn, pp. 1117f). Another indication of how well known and successful it was is the fact that the title was frequently imitated. One example is *The Young Man's Calling: or, The Whole Duty of Youth...* (8th edn 1726). Another is *The Whole Duty of A Christian. By Way of Question and Answer, exactly pursuant to the Method of the Whole Duty of Man, and design'd for the Use of Charity Schools...* (7th edn 1725). There was also *The Whole Duty of a Woman, The Whole Duty of a Mother*, etc..

When Hume mentioned in his autobiography that he had in his youth closely studied *The Whole Duty of Man* he was referring to the work attributed to Allestree. There can be no doubt that this is also the work Hume had in mind when, in his letter to Hutcheson 17.9.1739, he expressed a preference for Cicero over *The Whole Duty of Man*. Hume favoured ancient moralists over modern divines, and this would be an inoffensive way of making that point.

The threefold division of duties could be seen as having not only a rational, but also a scriptural foundation. Allestree's *The Whole Duty of Man* was organised according to 'the words of the Apostle Titus ii. 12: That we should live soberly, righteously, and godly in this present world; where the word soberly, contains our duty to our selves; righteously, our duty to our neighbour, and godly, our duty to God. These, therefore, shall be the heads of my discourse, our duty to God, ourselves, and our neighbour' (quoted from J. Spurr, *The Restoration Church*, p. 282).

Appendix 6 *A note on the choice of forum for philosophical discourses*

William Leechman's Preface to Hutcheson's posthumously published *System of Moral Philosophy* is the most important extant primary source of information about Hutcheson's life and work. On the subject of appropriate ways of communicating philosophical ideas, he wrote (pp. xxxviiif.):

> He particularly insisted upon the uselessness and impropriety of handling in the pulpit such speculative questions, as, whether human nature is capable of disinterested affections, whether the original of duty or moral obligation is from natural conscience, or moral sense, from law, or from rational views of interest, and such like enquiries [...] such disquisitions might be proper or even necessary in a school of philosophy, yet [...] they did not fall within the province of the preacher, whose office is not to explain the principles of the human mind, but to address himself to them and set them in motion.

This was a widespread custom. This remark about the practice of turning a sermon into a philosophy lecture would apply not only to Butler, but to many others as well, including the clergymen mentioned in the Introduction, i.e. Berkeley, Waterland, etc. There was a reaction against this style of preaching in the latter half of the century, no doubt due at least in part to the influence of Methodism. Thus, the compiler of *The English Preacher* (1773) commended the increasing taste for 'practical' preaching, and wrote

> In consequence of the taste for controversial, speculative, or critical preaching which formerly prevailed, we find in some of our best authors many discourses upon topics which are now pretty generally, and perhaps justly, considered as less useful, mixed with those which are moral or devotional.

Appendix 7 *A note on the similarity between Hutcheson and Hume*

Hume's *Treatise*, Book 3, Part 1, Section 1 is headed `Moral distinctions not deriv'd from reason' and is strongly influenced by Hutcheson's *Illustrations*.

Hume was quite explicit about this. Before the third last paragraph of chapter 1 of Hume's *Enquiry Concerning Human Understanding*, there was in the earliest editions (published under the title *Philosophical Essays Concerning Human Understanding*) a note, omitted from later editions for reasons unknown to me, in which Hume clearly indicated this. The quotation is from pp. 14f. of the first edition 1748, reproducing Hume's punctuation but not his use of capitals and italics:

> That faculty, by which we discern truth and falshood, and that by which we perceive vice and virtue had long been confounded with each other, and all morality was suppos'd to be built on eternal and immutable relations, which to every intelligent mind were equally invariable as any proposition concerning quantity or number. But a late philosopher (Mr. Hutcheson) has taught us, by the most convincing arguments, that morality is nothing in the abstract nature of things, but is entirely relative to the sentiment or mental taste of each particular being; in the same manner as the distinctions of sweet and bitter, hot and cold, arise from the particular feeling of each sense or organ. Moral perceptions therefore, ought not to be class'd with the operations of the understanding, but with the tastes or sentiments.

In the opinion of the reviewer in *Bibliothèque Raisonnée* 26 (1741) 411–27 at pp. 423f, Hume's *Treatise*, Book 3 (*Of Morals*) [1740] contains essentially the system proposed by Hutcheson in *Inquiry*.

The reviewer, incidentally, also complains that Hume ought to have made good Hutcheson's failure to reply to Gilbert Burnet's objections, presented in the correspondence that took place in *The London Journal* 1725. The complaint is obviously about the non-existence of a reply from Hutcheson, not of its inadequacy, so the reviewer must have been unaware of the fact that Hutcheson, in the preface to *T3&T4* (1st edn 1728) *ad fin.*, had written that he in this book `had endeavoured to leave no objections of [Burnet's] unanswered'. For details, see the bibliography.

The view that Hume's principles of morals were the same as Hutcheson's seems to have been commonly accepted, by, *inter alios*, the writer in *Beyträge zu den Leipziger Gelehrten Zeitungen*, vol. VII, pp. 549 ff. (not seen; the source for this is Trinius's *Freydencker-Lexicon*, p. 327).

Among recent writers who have reminded us of the similarities between Hutcheson and Hume and analysed them, especially as regards their moral epistemology, are Norman Kemp Smith, Arthur Prior, and David F. Norton. See the bibliography.

`Appendix 8 *Extract from a letter from Hume to Hutcheson*

The letter, dated 17.9.1739, is quoted (with spelling modernised) from *The Letters of David Hume*, ed. J.Y.T. Greig, Oxford: Clarendon Press, 1932, vol. I, pp. 32f.

[...] What affected me most in your remarks is your observing, that there wants a certain warmth in the cause of virtue, which, you think, all good men would relish, and could not displease amidst abstract enquiries. I must own, this has not happened by chance, but is the effect of a reasoning either good or bad. There are different ways of examining the mind as well as the body. One may consider it either as an anatomist or as a painter; either to discover its most secret springs and principles or to describe the grace and beauty of its actions. I imagine it impossible to conjoin these two views. Where you pull off the skin, and display all the minute parts, there appears something trivial, even in the noblest attitudes and most vigorous actions: nor can you ever render the object graceful or engaging but by cloathing the parts again with skin and flesh, and presenting only their bare outside. An anatomist, however, can give very good advice to a painter or statuary: and in like manner, I am persuaded, that a metaphysician may be very helpful to a moralist; though I cannot easily conceive these two characters united in the same work. Any warm sentiment of morals, I am afraid, would have the air of declamation amidst abstract reasonings, and would be esteemed contrary to good taste. And though I am much more ambitious of being esteemed a friend to virtue, than a writer of taste; yet I must always carry the latter in my eye, otherwise I must despair of ever being serviceable to virtue. I hope these reasons will satisfy you; though at the same time, I intend to make a new trial, if it be possible to make the moralist and metaphysician agree a little better.

I cannot agree to your sense of natural. It is founded on final causes; which is a consideration, that appears to me pretty uncertain and unphilosophical. [...]

Appendix 9 *A note on Hobbes's psychological egoism*

[Hobbes's] grand view was to deduce all human actions from *self-love*: by some bad fortune he has over-look'd every thing which is *generous* or *kind* in mankind; and represents men in that light in which a thorow knave or coward beholds them, suspecting all friendship, love, or social affection, of hypocrisy, or selfish design or fear.

(Hutcheson, `Reflections upon Laughter', in *Hibernicus's Letters*, p. 78. This is letter no. 10, dated 5 June 1725.)

Hume suggested a different reading in Appendix II of his *Enquiry Concerning the Principles of Morals*. He argued that Hobbes's theory need not be understood as an accusation against mankind of universal selfishness and hypocrisy. In his view, Hobbes and others deny that any passion can be disinterested; that the most generous friendship, however sincere, is a modification of self-love. In every action, the hero and the scoundrel are equally concerned about their own happiness and welfare. But, Hume continues, this is a *speculative* hypothesis:

> An Epicurean or a Hobbist readily allows, that there is such a thing as friendship in the world, *without hypocrisy or disguise*; though he may attempt, by *a philosophical chymistry*, to resolve the elements of this passion ... and explain every affection to be self-love, twisted and moulded, by a particular turn of the imagination, into a variety of appearances. (My italics.)

In recent years it has been argued that Hobbes was *not* a psychological egoist. This new reading of Hobbes is even said to have become generally accepted. Jean Hampton writes, in the *Philosophical Review* 98 (1990) on p. 410, with references to recent books and articles by B. Gert, G. Kavka, T. Sorell, etc., that 'Hobbes has now been so frequently defended against the charge of being a psychological egoist that perhaps we can take the issue as settled.'

At first sight, this assertion is certainly surprising. It seems to imply that nearly everyone who read Hobbes in the past three centuries had misread him. Perhaps some did: it is arguable that some of Butler's arguments do not really engage with Hobbes's view. But the general claim implies that for centuries the readers of Hobbes, many of whom must be supposed to have studied the texts with some care, would have had a blind spot on this matter. This is not impossible, but it seems improbable, and in order to make it plausible it would help to have the ubiquitousness of the supposed mistake explained.

Appendix 10 *Hutcheson's critique of Mandeville: some re-publication data*

Further editions of Mandeville's *Fable of the Bees* saw the light in 1728 and 1729, at which time the work again gained added publicity through prosecutions, initiated by the Grand Juries of Middlesex and of the City of London, aimed at suppressing the book. Their presentment is reproduced in *Fog's Weekly Journal* no. 18, 25 January 1729.

Also in 1729, a collection of essays from *The Dublin Weekly Journal*, edited by James Arbuckle, was published in London, on the 17th May, according to an advertisement in no. 511 of *The London Journal*. This is the collection whose second edition five years later was named *Hibernicus's Letters*. Included were Hutcheson's essays against Mandeville. These essays were of course particularly topical because of the re-editions and prosecutions of the *Fable of the Bees*, and were indeed put to further use. A fortnight later, in early June 1729, *The London Journal* commenced a three-week series of leading essays, which were devoted to an attack on Mandeville. In the polemic, the anonymous writer initially employs expressions like `the Nature and Reason of Things', `Virtue and Vice [being] founded on the Relation of Things': rationalistic turns of phrase for which Hutcheson is obviously not the source. It is rather Clarke's rationalism that springs to mind, although many other writers also used expressions of this kind, e.g. John Balguy, who could write: `Virtue consists in the Conformity of men's Actions to the Reasons of Things' (*The Foundation of Moral Goodness*, 1728, p. 60), and these locutions became indeed so common they could be used for effect even in popular works destined for a general readership, like Fielding's *Tom Jones*. In the sequel, however, the bulk of the instalments actually consists of direct quotations from Hutcheson, who is not named, but referred to as `a very great man' and as `an ingenious gentleman'. This eclectic performance appeared in *The London Journal* 514–16, 7, 14 and 21 June 1729. The anonymous author actually names his main source in no. 516, p. 1, col. 1, but the dependence of these essays on Hutcheson seems not to have been noticed previously. The only reference to them that I have seen is in Kaye's edition of *The Fable of the Bees* (vol. II, p. 424). He mentions nos. 514 and 515, but seems to have overlooked no. 516, in his chronological list of writings which contain references to *The Fable*.

Appendix 11   *An alleged recommendation of Hutcheson by Waterland*

According to R.T. Holtby, *Daniel Waterland 1683-1740: A Study in Eighteenth Century Orthodoxy*, p. 199, Waterland recommended Hutcheson in his *Advice to a Young Student*. It is a surprising statement, which stimulated a modest research effort yielding the following result.

There are various editions of this short work. An `Advice to a Student, 1706' by Waterland is mentioned by J.W. Adamson in a note on p. 76 of his edition of *The Educational Writings of John Locke* (London: Arnold 1912). No such edition is recorded in the *Eighteenth Century Short Title Catalogue* (2nd ed 1990). Adamson's information may nevertheless be correct. According to van Mildert's biographical memoir in the preface to his edition of Waterland's *Works*, Waterland tutored from 1704 and well into the 1710s:

His tract entitled `Advice to a Student', [was] written while he was engaged in that service, ...

Van Mildert was apparently unaware of any early edition, and of the earliest printed version which, no doubt without the author's permission, appeared in *The Present State of the Republick of Letters* 4 (1729) 412–443 under the heading: `Advice to a Young Student at the University; By a Divine of the Church of England.' Soon after, it was published as a pamphlet in Cambridge 1730, and again in Cambridge 1760.

No matter whether the very early version exists: it would have been written much earlier than any publication by Hutcheson and could not have recommended any writing of his. The curious fact is that none of the later versions mentioned so far do so either. There was, however, a `second edition, corrected', published in Oxford in 1755, and according to the preface, some amendments had been made by a `judicious friend'. This is the version that is reprinted in the nineteenth-century editions of Waterland's *Works*. And in this version the recommendation of Baronius for metaphysics in the fourth year has been changed in favour of Hutcheson's *Synopsis*, of which the first (unauthorised) edition was published in 1742. Waterland died in 1740. So the work recommended is not on moral philosophy, and the recommendation must have come from the judicious friend, and not from Waterland himself.

Appendix 12   *A note on Archibald Campbell's Enquiry*

The first edition of this work was published 1728 under the title *Aretelogia* ... and the name of the author was given as Alexander Innes.

Archibald Campbell (1691–1756) professor of ecclesiastical history at St Andrews from 1730, had sent the manuscript to a relative, Alexander Innes, a young clergyman, not yet settled, in London, asking him to help find a publisher. Innes succeeded but put his own name on the title-page, claiming authorship. He added a preface of his own which, arguably, shows an imperfect understanding of the body of the text. In this way he hoped to attract favourable attention from persons in high station, and to obtain preferment to a comfortable living. Eventually, Campbell became aware of what had happened and took strong exception to it. But when he confronted Innes, who had little to say in his defence, he nevertheless agreed to delay a public announcement concerning the authorship for a while, in order not to impair Innes's prospects, and Innes did in fact come into a profitable living. The subsequent editions, entitled *An Enquiry into the Original* ... were revised and expanded. The matter is briefly mentioned in Boswell's *Life of Johnson* (Aetat. 52, 1761, p. 254), but for further sordid detail see the long note by F.B. Kaye at p. 25 of vol. II of his edition of Mandeville's *Fable of the Bees*, or the *DNB*.

In the *Inquiry*, T2 2, 10, Hutcheson discusses parental love and illustrates it with the concern that an `honest farmer' would show for his children. In the fourth edition of the *Inquiry* (1738), a whole paragraph has been added. (In the copy I have used, this addition is not incorporated in the text but printed in an appendix.) It begins:

> Another author thinks all this easily deducible from Self-Love. `Children are not only made of our Bodies, but resemble us in Body and Mind; they are rational Agents as we are, and we only love our own Likeness in them.'[etc.]

Who is this author? The points to which Hutcheson here responds can be found in Archibald Campbell's *Aretelogia* (1728), pp. 240–50, slightly revised in *Enquiry* (1st edn 1733), pp. 336–46. Probably he is this unnamed `another author`.

Appendix 13 *The authorship of the review in* Bibliothèque Angloise

It has been suggested by David Raynor, in `Hutcheson's Defence Against a Charge of Plagiarism`, *Eighteenth-Century Ireland* 2 (1987) 177–181, that the review in *Bibliothèque Angloise* might have been written by Jean-Pierre Desmaizeaux (1673–1745) and not by La Chapelle himself. This is possible. But on the evidence available it does not seem probable.

In contrast to Le Clerc, in *Bibliothèque Ancienne et Moderne,* who suggests some similarity between Crousaz and Hutcheson only in passing, the author in *Bibliothèque Angloise* adopts quite an unpleasant tone and spends almost the whole of the short review on the complaint that Hutcheson has failed to acknowledge his indebtedness to Crousaz.

It is arguable that La Chapelle, in contrast to Desmaizeaux, would have had a motive for doing this. Hutcheson's theological sympathies went in a direction very different from the orthodox Calvinism to which La Chapelle staunchly adhered. Moreover, as shown by Margaret Thomas (`Michel de La Roche' pp. 111, 116, 167, etc.) there was tension between La Chapelle and La Roche. They had both been editors of the *Bibliothèque Angloise* until 1719, when La Roche was ousted. Differences of opinion on religious questions played their part. They were both Huguenots in exile, but whilst La Roche, having found refuge in England, soon joined the Church of England and consistently advocated tolerant latitudinarian views – he was also on friendly terms with Hoadly – , La Chapelle had followed a very different path. When La Roche's participation in the *Bibliothèque Angloise* was no longer desired, he entered into direct competition with his *Mémoires Littéraires de la Grande-Bretagne* 1720–1724. After their opening `Avertissements' the two writers never made direct mention of each other in their respective journals during this period of parallel activity, but eventually La Chapelle's pent-up hostility could be restrained no longer. So the opportunity to write a piece that would detract from the reputation of an author much admired by La Roche would not have been unwelcome to La Chapelle.

In contrast, Desmaizeaux, also a Huguenot in exile, had much in common with La Roche. Both of them had had an association with Bayle. They had worked together, especially on the English translation of Bayle's dictionary. Like La Roche, but in contrast to La Chapelle, Desmaizeaux was theologically quite liberal–minded, as were the people with whom he primarily was associated. When he first found refuge in England, Shaftesbury was among those who had given him support, and he maintained friendly contacts with deists and freethinkers like Anthony Collins (1676–1729).

There were, then, affinities of various kinds between Desmaizeaux, La Roche, and Hutcheson. La Chapelle, on the contrary represented a stricter, more traditional theology.

The suggestion that Desmaizeaux wrote the review for La Chapelle presupposes of course that they maintained contact. It is known that they did later in the decade, but there is not, to my knowledge, any evidence that there was contact at the relevant time.

A further conjecture merits exploration: there could have been a pecuniary interest. In 1724, a second edition of Crousaz's *Traité du Beau* (1st edn 1715) had been published in Amsterdam. The reviewer's statement that Hutcheson has written as a *copiste* of Crousaz might induce prospective buyers to prefer the latter.

None of these circumstances is conclusive, but until further evidence comes to light, La Chapelle seems a more likely author of the review than Desmaizeaux. He had reasons for wishing to discredit Hutcheson; Desmaizeaux had reasons for not wishing to do so.

Appendix 14 *Wollaston and Samuel Clarke*

In the *Reflections* Hutcheson refers frequently to 'our moralists' generally, but the only ones mentioned by name are Hobbes and Pufendorf.

According to Aldridge, Hutcheson had Samuel Clarke's *Discourse concerning the Being and Attributes of God* and Wollaston's *The Religion of Nature Delineated* particularly in mind, and suggests a series of parallels between Wollaston's work and the description Hutcheson gives of the views of the orthodox. See e.g. Aldridge, *A Preview*, p. 156. But the alleged parallels do not seem close, and the suggestion that these two theologians were orthodox is surprising.

A circumstance that suggests that Hutcheson did *not* have Wollaston particularly in his sights is a statement by James Arbuckle, a close friend and admirer of Hutcheson. In one of his contributions to *The Dublin Weekly Journal*, 7 May 1726 (*Hibernicus's Letters*, no. 58), he wrote that although, at the present, letters did not flourish as in the age of Socrates or the age of Cicero, when there was a constellation of great geniuses, nevertheless

> It must be owned that [the learned world] has lately produced some performances of great value and usefulness, on very important subjects, particularly in morality. My intelligent Readers will quickly perceive, that I have in my eye those two incomparable treatises, the *Religion of Nature delineated* and the *Inquiry into Beauty and Virtue*; works which cannot fail of being esteemed while mankind have any regard left for good sense, or useful knowledge.

We have already seen (p. 24) how vehemently Arbuckle reacted against the mercenary ethics of rewards and punishments. If he saw in Wollaston, the author of *Religion of Nature*, a typical representative of that outlook, the high praise of Wollaston – and of Hutcheson in the same breath – would not have been forthcoming. And there is no reason to believe that he and Hutcheson differed on this point.

On the other hand, Clarke could be a target, because of his Boyle lectures (see the bibliography). Aldridge mentions only the first set of these lectures, although the second is probably much more relevant.

When Hutcheson later criticised Wollaston and Samuel Clarke in *Illustrations*, it was for their rationalistic theories of ethics.

Appendix 15   *The origin of 'sociality'*

The noun 'sociality' itself and its ancestor *socialitas* were of recent currency. Seneca (*De beneficiis* 7, 1) had rendered Aristotle's *zoon politikon* by *animal sociale*, and this usage became firmly established in learned Latin, and was borrowed into vernacular languages. But the noun *socialitas* was rarely used before Pufendorf and it came into more general use through his major work. This is according to Schieder's article 'Sozialismus', p. 924, which draws on Hans Müller, *Ursprung und Geschichte des Wortes Sozialismus* (Hanover 1967). Towards the end of the eighteenth century, Hufeland wrote (*Lehrsätze des Naturrechts*, 2nd edn 1795, p. 28) that Pufendorf was the true father of natural law theory, and that he and many of his followers had based natural law on sociality and could therefore be called socialists.

Appendix 16   *Notes on Philopatris, Hutcheson and The London Journal*

All references in this appendix are to numbers and dates of *The London Journal*, except where otherwise indicated.

In the period when Hutcheson produced his major writings, *The London Journal* had a wide circulation, and was foremost among the periodicals that supported the Walpole administration. Below some observations are made on its political and theological anti-Catholicism; on the identity of Philopatris, Hutcheson's first reviewer; on the contact between Hutcheson and *The London Journal*; and on material in it relating to him.

A case of persecuting zeal

In late 1724 and early 1725, the time when Hutcheson published his *Reflections* and then his *Inquiry*, the editor of *The London Journal* used the signature Britannicus. He was the latitudinarian bishop Benjamin Hoadly (1676–1761). He is known to have been the 'author', i.e. editor, of *The London Journal* from 1722 to 1725, but it is known that he also wrote for it later. Theologically, he was quite undogmatic. Politically, he was a supporter of the Hanoverian succession and the Walpole administration.

In this period *The London Journal* contained many reports of misdeeds due to the intolerance and persecuting zeal of Roman Catholics. The news columns gave details about recent victims of the Spanish Inquisition, some of whom were burned alive in an act of faith (*auto-da-fé*) in Cuenca on 19 January 1725. Considerable attention was given to the persecution of Protestants in Thorn (Toruń) in Poland which had resulted in a number of bloody public executions.

Some of the reports in *The London Journal* on the events in Poland were also published separately. In no. 289, 6 Febr. 1725 there is an advertisement for 'Two letters by Britannicus on the persecutions at Thorn', published 'today' by Wilkins (the printer and bookseller, who also printed *The London Journal* and many other works which politically were in line with the Walpole administration). But these were by no means the only publications relating to the incident. A speech by the advocate for the Jesuits at Thorn was published in Dublin as well as in London, and so were the remarks signed Philopatris, originally published in a letter to Britannicus in *The London Journal*. Wilkins also published the two letters by Britannicus together with the advocate's speech, and with an anonymous *Authentick Narrative* ... whose author was Jean-François Bion (1668–c. 1741), a French priest who when ministering to Huguenot galley slaves had been so touched by their suffering, patience, and piety that he became a Protestant and moved via Geneva to England (where a book of his on the subject so affected Queen Anne that she intervened and secured the liberation of 136 of these prisoners) and later to Holland.

The executions at Thorn attracted attention well beyond the columns of *The London Journal*. Indeed, they affected international relations. The Czar and many Protestant powers prepared for mobilisation against Poland and were deliberating whether the incident should be regarded as a *casus belli*.

Who was Philopatris?

The signature Philopatris was affixed to many contributions to *The London Journal* in the early months of 1725. These contributions took the form of letters or articles addressed to the editor, i.e. Britannicus. They insist that the practice of justice and virtue, prompted by religion, is a great support of government, and warn frequently against the 'bigottry and Tyranny of the Church of Rome' (no. 292, 27 February 1725) and against the threat of popery. The Protestant (i.e. Anglican) clergy ought to be on its guard against the popish pretender to the crown. A whole series of reasons are given why they ought to be loyal. Many things of great value, such as the progress made in universities, and the increase in civil liberties, would be destroyed with the introduction of a popish establishment.

A number of these articles attacked the recently published *Life of Cardinal Wolsey* for its alleged favourable bias towards Roman Catholicism. Its author was Richard Fiddes (1671–1725). He had in this work 'taken a view of the reformation less unfavourable to the mediaeval church than most Protestant writers' (*DNB*).

In another article Philopatris thanks Britannicus, the pseudonym of the editor, for having drawn attention to the detestable affair at Thorn. He further explains, that he has to guard his anonymity since he lives far from the metropolis and in a country where he is 'surrounded too much with such Persons as I am speaking of' (i.e. papists); this is why he does not even name the place from which he writes. Further on in the same article (no. 290, 13 February 1725) he complains that in Ireland popery is increasing. This is a matter of concern, since it is in his view incompatible with allegiance to the reigning monarch. A month later, Philopatris presents a translation from High–Dutch (i.e. German) of an account of the recent execution at Thorn. As already mentioned, some of Philopatris's comments on this affair were also published separately by Wilkins.

After this, Philopatris disappears for a while, but about a year later (no. 351, 16 April 1726) a letter with this signature recommends `Mr Ollyffe's Book, entitled *The Madness of Disaffection against the Present Government'* [!], and warns against the designs of the Jesuits against our happy Establishment; again there is a reference to the events in Poland, but it is pointed out that the Pope is highly displeased with the excessive zeal displayed by the Jesuits.

Philopatris was of course not alone in expressing strong anti-Catholic sentiments. On the contrary, there was continuing anti-Catholic agitation from the supporters of the Anglican Church and the Hanoverian succession, springing from motives both religious and political. To take just one example (no. 380, 5 November 1726), Anti-Papius, who mentions one of Philopatris's letters from the previous year, elaborates on the remarks in it on the arts used to seduce the meaner sort of people in the part of England where he lives, and complains of the complacency of the Protestants, who ought to counteract papist influence by giving more help to the indigent needy. A popish neighbour, a gentleman, uses the art of charity for purposes of conversion, drawing his arguments from the cellar and the pantry rather than from the Bible: in his house his table is laid as a snare. Worse still, Catholic maids tempt the lads `to embrace them and their religion together'. They marry, and outbreed the Protestants.

A contemporary advertisement (in no. 457, 4 May 1728) presents a neat summary of the standard anti-Catholic objections current in the theological-political discourse of the time:

This Day is published, A True Representation of Popery, as it appears in Foreign Parts: Design'd as a Preservative against its Contagion; particularly recommended to British Protestants during their Residence in Popish Countries. In Ten Discourses, Being the Substance of several Sermons preach'd before the Factory at *Oporto* in *Portugal* on

The Doctrine of Merit;	Death-Bed Confession;
Transubstantiation;	Invocation of Saints;
Prayers in an unknown Tongue;	Invention of New Sacraments;
Denying the Cup to the Laity;	Superstitious Ceremonies;
Popery destructive of the Love of	Artifices and Sophistry of their
our Country;	Priests in making Converts &c.;
Romish Cruelty in their Act of Faith;	Infallibility;
Purgatory;	Pope's Supremacy;

By Henry Stephens, M.A., Vicar of *Malden* in *Surrey*, 2nd Chaplain to the Rt. Rev. the Lord Bishop of St. *David*'s. Printed for *James* and *John Knapton*, at the Crown in St. Paul's Church-Yard.

The reason for this search for Philopatris is that this is also the signature of the reviewer of Hutcheson's *Inquiry*. He begins his review (in no. 296, 27 March 1725 and reprinted in *Letters*) by noting the complaint that philosophy and religion are no longer seen as fit pursuits for gentlemen. In contrast, among the ancients, it was their recreation after the hurry of public affairs. He then quotes from pp. 125 and 129, on egoism, and from p. 147 on love of country. He praises `this treatise, and another, which has lately appeared with so great and just an Applause'. The other work was no doubt Wollaston's *Religion of Nature*. The two works were similarly juxtaposed in an article by Arbuckle some time after (see appendix 14 above) and in other contexts. For instance, reviews of the two adjoin each other in *Bibliothèque Ancienne et Moderne* 26 (1726)

Was this Philopatris, the reviewer, identical with the commentator on the events in Poland? And with the reviewer of Fiddes's Life of Wolsey?

It was not unusual for the same pseudonym to be used by different writers, though not indiscriminately. In the same period and in the same publication, different writers using the same signature could be supposed to have much in common: an example is offered by Cato, to whom we shall return.

One detail to be noticed is that this is the only early discussion of Hutcheson that reveals an interest in politics: the reviewer mentions with praise Hutcheson's view that national love, love of country, cannot arise if there is tyranny, faction, etc.

In the search for clues as to the identity of the writers behind the pseudonyms, something may be gained by following Fiddes's track. He did not leave the attack on himself unanswered. For his answer, BLC vol. 43, p. 57 has the following entry, which reproduces his title-page and is followed by a comment by the cataloguer:

An Answer to Britanicus [sic], compiler of the London-Journal. By the compiler of Cardinal Wolsey's Life, lately published. {A reply to a letter in the `London Journal' written to `Britannicus', i.e. Benjamin Hoadly, by `Philopatris', possibly a pseudonym for Hoadly.}

This title suggests that Fiddes simply addressed his reply *to* the editor in the same way that Philopatris, his critic, had addressed his remarks *to* the editor. So the title by itself cannot support the cataloguer's comment. But there is evidence elsewhere: although it was common for title-pages to carry the same wording as advertisements, this case is an exception. The wording of an advertisement for Fiddes's pamphlet (in no. 300, 24 April 1725) suggests something more:

A vindication of the life of Cardinal Wolsey, from the Reflections of Britannicus, Compiler of the London Journal. By Richard Fiddes, D.D.

Here, the formulation is `the reflections *of* Britannicus'. The implication of the advertisement is clearly that Philopatris is another pseudonym used by Hoadly. This gives some justification for the note in the BLC. On closer scrutiny, however, the grounds for the conjecture that Philopatris is Hoadly seem insufficient. That Britannicus is Hoadly seems to have been common knowledge, and Fiddes must have been aware of it. It is also obvious that he would find Hoadly, who was a very prominent representative of latitudinarian and Whig standpoints in the public debate, a much more inviting target than some other, possibly much less important, writer. So, probably uncertain of the identity of his assailant Philopatris, and in any case more interested in taking on a leader rather than a follower, Fiddes writes, addressing himself to Britannicus (*An Answer*, p. 10):

> It is probable you may here endeavour to defend yourself, as well you can, by saying, you were only the publisher, not the writer, of the letter, to which I refer, and that you took it out of the collection, or common place, as it came to hand, from which your Journal of Saturday last [20 February 1725] was to be furnished. This excuse will not serve: every man knows, who knows any thing, that he who propagates a scandal, is, in common construction, and the reason of the thing, to be treated as the author of it: so that I am not in the least concerned to enquire, whether the letter in your news-paper was really communicated by a friend, or whether, according to a common modern practice, Britanicus [sic] wrote that letter under another fictitious name to himself;

and in a second letter, dated three days later, in response to the second instalment of Philopatris's review, Fiddes again addresses himself to Britannicus (*An Answer*... p. 34):

> The letter at present before me, whether from yourself or your friend, for I make no distinction in the case...

The question is, then, whether Hoadly, alias Britannicus, in this instance had followed the `modern practice' mentioned by Fiddes. On the evidence, the answer must be negative. We are not aware of any circumstance that would have given him a reason for hiding. Also, Philopatris had given quite a few hints about his own location and circumstances; the description does not fit Hoadly; there is no reason why Hoadly should have engaged in such an elaborate game of hide-and-seek.

There is also an article over the same signature, which may well be by the same author, in *The Dublin Weekly Journal* 100, 25 February 1727. Like many articles in *The London Journal* during this decade, it uses a rhetoric which closely follows Locke's *Second Treatise* to urge support for the Whig establishment, to warn against any changes to the political system, and to assure the readers that they have never had it so good. For instance: `We have the happiness to live in a flourishing country; a country where we enjoy our Religion in its purity; our properties with security, and all the ornaments as well as common conveniencies of human life, and at the same time too, we have the happiness to hear our king from the throne exhorting us to be zealous asserters of all our liberties' etc. As far as style and content goes, it could well be written by the same author.

As it happens, this is, as noted by Bryan Coleborne (Appendix F of his *Jonathan Swift and the Dunces of Dublin*), one of the two articles (out of 103) which Arbuckle did *not* include in his collection of essays from *The Dublin Weekly Journal*. Whilst the other one was probably omitted because it was too slight, the reason why Philopatris's piece was not included was probably that it was an essay in politics, whilst the essays collected dealt with more general topics of a moral or literary kind.

The Philopatris who wrote the short review is, then, probably an acquaintance of Hoadly's, living in Ireland, a strong supporter of the established church, strongly against popish tendencies, and in favour of a broad and quite undogmatic approach to questions of religion and morality; his opinions would have been very similar to Hoadly's. It is by no means unlikely that he can be found among persons associated with the Molesworth circle.

This is of course quite inconclusive. As yet, we do not have information that would allow a secure identification of the first reviewer of Hutcheson, though the particulars reviewed may help in the search. One conclusion that may be drawn is that Hoadly himself probably was not Hutcheson's reviewer.

On the whole, the Irish presence in *The London Journal* in this period is notable and merits closer study. There is a great deal of Irish material in this newspaper. Of the poetical material can be mentioned, for instance, verses from Philo-musus, `already much applauded in Dublin', in homage to the honourable Miss Carteret, daughter of the Lord-Lieutenant; and to Miss Georgina, the younger daughter, homage is paid in further poems from Mr Ph– [i.e. Ambrose Philips] in Dublin. In a subsequent issue another Dublin correspondent complains of Ph–'s bad verse. From Dublin comes also verse by Jonathan Swift, Dean of St Patrick's, including, some years later, a vicious attack on Arbuckle (in no. 552, 28 February 1730).

It was not a one-way traffic. During Arbuckle's editorship of *The Dublin Weekly Journal* (1725–27), he leading essays were written for that purpose by himself or other authors, including, of course, Hutcheson. Once he had left, in spring 1727, many of the leading articles were no longer original, but simply reprinted from *The London Journal*. This was done without acknowledgment, which would not have been considered improper at the time, although the cases when the reprinted article appears over a different signature seem somewhat dubious.

How was Hutcheson introduced to The London Journal?

It would be tempting to suppose that Hutcheson's initial contact with *The London Journal*, which led to the publication of the *Reflections*, was mediated by Robert Molesworth, a Whig opponent of Walpole in the early 1720s. He maintained contact with John Trenchard (1662–1723) and Thomas Gordon (c. 1690–1750), the authors of the letters signed `Cato' which in the early 1720s were published in *The London Journal*. Many of these letters sharply criticised those responsible for the major financial crash known as the South Sea Bubble, insisted that they be punished for their misdeeds, attacked the government for failing to do so, and deplored the decline in political culture and public spirit. They extolled, as can be expected over such a signature, the civic virtues of republican Rome, with special emphasis on probity and incorruptibility. Molesworth shared these views, and was even believed to be the author of some of these letters, mistakenly, according to Gordon's dedication of the 1733 edition of the collected *Cato's Letters* (at pp. xvi–xviii).

There is, however, an important circumstance that might seem to rule out the possibility that Hutcheson's contact with *The London Journal* could have been mediated by Molesworth. After mid-September 1722, Cato's letters, to which this newspaper had owed its remarkable popularity, were evicted. A sudden reversal of the political direction of *The London Journal* took place. From being critical of the government, it became a consistent defender of government policies. The proprietor, called Elizée Dobrée in documents extant, had been persuaded to change the political line of the paper by means of a very powerful argument, formulated by Walpole's agent in terms of pounds sterling. The result was a complete political turnaround, and, as anticipated, a drop in circulation, handsomely compensated by a generous government subsidy. This is the story as told in Realey ('The London Journal and its Authors 1720-1723', *Bulletin of the University of Kansas* 5, no.3, (1935), p. 34), who remarks that Walpole preferred winning men by finding their price.

With Cato's letters unwelcome, one might suppose that the authors and their like-minded friends, including Molesworth, would also be *personae non gratae* with the politically reformed *London Journal*, and that therefore Hutcheson could not have gained access for his *Reflections* through these channels.

Such an inference would be premature. An involvement with Cato's letters or their authors was in fact compatible with a continued association with *The London Journal*. (On this, see also Harris, *London Newspapers in the Age of Walpole*, London: Associated University Presses 1987, p. 104.) Hanson takes the view (*Government and the Press* 1695–1763, London: Oxford University Press/Humphrey Milford 1936, p. 107) that on Trenchard's death (1723) Gordon seems to have decided that compliance with those in government was the best means to fortune. Four years later, in 1727, his translation of Tacitus was dedicated to Walpole. So, the fact that the letters signed Cato were no longer published in *The London Journal* need not have prevented Gordon from remaining associated with it. This way of telling the story, like Realey's, makes it seem as if Gordon was more flexible than principled. There are, however, reasons to doubt this, at least if it is taken to imply that he was induced to change sides in politics. As argued by Marie P. McMahon in *The Radical Whigs, John Trenchard and Thomas Gordon: Libertarian loyalists to the new house of Hanover* (Lanham, MD: University Press of America 1990) 'the conventional view that *Cato's Letters* constitute a major critique of the ministry of Robert Walpole is incorrect'(p. 100); Trenchard and Gordon did not belong to the class of opposition writers (p. 119). She suggests that it was Cato's attack on

Walpole's having soldiers at the ready for fear of a possible and suspected Jacobite conspiracy (in which Atterbury played a prominent part) that precipitated the removal of Cato. Less than a year later Cato recanted on this matter, and may well have been sincere (pp. 184ff.). It is, however, more likely that as suggested by Joshi ('The London Journal, 1719–1738', *Journal of the University of Bombay* 9 (1940) 33–66), it was the persistence and the vehemence of Cato's earlier attacks on the guilty parties in the South Sea swindle and on the ministers who failed to take action against them that led to the eviction of Cato. In any case, Cato was evicted because he was a troublesome critic, but not because he belonged to the opposition against Walpole's Whig administration. Hoadly became editor because he could be expected to toe the government line much more faithfully.

This explains the fact that although *The London Journal* continued to receive generous government subsidies and frequently engaged in polemics against the Tory critics of the Walpole administration, who were writing in *Mist's Weekly Journal, Fog's Weekly Journal, The Craftsman*, etc., one can find in it high praise for Gordon some years later: 'the excellent advocates for civil and religious liberty, among whom the author of Cato's Letters and the *Independent Whig* (written by Gordon] stands foremost' (no. 498, 15 February 1729). The statement occurs in an article on superstition and false religion by Publicola, over whose signature readers were often told that they had never had it so good and that criticising the government was sheer folly. This Publicola might well have been Hoadly: Joshi has shown ('The London Journal, 1719–1738', p. 57) that eight weeks earlier the signature Publicola was used by Hoadly.

Drawing these facts together, and considering also that Gordon had written on Hoadly's behalf in the Bangorian controversy 1717–20, it is natural to infer that although *Cato's Letters* had to leave, their author could still be admitted after September 1722, when Hoadly had been put in charge.

Given the affinities of opinion between Molesworth, Hoadly, and Gordon, together with the obvious Irish presence in the contents of *The London Journal*, the conjecture that Hutcheson was introduced by his noble friend seems plausible indeed.

A survey of material in The London Journal relating to Hutcheson

Shortly after Philopatris's review of *Inquiry*, there appeared a letter from Philaretus (= Gilbert Burnet Jr, d. 1726), the first of the correspondence between him and Hutcheson, which continued until December 1725. It was later republished, together with Philopatris's review. See under *Letters* in the bibliography.

A little more than two years later, an advertisement in no. 441, 13 January 1728, announced that Hutcheson's *Essay* and *Illustrations* was 'this day published', and six weeks later, in no. 447, the signature Zeno referred to the earlier learned correspondence and expressed the hope that another Philaretus, a friend of virtue, would provoke the friend of mankind Philanthropus (i.e. Hutcheson) again to write in the journal. This hope was partly fulfilled in no. 450, 16 March, with a contribution from a Philaretus, on which a comment, perhaps somewhat facetious, came from Eurydice in no. 454, 13 April: the theories of a moral sense may satisfy a few people of particularly noble disposition, but it is to be wished that the systems of morality could be presented more attractively, so that they could have a beneficial influence on people's conduct more generally. In no. 463, 15 June, a friend of truth, signing himself Aletheiophilos, joined the fray, courteously referring to Hutcheson as a scholar and a gentleman, but rising to the defence of Wollaston against some of Hutcheson's objections in the *Illustrations*, whereupon the friend of beauty Philocalus, the only one of these correspondents who refers to Hutcheson by name, springs to his defence in no. 468, 20 July, in a rather polemical tone. These letters, except Eurydice's, are reproduced in *Collected Works*, vol. II.

This is not the end of the story. As noted above in appendix 10, the attack on Mandeville, in nos. 514–16, 7, 14, and 21 June 1729, was conducted to a very large extent with borrowings from Hutcheson.

Appendix 17   *The Letter to William Mace*

Wodrow's sympathies were with the evangelicals, and he would have suspected Hutcheson of being too much beholden to the opposite party. He was, however, prepared to give him the benefit of the doubt. In his *Analecta* (vol. IV, p. 185), he wrote:

> About this time, Mr Hutcheson came to Glasgou, and about eighteen or twenty of his former students with him. He is well spoke of. He teaches Mr. Carmichael's Compend and Puffendorf, and speaks with much veneration of him, which at least is an evidence of his prudence.

As it happens, Wodrow was quite right. Hutcheson did feel obliged to be cautious. A letter dated 6 September 1727 from him to William Mace (lecturer in civil law at Gresham College in London, d. 1767), published in *European Magazine and London Review* 14 (1788), pp. 158–60 shows his awareness of the need to be circumspect in order not to offend the orthodox in his church, especially on the very sensitive question of freedom of the will, with its implications for the doctrine of predestination.

The first two-thirds of the letter to Mace, in which epistemological matters are discussed, was published with an introduction by David Berman: 'Francis Hutcheson on Berkeley and the Molyneux Problem', pp. 259–65, in *Proceedings of the Royal Irish Academy* 74, Section C, no. 8 (1974). More recently the full text has been republished in vol. I of S. Deane (ed.), *The Field Day Anthology of Irish Writing*, pp. 786–8.

Of interest in the present context is the conclusion of the letter, reproduced below, where Hutcheson openly acknowledges the need for caution:

> As to the main point in your letter about our activity, we are very much of the same opinion. But you know how sacred a point human

liberty and activity, in the common notions, are to the generality of men, and how prejudicial any singularity on these heads might be to one whose business depends upon a character of orthodoxy. I am very sensible that the truest ideas of human virtue and of the divine goodness may be given on your scheme; but how few are there whom we could convince on these points.

Vel quia turpe putant parere minoribus, et quæ
imberbes didicere, senes perdenda fateri.

[because they regard it as shameful to take advice from those younger than themselves, and to acknowledge, when in old age, that what they learnt when they were beardless youths ought to be repudiated. Horace, Epist. 2, 1, 85–86.]

I have some nearer touches at these points in another set of papers, which I shall send over very soon to be joined with the other. But I am still on my guard in them. [...]

I am, Sir,
Your most obliged humble servant,
Francis Hutcheson.

To Mr. William Mace, at Mr. Osborn's, bookseller, Pater-noster-Row.

Bibliography

The lengthy descriptive titles of eighteenth-century works are often very informative and for this reason some of them have been reproduced in the following; the original use of capitals and italics has, however, been adopted only in part.

Works by Hutcheson

This is not a complete bibliography of Hutcheson's works. It covers the philosophical works published in his lifetime. Detailed information has been given about the various editions of the four treatises published in that period, together with a listing of all the modern editions and facsimile reprints of these that have come to light. If a definitive bibliography of Hutcheson were to be prepared, the information here collected could be of some use. Two recent translations, one with a useful introduction and one with useful textual comparisons of the four earliest editions of *Inquiry* are also listed. Further bibliographical information, some of which needs revision, can be found in Jessop, in Peach, and in the prefaces by Bernhard Fabian to the volumes of the *Collected Works*.

Collected works

Collected Works of Francis Hutcheson. Facsimile edition prepared by B. Fabian. 7 vols. Hildesheim: Olms 1969, 1971.

> This is the first collection ever made of Hutcheson's works. Of *T1&T2* and *T3&T4*, it is the first editions that have been reprinted, rather than later ones revised by Hutcheson. According to the preface in vol. I, p. vii, the collection is complete (except for the translation of Marcus Aurelius, undertaken jointly with James Moor and published originally in 1742). This has to be qualified in the light of the information on p. ix above.

T1&T2 (Inquiry)

1st edn 1725 (A)
An Inquiry into the Original of our Ideas of Beauty and Virtue; In Two Treatises. In which The Principles of the late Earl of Shaftsbury are explain'd and defended, against the Author of the *Fable of the Bees*: and the

Ideas of Moral Good and Evil are establish'd, according to the Sentiments of the antient Moralists. With an Attempt to introduce a Mathematical Calculation in Subjects of Morality.

This is the only edition in which the sentences referring to Shaftesbury, Mandeville, and mathematics appear on the title-page. They are followed by a motto from Cicero:

Itaque eorum ipsorum qui aspectu sentiuntur, nullum aliud animal pulchritudinem, venustatem, convenientiam partium sentit. Quam similitudinem natura ratioque ab oculis ad animum transferens, multo etiam magis pulchritudinem, constantiam, ordinem in consiliis, factis*ve* conservand*um* putat. Quibus ex rebus conflatur & efficitur id quod quaerimus honestum: Quod etiamsi nobilitatum non sit, tamen honestum sit: quodque etiamsi à nullo laudetur, naturâ est laudabile. Formam quidem ipsam & tanquam faciem honesti vides, quae si oculis cern*eretur*, miràbiles amores excitaret sapientiae. Cic. de Off. lib. 1.c.4.

(And so no other animal has a sense of beauty, loveliness, harmony in the visible world; and Nature and Reason, extending the analogy of this from the world of sense to the world of spirit, find that beauty, consistency, order are far more to be maintained in thought and deed. It is from these elements that is forged and fashioned that moral goodness which is the subject of this inquiry – something that, even though it be not generally ennobled, is still worthy of all honour; and by its own nature, we correctly maintain, it merits praise, even though it be praised by none. You see here the very form and, as it were, the face of Moral Goodness; `and if`, Plato says [*Phaedrus* 250 D] `it could be seen with the physical eye, it would awaken a marvellous love of wisdom'.) (Transl. Walter Miller; Loeb edn.)

London: Printed by J. Darby in Bartholomew-Close for Wil. and John Smith on the Blind Key in Dublin; and sold by W. and J. Innys at the West-End of St. Paul's Church-Yard, J. Osborn and T. Longman in Pater-Noster-Row, and S. Chandler in the Poultry. MDCCXXV.

The text of *T1* has the heading: `Treatise I viz. An Inquiry concerning Beauty, Order &c.' and the text of *T2* has the heading: `An Inquiry concerning Moral Good and Evil' and is separated from *T1* by a title-page with the following text:

Treatise II. viz. An Inquiry Concerning the Original of our Ideas of Virtue or Moral Good. – quod magis ad nos pertinet, & nescire malum est, agitamus: utrumne Divitiis homines, an sint Virtute beati: Quidve ad Amicitias, Usus, Rectumne, trahat nos Et quae sit natura Boni, summumque quid ejus. Hor. Sat. 6. Lib. 2. v. 72.

(But we discuss what more concerns us and is an evil not to know; whether it is wealth or virtue that makes men happy; what it is that draws us to friendship, convenience or the truly right; and what is the nature of the good, and what its highest form.)

The entry above follows the copy in the British Library. The title-page of the copy in the Bodleian Library, Oxford, differs in that the word *tanquam* is missing. But two misprints, indicated by italics in the Latin quotation above (it should be *factisque* and *cerneretur*) are corrected, as they also were in the later editions. The misprinted ending in *conservandum* (replace u by a) was never corrected.

This edition was published anonymously, probably 1 March 1725. Not much later is the date of Hutcheson's preface to the second edition, June 1725. It can be inferred that the work was favoured by the reading public.

Reprints
New York: AMS Press (according to Saur's reprint catalogue; not seen). Vol. I of the *Collected Works*.

1st edn 1725 (B)
An Inquiry into the Original of our Ideas of Beauty and Virtue; In Two Treatises. I. Concerning Beauty, Order, Harmony, Design. II. Concerning Moral Good and Evil.

The title-page differs from 1st edn 1725 (A). There is no mention of Shaftesbury Mandeville etc. The motto from Cicero follows, and then a different list of booksellers:

London: Printed by John Darby in Bartholomew-Close, for William and John Smith on the Blind Key in Dublin; and sold by William and John Innys at the West-End of St. Paul's Church-Yard, John Osborn in Lombard Street and Sam. Chandler in the poultry. MDCCXXV.

2nd edn 1726
An Inquiry into the Original of our Ideas of Beauty and Virtue; In Two Treatises. I. Concerning Beauty, Order, Harmony, Design. II. Concerning Moral Good and Evil. The Second Edition, Corrected and Enlarg'd.

As in 1st edn 1725 (B), there is no mention of Shaftesbury, Mandeville etc. The motto from Cicero follows, and then a different list of booksellers:

London: Printed for J. Darby, A Bettesworth, F. Fayram, J. Pemberton, C. Rivington, J. Hooke, F. Clay, J. Batley, and E. Symon. 1726.

As in the first edition, the text of T1 has the heading: `An Inquiry concerning Beauty, Order &c.' but the text of T1 is now also, like that of T2, preceded by a title-page which reads: `Treatise I. viz. An Inquiry concerning Beauty, Order, &c.' T2 is, as before, preceded by a title-page, p. 109, with unchanged text, and the heading of the text, now on p. 111, is also unchanged.

To this edition is added Hutcheson's signed dedication to his Excellency the Lord Carteret. The preface is dated June 1725. The book was published on 30 October 1725, according to *The London Journal* no. 327. The year of imprint is 1726, in keeping with the practice of booksellers to anticipate the new year, in order to make the product look fresher. A pamphlet containing the revisions to the text of the first edition was also for sale. It is reprinted in vol. I of the *Collected Works*.

Reprint
New York: Garland 1971.

3rd edn 1729

An Inquiry ... Good and Evil. The Third Edition, Corrected. [Motto from Cicero] London: Printed for J. and J. Knapton, J. Darby, A Bettesworth, F. Fayram, J. Pemberton, J. Osborn and T. Longman, C. Rivington, F. Clay, J. Batley and A. Ward. M.DC. XXIX.

> The wording of the title-page is the same as for 2nd edn 1726, with a different list of booksellers. P. 1 of *T1* has the heading `An Inquiry concerning Beauty, Order &c. *T2* begins on p. 104 with the heading `An Inquiry concerning Moral Good and Evil'.

4th edn 1738

An Inquiry ... Good and Evil. The fourth edition, corrected. [Motto from Cicero] London: Printed for D. Midwinter, A Bettesworth and C. Hitch, J. and J. Pemberton, R. Ware, C. Rivington, F. Clay, A. Ward, J. and P. Knapton, T. Longman, R. Hett, and J. Wood. MDCCXXXVIII.

> P. 1 of *T1* begins with the full title of the work, followed by a heading which reads: Treatise I. Of Beauty, Order, Harmony, Design. *T2* begins on p. 105 with the heading: Treatise II. An inquiry concerning Moral Good and Evil.

> This is a revised edition: there are a number of important additions and changes, and the attempt to introduce a mathematical calculation in subjects of morality has been abandoned.

Reprint
Farnborough: Gregg 1969.

A modern edition
> *Recherche sur l'origine de nos idées de la beauté et de la vertu.* Transl. and ed. Anne-Dominique Balmès. Paris: Vrin 1991.

T1 (Inquiry concerning Beauty)

Reprint
> (2nd edn 1726) in Paul McReynolds (ed.), *Four Early Works on Motivation.* Gainesville, Fla.: Scholars' 1969.

A modern edition
> *An Inquiry concerning Beauty, Order, Harmony, Design.* Edited, with an introduction and notes by Peter Kivy. The Hague: Nijhoff, 1973 (= International Archives of the History of Ideas. Series Minor. 9).

> The text is based on 4th edn 1738, but is collated with the earlier editions. Included is also the `Reflections Upon Laughter'.

T2 (Inquiry concerning Virtue)

A modern edition
Eine Untersuchung über den Ursprung unserer Ideen von Schönheit und Tugend. Ueber moralisch Gutes und Schlechtes. Transl. and ed. Wolfgang Leidhold. Hamburg: Meiner 1986 (= Philosophische Bibliothek 316).

T3&T4 (Essay and Illustrations)

1st edn 1728 (A)
An Essay on the Nature and Conduct of the Passions and Affections. With Illustrations On the Moral Sense. By the Author of the Inquiry into the Original of our Ideas of Beauty and Virtue.

> Hoc opus, hoc studium, parvi properemus, & ampli.
> Si Patriae volumus, si Nobis vivere chari. Hor.

> [Let us hasten, small and great alike, to this task, this concern (scil. heavenly wisdom], if we want to live dear to our country or dear to ourselves. Horace, *Epistulae* 1, 3, 28–29.]

London: printed by J. Darby and T. Browne, for John Smith and William Bruce, Booksellers in Dublin; and sold by J. Osborn and T. Longman in Pater Noster-Row, and S. Chandler in the Poultrey, M.DCC.XXVIII.

> `This day published' according to an advertisement in *The London Journal*, no. 441, 13 January 1728, which names John Darby in Bartolomew [*sic*] Close as printer, and adds to the above list of booksellers James Warrender, Bookseller in Bath.

> This work was discussed in *The London Journal* 1728, in letters reproduced in *Collected Works*, vol. II. For details, see p. 167.

Reprints
Vol. II of the *Collected Works*.
New York: Garland 1971.
Menston, Yorkshire: Scolar Press 1972.

1st edn 1728 (B)
An Essay ... Moral Sense. [As 1st edn 1728 (A), but reset, with more errors than previously. The motto from Horace is followed by:] London: printed and Dublin re-printed by S. Powell for P. Crampton, at Addison's Head, opposite the Horse-Guard in Dame's-street, and T. Benson, at Shakespear's Head in Castle-Street, MDCCXXVIII.

> Peach suggests that this is the earlier printing, because it has more errors than 1st edn 1728 (A). But the text above: `London printed and Dublin re-printed' seems to rule this out.

2nd edn 1730

An Essay ... Moral Sense. By Francis Hutcheson, Professor of Moral Philosophy in the University of Glascow [*sic*]; and Author of the Inquiry into the Original of our Ideas of Beauty and Virtue. [The motto from Horace.] London: Printed for James and John Knapton, and John Crownfield in St. Paul's Church-Yard; John Darby in Bartholomew-Close; Thomas Osborne Jun. at Greys Inn; and Lauton Gulliver in Fleetstreet. M.DCC.XXX.

> This seems to be a re-issue (as this term is defined in Gaskell, p. 316) of 1st edn 1728 (A), with a different title-page only. `Apparently a title edition consisting of sheets of the first edition', according to the editor's preface, at p. vii in vol. II of *Collected Works*. Of the works in moral philosophy by Hutcheson published in his lifetime, this is the only edition that carries his name on the title-page. In the other ones (except 1st edn 1725, which is anonymous) his name appears only under his dedication or preface. This is the title-page reproduced on p. 103 of Peach's edition of *T4* (see below).

3rd edn 1742

An Essay on the Nature and Conduct of the Passions and Affections. With Illustrations On the Moral Sense. By the Author of the Inquiry into the Original of our Ideas of Beauty and Virtue. The third edition. With additions. [The motto from Horace.] London: Printed for A. Ward, J. and P. Knapton, T. Longman, S. Birt, C. Hitch, L. Gilliver, T. Astley, S. Austen, and J. Rivington. MDCCXLII.

> There are many additions and revisions. Some were not incorporated in the text, but occur in an appendix.

Reprint

(Ed. Paul McReynolds), Gainesville, Fla.: Scholars' 1969.

T4 (*Illustrations*)

Illustrations on the Moral Sense

Edited [with an introduction and notes] by Bernard Peach. Cambridge, Mass.: Harvard University Press, 1971.

> The text is based on a posthumous edition, but collated with the previous ones. Included is also the correspondence between Hutcheson and Gilbert Burnet, listed below under *Letters*.

* * *   * * *   * * *

Note: The anthologies on moral philosophy edited, respectively, by L. A. Selby-Bigge, D. D. Raphael, and J. Schneewind, contain extensive selections from the works mentioned above.

`Reflections on our Common Systems of Morality', *The London Journal* 1724. For details, see p. 95.

Correspondence in with Gilbert Burnet in *The London Journal* 1725: see *Letters* ... 1735 below.

`Reflections Upon Laughter', *The Dublin Weekly Journal*, 5, 12, and 19 June 1725. Reprinted in Arbuckle's *Hibernicus's Letters* nos. 10, 11, and 12, pp. 77–107.

Reprints (from *Hibernicus's Letters*)
    In vol. VII of the *Collected Works*.
    New York: Garland 1971.
    Bristol: Thoemmes 1989.
    In Kivy's edition of *T1* (*Inquiry into Beauty*), *q.v. supra*.

`Remarks upon the Fable of the Bees', *The Dublin Weekly Journal*, 4, 11, and 19 February 1726. Reprinted in Arbuckle's *Hibernicus's Letters*, nos. 45–47, pp. 370–407.

Reprints (from *Hibernicus's Letters*)
    In vol. VII of the *Collected Works*.
    New York: Garland 1971.
    Bristol: Thoemmes 1989.

De naturali hominum Socialitate Oratio Inauguralis. [Device]. Glasgoviae. Typis Academicis M.DCC.XXX. For details, see p. 123.

Letters between the late Mr. Gilbert Burnet, and Mr. Hutchinson, Concerning The true foundation of Virtue and Moral Goodness. Formerly published in the London Journal. To which is added, a preface and a postscript. Wrote by Mr. Burnet some time before his Death. [Motto from Cicero] London: Printed by W. Wilkins in Lombard-Street, 1735.

> The letters from Philaretus [i.e. Burnet] are dated 10 April, 31 July, 7 August, 27 November, and 25 December; those from Philanthropus [i.e. Hutcheson] 12 June, 19 June, and 9 October. Also included is the review by Philopatris of 27 March. They were all published in 1725.

> David Norton notes in his *David Hume*, p. 60, n. 9, that the repeated misdating of these letters to 1728 was corrected by Bernard Peach in *Journal of the History of Philosophy* 8 (1970) 87–91. Peach was, however, anticipated by John McManmon 1965 (see entry under his name). McManmon further claimed that the 1735 edition had omitted two letters but this is not correct. There is also a letter from Philanthropos in *The London Journal* 372, 10 September 1726 on law reform, which is not by Hutcheson.

Reprints
    In vol. VII of the *Collected Works*.

In Peach's edition of *T4* (*Illustrations*) 1971, pp. 197–247. Philopatris' review is not included.

The Meditations of Marcus Aurelius Antoninus. Newly translated from the Greek. With Notes, and an Account of his Life. Glasgow: Printed by Robert Foulis; and sold by him at the College; by Mess. Hamilton and Balfour, in Edinburgh; and by Andrew Millar, over against St. Clements Church, London. MDCCXLII.

> James Moor translated books 1 and 2, Hutcheson the rest. The introduction and annotations are probably Hutcheson's. Their general tendency is to demonstrate that Stoicism and Christianity, if properly understood, agree on many matters of moral significance.

Metaphysicae synopsis: ontologiam et pneumatologiam complectens. Glasguae: ex officina Roberti Foulis venales prostant Londini apud Andream Miller, ex adversum D. Clementis Aedem, in vico vulgo dicto the Strand. Oxonii apud Jacobum Fletcher, Bibliopolam. MDCCXLII.

Synopsis metaphysicae, ontologiam & penumatologiam complectens. Editio altera auctior. [Glasgow: Foulis] MDCCXLIV.

Philosophiae moralis institutio compendiaria, Ethices & Jurisprudentiae Naturalis elementa continens Lib. III. Glasgow: Foulis 1742.

[The same.] 2nd edn, `auctior & emendatior', Glasgow: Foulis 1745.

Philosophiae moralis institutio compendiaria, etc. Rotterdam: Bradshaw 1745.

> An unrevised reprint of the first edition of the Compend.

A Short Introduction to Moral Philosophy 1747.

> A translation by another hand (James Moor?) of the Compend.

A System of Moral Philosophy, in three books; written by the late Francis Hutcheson, L.L.D., Professor of Philosophy in the University of Glasgow. Published from the original manuscript, by his son Francis Hutcheson, M.D. To which is prefixed some account of the life, writings and character of the author, by the reverend William Leechman, D. D. Professor of Divinity in the same university. [2 vols.] Glasgow: printed and sold by R. and A. Foulis, printers to the university. London, sold by A. Millar over-against Katharine-Street in the Strand, and by T. Longman in Pater-Noster Row. M.DCC.LV.

Other Works

Periodicals, series, etc.

Acta Eruditorum (Leipzig) 1727

Bibliothèque Ancienne et Moderne 24 (1725), 26 (1726)

Bibliothèque Angloise ou Histoire Litteraire de la Grande Bretagne 13 (1725)

Bibliothèque Germanique ou Histoire Littéraire de l'Allemagne et des pays du Nord 9 (1725)

Bibliothèque Raisonnée des Ouvrages des Savans de l'Europe 1 (1728), 14 (1735),16 (1736), 26 (1741), 29 (1742)

The British Library. *General Catalogue of Printed Books*

The Dublin Weekly Journal (1725–1731)

European Magazine and London Review 14 (1788)

Fog's Weekly Journal (1729)

Historical Manuscripts Commission. *Reports on Manuscripts in Various Collections.* Vol. VIII. London: H.M. Stationery Office. 1913.

Journal de Trévoux (= *Mémoires pour l'Histoire des Sciences & des Beaux Arts*) (1726)

Journal Litéraire 17 (1731)

The London Journal (1724–1730)

Neue Zeitungen von gelehrten Sachen (Leipzig) 18.12.1727

New Memoirs of Literature 1 (1725), 4 (1726)

The Present State of the Republick of Letters, 4 (1729), 6 (1730), 7 (1731), 9 (1732)

The Spectator (ed. D. Bond). 5 vols. Oxford: Oxford University Press 1965

Books and articles

[Anon.] *The English Preacher: or sermons on the principal subjects of religion and morality*, vol. I. London 1773.

[Anon.] *An Essay upon Modern Gallantry*. London 1726.

[Anon.] `A Letter written from Copenhagen. October 31. 1724' in *New Memoirs of Literature* 3 (1726) 177–9.

[Anon.] *A Letter to Mr. John Clarke, Master of the Publick Grammar-School in Hull. Wherein is shew'd, that he hath treated the Learned Dr. Clarke very unfairly. That he hath carry'd the Principle of Self-Love much too far. And, That his heavy Charge against the Author of Beauty and Virtue, may, with more Reason, be retorted upon himself.* LNDDON [sic] Printed for J. Roberts near the Oxford-Arms in Warwick-Lane MDCCXXVII.

[Anon.] *Variorum opuscula ad cultiorem jurisprudentiam adsequendam pertinentia*, Tom.1., Pisa: Aug. Pizzorno MDCCLXIX.

> In the preface, the editor explains that the first item, De animi cultura, is an exercitatio by Hutcheson, published separately in Glasgow 1740 but subsequently incorporated as ch. 6 of his *Philosophiae moralis institutio compendiaria*, and reprinted from the Rotterdam 1745 edition of that work. This item is mentioned s.v. Hutcheson in BLC and in Jessop. No copy of the original pamphlet seems to be extant.

Advice to a Young Student: see Waterland.

Aldridge, Alfred Owen, `A Preview of Hutcheson's Ethics', *Modern Language Notes* 46 (1946) 153–161.

Arbuckle, James, *Glotta, A Poem*. Glasgow: William Duncan 1721.

(ed.), *A Collection of Letters and Essays on Several Subjects, Lately Publish'd in The Dublin Journal*. 2 vols. London: 1729.

(ed.), *Hibernicus's Letters: or, a Philosophical Miscellany*. 2 vols. London: 1734. The second edition of the preceding item.

> The essays collected had been published in *The Dublin Weekly Journal* 1725–1727. Most of the 101 `letters' here reprinted were written by Arbuckle, but others also contributed. For details, see his postscript, (also originally in the journal, no. 104). For Hutcheson's contribution, see the editorial introduction to vol. VII of the *Collected Works*.

Aretelogia: see A. Campbell and appendix 12.

Aristotle, *Categories and De Interpretatione* (ed. J. Ackrill). Oxford: Oxford University Press 1963.

Politics (ed. T.J. Saunders). London: Penguin 1981.

[Balguy, John] (1686–1748), *A Letter to a Deist, concerning the beauty and excellency of moral Virtue, and the support and improvement it receives from the Christian Revelation. By a Country-Clergyman.* London: J. Pemberton, 1726.

[Balguy, John], *The Foundation of Moral Goodness: or a Further Inquiry into the Original of our Idea of Virtue*. By a Clergyman. London: J. Pemberton, 1728 (Facsimile reprint. New York: Garland 1976).

Balmès, Anne-Dominique, `Avant-propos' in Francis Hutcheson, *Recherche sur l'origine de nos idées de la beauté et de la vertu*. Paris: Vrin 1991.

[Bayle, Pierre] (1647–1706), *Penseés diverses écrites à un Docteur de Sorbonne à l'occasion de la comète qui parut au mois de décembre 1680*. Rotterdam: Leers 2nd edn 1683.

Dictionnaire Historique et Critique, 3 vols. (1697) Rotterdam: Leers 2nd edn 1702.

The Dictionary Historical and Critical of Mr Peter Bayle (transl. P. Desmaizeaux et al.) 2nd edn London 1734–38.

Historical and Critical Dictionary. Selections. Transl. and ed. R. Popkin and C. Brush. Indianapolis, Ind.: Bobbs-Merrill 1965.

Beardsley, Monroe C., `Aesthetics', *The Encyclopedia of Philosophy* (ed. P. Edwards). New York: Collier-Macmillan 1967.

[Benezet, Antoine (Anthony)] (1713–1784), *A Short Account of that Part of Africa Inhabited by the Negroes*. [...] Philadelphia 2nd edn 1762.

Berkeley, George (1685–1753), *Alciphron* (1732); reprinted in *The Works of George Berkeley* (eds. A. Luce and T. Jessop), vol. III. London: Nelson 1950.

Passive Obedience, Or, the Christian doctrine of not resisting the Supreme Power, proved and vindicated upon the principles of the Law of Nature (1712); reprinted in *The Works of George Berkeley* (eds. A. Luce and T. Jessop), vol. VI. London: Nelson 1953.

Essay towards Preventing the Ruin of Great Britain (1721), reprinted ibid.

Berman, David, `Francis Hutcheson on Berkeley and the Molyneux Problem', *Proceedings of the Royal Irish Academy* 74 (1974), Section C, no. 8, pp. 259–65.

`Dr Berkly's books', in Damian Smyth (ed.), *Francis Hutcheson*, p. 23.

Blackstone, William T., *Francis Hutcheson and Contemporary Ethical Theory*, Athens, Ga.: University of Georgia Press 1965.

Boswell, James, *The Life of Samuel Johnson, LL.D.*, Oxford: Oxford University Press (The World's Classics) 1980.

Buddeus, J.F., *Theses theologicae de atheismi et superstitione* (1716) (ed. H. Buurt). Utrecht 1737.

Burleigh, H.C., *A Church History of Scotland*. London: Oxford University Press 1960.

Butler, Joseph (1692–1752), *Fifteen Sermons...and a Dissertation on the Nature of Virtue* (ed. T.A.Roberts). London: S.P.C.K. 1970.

The *Fifteen Sermons* were first published in June 1726.

Butler, Joseph, *The Works of the Right Reverend Father in God Joseph Butler D.C.L. Late Lord Bishop of Durham. To which is prefixed a preface by Samuel Halifax D.D. Late Lord Bishop of Gloucester*. 2 vols. Oxford: Clarendon Press 1874.

[Campbell, Archibald (1691–1756)], *Aretelogia Or an Enquiry into the Original of Moral Virtue*, wherein the false Notions of Machiavel, Hobbs, Spinosa, and Mr. Bayle, as they are collected and digested by the author of *the Fable of the Bees*, are examined and confuted; and the eternal and unalterable Law of Nature and obligation of moral virtue is stated and vindicated; to which is prefixed a prefatory introduction in a letter to that author. By *Alexander Innes*, D.D. Preacher-Assistant at St. *Margaret's Westminster*.

On the authorship of this, see appendix 12.

Campbell, Archibald, *An Enquiry into the Original of Moral Virtue wherein it is shown (against the Author of the Fable of the Bees etc.) that virtue is founded in the nature of things, is unalterable, and eternal, and the great means of private and publick happiness. With some reflections on a late book intitled, An Enquiry into the Original of our Ideas of Beauty and Virtue ...* Edinburgh: Printed for Gavin Hamilton by R. Fleming and Company. 1733.

The Report of the Committee for Purity of Doctrine, At Edinburgh March 16, 1736. With Professor Campbell's Remarks upon it. To which is subjoin'd, by way of conclusion, a short account of the orthodoxy of both sides. He that walketh uprightly walketh surely; But he that perverteth his way shall be known. Prov. x. 9. Edinburgh: Lumsden & Robertson 1736.

Campbell, R.H. and A.S. Skinner (eds.), *The Origins and Nature of the Scottish Enlightenment*. Edinburgh: Donald 1982.

Campbell, T.D., `Francis Hutcheson, "Father" of the Scottish Enlightenment', in R.H. Campbell and A.S. Skinner (eds.), pp. 167–185.

Carmichael, Gerschom (1672–1729), *Synopsis Theologiae Naturalis*. Edinburgh: J. Paton 1729.

Cato's Letters: see Trenchard.

Cicero, *The Nature of the Gods* (ed. J.M. Ross), London: Penguin (1972) 1984.

Clarke, John (1687–1734), *An Examination of the Notion of Moral Good and Evil, advanced in a late book, entitled, The Religion of Nature Delineated ...* London: Printed for A. Bettesworth. 1725.

An attack on Wollaston, published 1 May 1725, according to an advertisement in *The London Journal*, no. 301.

Clarke, John, *The Foundation of Morality in Theory and Practice considered*, in an examination of the learned Dr. Samuel Clarke's opinion, concerning the original of moral obligation; and also of the notion of virtue, advanced in a late book, entituled, An Inquiry into the

Original of our Ideas of Beauty and Virtue. By John Clarke, Master of the Publick Grammar-School in Hull. York. Printed by Thomas Gent: [...] n.d. [1726].

Pp. 3–40 deal with Samuel Clarke, pp. 41–112 with Hutcheson.

Clarke, Samuel (1675–1729), *A Demonstration of the Being and Attributes of God: more particularly in answer to Mr. Hobbs, Spinoza, and their followers. Wherein the notion of liberty is stated, and the possibility and certainty of it proved, in opposition to necessity and fate. Being the substance of eight sermons preache'd at the Cathedral-Church of St. Paul, in the Year 1704, at the Lecture founded by the Honourable Robert Boyle Esq; By Samuel Clark,* M.A. Chaplain to the Right Reverend Father in God John, Lord Bishop of *Norwich.* Rom I. 20. For the invisible things of Him from the creation of the world, are clearly seen, being understood by the things that are made; even his eternal power and God-head: So that they are without excuse. London. Printed by Will. Botham, for James Knapton at the *Crown* in St. *Paul's* Church Yard. 1705.

Facsimile reprint Stuttgart-Bad Cannstatt: Frommann 1964. In one volume, bound with:

A Discourse Concerning the Unchangeable Obligations of Natural Religion and the Truth and Certainty of the Christian revelation. Being eight sermons preach'd at the Cathedral-Church of St Paul, in the year 1705, at the Lecture founded by the honourable Robert Boyle Esq; By Samuel Clark, M.A. Chaplain to the Right Reverend Father in God John, Lord Bishop of *Norwich.* Isa. 5, 20. Wo unto them that call evil good, and good evil; that put darkness for light, and light for darkness; that put bitter for sweet, and sweet for bitter. Rom. I,22. Professing themselves to be wise, they became fools. I Cor. 2, 10. But God hath revealed them unto us by his spirit. London. Printed by Will. Botham, for James Knapton at the *Crown* in St. *Paul's* Church Yard. 1706.

Facsimile reprint Stuttgart-Bad Cannstatt: Frommann 1964. In one volume, bound with the previous item.

Cohen, Mendel F., 'Obligation and Human Nature in Hume's Philosophy', *Philosophical Quarterly* 40 (1990) 316–340.

Coleborne, Bryan, *Jonathan Swift and the Dunces of Dublin* (Dublin: National University of Ireland. Diss. 1982)

Cousin, Victor, *Philosophie Ecossaise*, 3rd edn. Paris: Librarie Nouvelle 1857.

Cranfield, C.E.B., *A Critical and Exegetical Commentary on The Epistle to the Romans*, Edinburgh: T. & T. Clark (1979) 2nd edn 1983.

Crescenzo, G. de: see de Crescenzo.

Cumberland, Richard (1632–1718), *A Treatise of the Laws of Nature* (transl. John Maxwell) London 1727. Facsimile reprint: New York: Garland 1978.

According to an advertisement in *The London Journal* of 20 May 1727, the work was published 'this day'. As usual, claims of this kind are not to be taken too literally: it could have been earlier.

Deane, Seamus (ed.), *The Field Day Anthology of Irish Writing*. 3 vols. Derry, Northern Ireland: Field Day Publications/ W.W. Norton 1991.

de Crescenzo, G., *Francis Hutcheson e il suo tempo*. Turin: Taylor 1968.

Derathé, Robert, *Jean-Jacques Rousseau et la science politique de son temps*. (1950; 2nd edn 1970) 1979.

Dodwell, Henry (Jr) (d.1784), *Christianity not Founded on Argument*. London (1741) 2nd edn 1743.

Drummond, Andrew and Bulloch, James, *The Scottish Church 1688–1843*. Edinburgh: The Saint Andrew Press (1973) 1981.

Duncan, Richard, *Notices and Documents illustrative of the Literary History of Glasgow*. Glasgow [Maitland Club] 1831.

Eighteenth-Century Ireland: see D. Raynor; M.A. Stewart.

Elliot, R. and A. Gare (eds.), *Environmental Philosophy*. St. Lucia, Queensland: University of Queensland Press 1983.

Ferguson, James P., *The Philosophy of Dr. Samuel Clarke and its Critics*. New York: Vantage Press 1974.

Feuerbach, Ludwig (1804–72), *The Essence of Christianity*. Transl. by Marian Evans of *Das Wesen des Christentums* (1841). New York: Harper 1957.

[Fiddes, Richard (1672–1725)], *An Answer to Britanicus*, [sic] *Compiler of the London-Journal*. By the Compiler of Cardinal Wolsey's Life, Lately published. London: Printed for S. Billingsley, at the Judge's Head in Chancery Lane, 1725.

Field Day Anthology: see Deane, S. (ed.).

[Fielding, Henry (1707–54)], *An Apology for the life of Mrs. Shamela Andrews. In which, the many notorious falshoods and misrepresentations of a book called Pamela, are exposed and refuted; and all the matchless arts of that young politician, set in a true and just light. Together with a full account of all that passed between her and Parson Arthur Williams; whose character is represented in a manner something different from what he bears in Pamela...* M DCC XLI. Ed. Douglas Brooks-Davies. Oxford: Oxford University Press 1980.

Fielding, Henry, *The History of Tom Jones, A Foundling*. (1749) 2 vols. Oxford: Oxford University Press 1974.

Fortnight: see Smyth, Damian (ed.).

Francis Hutcheson: see Smyth, Damian (ed.).

Gaskell, Philip, *A New Introduction to Bibliography*. Oxford: Clarendon Press 1979.

Gay, John (1699–1745), *Preliminary Dissertation Concerning the Fundamental Principle of Virtue or Morality* in: William King, *Essay on the Origin of Evil* 1731.

Gibson, Edgar C.S., *The Thirty-nine Articles of the Church of England*. 2 vols. London: Methuen 1897.

Gigas, E. (ed.), *Briefe Samuel Pufendorfs an Christian Thomasius (1687–1693)* (= Historische Bibliothek hrsg. von der Redaktion der Historischen Zeitschrift. Vol. II.), Munich and Leipzig: Oldenbourg 1897. Facsimile reprint in *Samuel Pufendorf, Briefe Samuel Pufendorfs und Christian Thomasius. Pufendorf-Briefe an Falaiseau, Frise und Weigel*. [Königstein]: Scriptor 1980.

Gordon, Thomas (c.1690–1750): see Trenchard.

Gracián, Baltasar (1601–58), *El discreto* (1646), translated as *The Compleat Gentleman* (2nd edn 1730)

Grotius, Hugo (1583–1645), *De jure belli ac pacis* (1625) (ed. J. Barbeyrac). Amsterdam: Jansson & Waesberg 1712.

   Le Droit de la guerre et de la paix (ed. and transl. J. Barbeyrac). Basle: Thourneisen 1746.

Grove, Henry (1684–1738), *System of Moral Philosophy*. London: Thomas Amory 1749.

Haakonssen, Knud, `Natural Law and Moral Realism: the Scottish Synthesis', in M.A. Stewart (ed.), *Studies ...* pp. 61–85.

Hamilton, Thomas, *History of the Irish Presbyterian Church*. Edinburgh: T. & T. Clark 1887.

Hampton, Jean, Review of Tom Sorell, *Hobbes* in *Philosophical Review* 98 (1990) 408–411.

Hanson, Laurence, *Government and the Press 1695–1763*. London: Oxford University Press/Humphrey Milford 1936.

Harris, Michael, *London Newspapers in the Age of Walpole*. London: Associated University Presses 1987.

Harrison, Bernard, *Henry Fielding's Tom Jones. The Novelist as Moral Philosopher*. London: Sussex University Press/Chatto & Windus 1975.

Hibernicus's Letters: see Arbuckle.

Hobbes, Thomas (1588–1679), *De cive* (1642) (ed. H. Warrender). Oxford: Oxford University Press 1983.

   Philosophicall Rudiments Concerning Government and Society (1651) [translation of *De Cive*] (ed. H. Warrender). Oxford: Oxford University Press 1983.

Hobbes, Thomas, *Leviathan* (1651) (ed. C.B. MacPherson). Harmondsworth: Penguin 1968.

Holtby, R[obert] T[insley], *Daniel Waterland 1683-1740. A Study in Eighteenth Century Orthodoxy.* Carlisle[: C. Thurnan] 1966.

Hont, Istvan and M. Ignatieff (eds.), *Wealth and Virtue.* Cambridge: Cambridge University Press 1983.

Horace, *Opera* (ed Wickham and Garrod). Oxford: Oxford University Press 1901.

Q. *Horati Flacci Opera* (ed. S. Borzsak). Leipzig: Teubner 1984.

Satires, Epistles and Ars Poetica (transl. H.R. Fairclough). Loeb Classical Library. London: Heinemann; New York: Putnam 1926.

The Complete Works (transl. C.Passage). New York: Ungar 1983.

Hudson, W.D. (ed.), *The Is–Ought Question.* London: Macmillan 1969.

Hufeland, Gottlieb, *Lehrsätze des Naturrechts.* Jena (1790), 2nd edn 1795.

[Hume, David (1712–76)], *A Treatise of Human Nature, Book III, Of Morals* (1740), in *Hume's Treatise of Human Nature* (ed. L.A. Selby-Bigge and P. Nidditch). Oxford: Oxford University Press 1978.

Philosophical Essays Concerning Human Understanding. By the Author of the Essays Moral and Political. London: Printed for A. Millar, opposite Katharine-Street in the Strand. MDCCXLVII.

Enquiry concerning the Principles of Morals (1751) in *Hume's Enquiries* (ed. L.A. Selby-Bigge and P. Nidditch). Oxford: Oxford University Press 1975.

Dialogues Concerning Natural Religion (1779), (ed. N. Kemp Smith), 2nd edn. London: Nelson 1947.

The Letters of David Hume, vol. I (ed. J.Y.T. Greig). Oxford: Clarendon Press 1932.

Innes, A.: see Campbell, Archibald.

Jensen, Henning, *Motivation and the Moral Sense in Francis Hutcheson's Ethical Theory.* The Hague: Nijhoff 1971.

Jessop, T.E., *A Bibliography of David Hume and of Scottish Philosophy from Francis Hutcheson to Lord Balfour.* London: Brown 1938.

Johnson, Thomas (c.1703–37), *Essay on Moral Obligation: With a view towards settling the controversy, concerning moral and positive duties. In answer to two late pamphlets; The one entitled; the true foundation of natural and revealed religion asserted; being a reply to the supplement to the Treatise on the Christian Sacraments. The other – Some Reflections upon the Comparative Excellency and Usefulness of Moral and Positive Duties: by Mr. Chubb.* London 1731.

Johnson, Thomas *A Summary of Natural Religion. Containing a proof of the being and attributes of God: And a particular deduction of the laws of nature: with an enquiry into the ground of their obligation: In which the relations of things are distinctly considered, both as an objective rule to the*

Divine Mind, and as the foundation of morality. Cambridge: Thurlbourn 1736.

Joshi, K.L., `The London Journal, 1719–1738', *Journal of the University of Bombay* 9 (1940) 33–66.

Kant, Immanuel (1724–1804), *The Moral Law.* Transl. by H. Paton of *Grundlegung zur Metaphysik der Sitten* (1785). London: Hutchinson 1948.

Kavka, George S., *Hobbesian Moral and Political Theory*, Princeton, N.J.: Princeton University Press 1986

Kaye, F.B.: see Mandeville.

Kemp Smith, Norman, *The Philosophy of David Hume.* London: Macmillan 1941.

Kirk, Linda, *Richard Cumberland and Natural Law.* Cambridge: James Clarke 1987.

Lecky, William Edward Hartpole, *A History of England in the Eighteenth Century.* 7 vols. London: Longmans Cabinet edition (1892) 1910.

Leechman, William (1706–1785), Preface to Hutcheson's *System of Moral Philosophy.* Glasgow and London 1755.

Leibniz, Gottfried Wilhelm (1646–1716), *Theodicy. Essays on the Goodness of God, the Freedom of Man, and the Origin of Evil* (1710) (ed. A. Farrer; transl. E.M. Huggard). London: Routledge 1952.

  The Political Writings (ed. P. Riley). Cambridge: Cambridge University Press (1972) 2nd edn 1988.

Leidhold, Wolfgang, *Ethik und Politik bei Francis Hutcheson.* Munich: Alber 1985.

  `Einleitung' in Hutcheson, Francis, *Eine Untersuchung* ... Hamburg: Meiner 1986.

Locke, John (1632–1704), *Essay Concerning Human Understanding,* (1690) (ed. P. Nidditch). Oxford: Oxford University Press 1975.

  Two Treatises of Government (1690) (ed. P. Laslett). Cambridge: Cambridge University Press (1st edn 1960, 2nd edn 1970), 3rd edn 1988.

  The Educational Writings of John Locke (ed. J.W. Adamson). London: Arnold 1912.

Luig, Klaus, `Zur Verbreitung des Naturrechts in Europa', *Tijdschrift voor Rechtsgeschiedenis/Revue d'histoire du droit* 60 (1972) 539–57.

McCosh, James, *The Scottish Philosophy.* London 1875. Facsimile reprint Hildesheim: Olms 1966).

Mackie, J. D., *The University of Glasgow 1451–1951.* Glasgow: Jackson 1954.

McMahon, Marie P., *The Radical Whigs, John Trenchard and Thomas Gordon: Libertarian loyalists to the new house of Hanover*. Lanham, MD: University Press of America 1990.

McManmon, John, `Some Problems regarding a Series of Letters between Francis Hutcheson and Gilbert Burnet', *Studies in Scottish Literature* 3 (1965).

McReynolds, Paul (ed.), *Four Early Works on Motivation*. Gainesville, Fla.: Scholars' 1969.

Maitland Club: see Duncan; *Munimenta*; Wodrow.

Mandeville, Bernard (1670–1733), *The Fable of the Bees* (ed. F.B. Kaye), 2 vols. Oxford: Oxford University Press 1924.

Midgley, Mary, `Duties concerning Islands', in R. Elliot and A. Gare (eds.), *Environmental Philosophy*. St Lucia, Queensland: University of Queensland Press 1983, pp. 166–81.

Mill, John Stuart (1806–73), Review of R. Blakey, *History of Moral Science*, in J. B. Schneewind (ed.), *Mill's Ethical Writings*. New York: Collier 1965, pp. 69–74.

On Liberty (1859). London: Dent (Everyman edn) 1910; London: Penguin 1974; Cambridge: Cambridge University Press 1989.

Moore, James, `The Two Systems of Francis Hutcheson' in M.A. Stewart (ed.), *Studies* ... pp. 37–59.

Müller, Hans, *Ursprung und Geschichte des Wortes Sozialismus und seiner Verwandten*. Hanover 1967.

Munimenta almae universitatis Glasguensis. Vol. III. Glasgow: [Maitland Club] 1854.

Murray, David, *Memories of the Old College of Glasgow* [=Glasgow University Publications no. 3]. Glasgow: 1927.

Norton, David Fate, *David Hume, Common-Sense Moralist, Sceptical Metaphysician*. Princeton, N.J.: Princeton University Press 1982.

`Francis Hutcheson in America', *Studies on Voltaire and the Eighteenth Century* 154 (1976) 1547–1568.

[Nyblæus, Axel], *Om Puffendorfs plats i nyare praktiska philosophiens historia*. Inbjudningsprogram till den philosophiæ doktorspromotion hvilken i philosophiska faculteten vid Lunds universitet kommer att förrättas den 29 maj 1868 af promotor [= Axel Nyblæus]. (On Pufendorf's place in the modern history of practical philosophy. Invitation programme for a Ph. D. graduation ceremony.) Lund 1868.

O'Keefe, Cyril B., S.J., *Contemporary Reactions to the Enlightenment (1728–1762)*. Geneva: Slatkine 1974.

Pacchi, Arrigo, `Hobbes e l'epicureismo', *Rivista critica di storia della filosofia* 33 (1978) 55–72.

Palladini, Fiammetta, *Discussioni seicentesche su Samuel Pufendorf.* [Bologna:] Il Mulino 1978.

`Lucrezio in Pufendorf`, *La Cultura* 19 (1981) 110–49.

Samuel Pufendorf, discepolo di Hobbes. Per una reinterpretazione del giusnaturalismo moderno. Bologna: Il Mulino 1990.

Pascal, Blaise (1623–62), *Oeuvres complètes* (ed. J. Chevalier) [=Bibliothèque de la Pléiade t. 34]. Paris: Gallimard 1962.

Pensées (ed. Z. Tourneur and D. Anzieu). Paris: Colin (1960) 1965

Peach, Bernard, `Editor's Introduction', to his edition of Hutcheson's *Illustrations,* q.v. *supra.*

Prior, Arthur, *Logic and the Basis of Ethics.* Oxford: Oxford University Press 1949.

Pufendorf, Samuel (1632–94), Letters to C. Thomasius: see Gigas.

De jure naturae et gentium. Lund 1672; Frankfurt 2nd edn 1684.

On the Law of Nature and Nations, transl. B. Kennett. Oxford 1703.

Du droit de la nature et des gens, transl. Jean Barbeyrac. (1706) Amsterdam 2nd edn 1712.

De Officio hominis et civis, ed. Immanuel Weber. Frankfurt (1700) 1719.

De officio hominis et civis, ed. Gottlieb Gerhard Titius. Leipzig 3rd edn 1715.

De Officio hominis et civis, ed. Gerschom Carmichael. (Glasgow 1718); Edinburgh 2nd edn 1724.

On the Duty of Man and Citizen, transl. F.G. Moore. Oxford University Press 1927.

On the Duty of Man and Citizen, ed. J. Tully, transl. Michael Silverthorne. Cambridge: Cambridge University Press 1991.

On the Natural State of Men. The 1678 Latin Edition and English Translation. Translated, annotated and introduced by Michael Seidler. Lampeter: Mellen Press 1990.

Raphael, D. Daiches, *The Moral Sense.* London: Oxford University Press 1947.

`A New Light', in Smyth (ed.), *Francis Hutcheson,* pp. 2–3.

Raynor, David R., `Hutcheson's Defence Against a Charge of Plagiarism', *Eighteenth-Century Ireland* 2 (1987) 177–81.

Realey, Charles B., `The London Journal and its Authors 1720–1723', *Bulletin of the University of Kansas* 5, no. 3 (1935). Lawrence, Kans. 1935.

Realey, Charles B., *The Early Opposition to Sir Robert Walpole 1720–1727* [= University of Kansas Humanistic Studies 4, nos 2–3]. Lawrence, Kans. 1931.

Reid, James Seaton (1798–1851), *History of the Presbyterian Church in Ireland*, vol. III. New edn Belfast 1867.

Pp. 236ff. of this volume were written by D.D. Killen on the basis of Reid's posthumous notes.

Rétat, Pierre, *Le Dictionnaire de Bayle et la lutte philosophique au XVIIIᵉ siècle* (= Bibliothèque de la faculté des lettres de Lyon. XXVIII). Société d'édition "Les Belles Lettres". Paris 1971.

Robbins, Caroline, `When it is that Colonies May Turn Independent: An Analysis of the Environment and Politics of Francis Hutcheson (1694–1746)', *William and Mary Quarterly 3rd series* 11 (1954) 214–51. Reprinted in Caroline Robbins, *Absolute Liberty* (ed. B. Taft), Hamden, Conn.: Archon 1982.

The Eighteenth-Century Commonwealthman. Cambridge, Mass.: Harvard University Press 1959.

Robertson, John Mackinnon (1856–1933), *A History of Freethought*, vol. II. 4th edn. London: Watts 1936.

Rydberg, Viktor (1828–95), *Filosofiska föreläsningar II. Leibniz' Teodicé* [Philosophical Lectures: Leibniz's Theodicy (given 1876 in Swedish)]. Stockholm: Bonniers 1900.

Schaff, Philip, *The Creeds of Christendom, with a history and critical notes*, vol. III: *The Evangelical Protestant Creeds, with translations*. New York: Harper 1877.

Schieder, Wolfgang, `Sozialismus', in Otto Brunner (ed.), *Geschichtliche Grundbegriffe*, vol. V. Stuttgart: Klett/Cotta 1984.

Schneewind, Jerome (ed.), *Mill's Ethical Writings*. New York: Collier-Macmillan 1965

(ed.) *Moral Philosophy from Montaigne to Kant*. 2 vols. Cambridge: Cambridge University Press 1990.

Scott, William Robert, *Francis Hutcheson. His Life, Teaching and Position in the History of Philosophy*. Cambridge: Cambridge University Press 1900. Facsimile reprint New York: Kelley 1966.

Seidler, Michael, `Introductory essay' to Samuel Pufendorf, *On the Natural State of Men*.

Sgard, Jean (ed.), *Dictionnaire des journalistes*. Grenoble: Presses Universitaires de Grenoble 1976.

Shaftesbury, (Anthony Ashley Cooper), Earl of (1671–1713), *Characteristics of Men, Manners, Opinions, Times* (1711). Ed. John M. Robertson (1900). Indianapolis, Ind.: Bobbs-Merrill 1964.

Smith, Adam (1723–90), *Theory of Moral Sentiments* (1759) (eds. D. D. Raphael and A.L. Macfie). Oxford: Oxford University Press 1976.

Smith, Norman Kemp, see: Kemp Smith.

Smyth, Damian (ed.), *Francis Hutcheson* [= Supplement to *Fortnight* no. 308 July/August 1992]. Belfast 1992.

Sorensen, Roy A., `Vagueness Implies Non-Cognitivism' *American Philosophical Quarterly* 27 (1990) 1–14.

Sorley, W.R., *A History of English Philosophy*. Cambridge: Cambridge University Press (1920) 1951.

Spitz, J.-F., `Le Concept d'état de nature chez Locke et chez Pufendorf', *Archives de Philosophie* 49 (1986) 437–52.

Sprague, Elmer, `Butler, Joseph', *Encyclopedia of Philosophy* (ed. Paul Edwards). New York: Collier-Macmillan 1967.

Spurr, John, `"Latitudinarianism" and the Restoration Church', *Historical Journal* 31 (1988) 61–82.

   The Restoration Church of England, 1646–1689. New Haven and London: Yale University Press 1991

Stewart, M.A., `John Smith and the Molesworth Circle', *Eighteenth-Century Ireland* 2 (1987) 89–102.

   (ed.), *Studies in The Philosophy of the Scottish Enlightenment* (= Oxford Studies in the History of Philosophy, Vol. I). Oxford: Oxford University Press 1990.

   `Academic Freedom: Origins of an Idea', *Bulletin of the Australian Society of Legal Philosophy* vol. 16, no. 57, (1991/92) 1–31.

   `The Stoic Legacy in the Early Scottish Enlightenment', in Osler, Margaret J. (ed.), *Atoms, Pneuma, and Tranquillity: Stoic themes in European thought*. Cambridge: Cambridge University Press 1991, pp. 273–296.

   `Abating bigotry and hot zeal', in Smyth (ed.), *Francis Hutcheson*, pp. 4–6.

Sykes, Norman, `Benjamin Hoadly, Bishop of Bangor', in F.J.C. Hearnshaw (ed.), *The Social and Political Ideas of some English Thinkers of the Augustan Age*. London: Harrap 1928.

Thomas, Margaret D., `Michel de La Roche', in J. Sgard (ed.), *Dictionnaire*, pp. 225–8.

   `Michel de La Roche: A Huguenot critic of Calvin', *Studies on Voltaire and the Eighteenth Century* 238 (1985) 97–195.

[Trenchard, John (1662–1723) and Gordon, Thomas (c.1690–1750] *Cato's Letters; or, Essays on Liberty, Civil and Religious, And other important*

Subjects. 3rd edn. London 1733. Facsimile reprint New York: Russell & Russell 1969.

Trinius, Johann Anton, *Freydencker-Lexicon oder Einleitung in die Geschichte der neueren Freygeister ihrer Schriften, und deren Widerlegungen* ... Leipzig and Bernburg: C.G. Córner 1759.

Turco, Luigi, `La prima Inquiry morale di Francis Hutcheson', *Rivista critica di storia della filosofia* 23 (1968) 39–60; 297–329.

Veitch, John, `Philosophy in the Scottish Universities', *Mind* 2 (1877).

Waterland, Daniel, *The Works of The Rev. Daniel Waterland*, D.D. formerly Master of Magdalen College, Cambridge, Canon of Windsor, and Archdeacon of Middlesex; now first collected and arranged. Ed. William van Mildert, D.D. Lord Bishop of Llandaff. Oxford: Clarendon Press MDCCCXXIII. 10 vols.

[The same] 3rd edn 1856. 6 vols.

[Waterland, Daniel], *Advice to a Young Student, with a method of study for the first four years*. London: Printed for John Crownfield ... and sold by Cornelius Crownfield ... Cambridge. 1730.

For further bibliographical information, see appendix 11.

The Nature, Obligation, and Efficacy of the Christian Sacraments considered, in *Works*, (1823) vol. V; (3rd edn 1856), vol. IV.

Sermons on several Important Subjects of Religion and Morality. To Which are added Two Tracts: [etc.] In two volumes. By Daniel Waterland, D.D. Late Arch-Deacon of Middlesex, Master of Magdalen-College in Cambridge, &c. and Chaplain in ordinary to His Majesty. Publish'd from His Original MSS. With a Preface, by Joseph Clarke, M.A. Fellow of Magdalen-College in Cambridge. (1742).

Welzel, Hans, *Die Naturrechtslehre Samuel Pufendorfs*. Berlin: de Gruyter 1958.

Willey, Basil, *The English Moralists*. London: Chatto & Windus 1964.

Wills, Gary, *Inventing America*, (1978) London: Athlone Press 1980.

Witherspoon, John (1723–94), `Ecclesiastical Characteristics' (1753) in *Selected Writings* (ed. Thomas Miller). Carbondale, Ill.: Southern Illinois University Press 1990, pp. 57–102.

Wodrow, Robert (1679–1734), *Analecta or Materials for a History of Remarkable Providences*, vol. IV, ed. M[atthew] L[eisman]. Edinburgh [Maitland Club] 1843.

Wollaston, William (1660–1724), *The Religion of Nature Delineated*. London, 1724.

There was also an earlier edition 1722, privately printed.

Wood, Gordon S., `Heroics', *New York Review of Books* 28, no. 5 (1981).

Index

For EU product safety concerns, contact us at Calle de José Abascal, 56–1°, 28003 Madrid, Spain or eugpsr@cambridge.org.

www.ingramcontent.com/pod-product-compliance
Ingram Content Group UK Ltd.
Pitfield, Milton Keynes, MK11 3LW, UK
UKHW020807190625
459647UK00032B/2364